Praise for KILLING THE BUDDHA

"This collection proves that fear and trembling are human, but a sense of humor is divine."

—*O, The Oprah Magazine*

"Daring and delightful. . . . Heretics and skeptics, as well as true-blue believers, will find *Killing the Buddha* refreshing, inspiring and downright invigorating."

—Lauren Winner, *Newsday*

"The editors manage to pull off a most impressive work. This is perhaps the most original and insightful spiritual writing to come out of America since Jack Kerouac first hit the road."

—*Publishers Weekly*

"Shot through with epiphanies and controversy."

—"Hot Type," *Vanity Fair*

"*Killing the Buddha* is, without question, one of the most eccentric and fascinating books of the year. . . . This much is reasonably certain: you're unlikely to have encountered anything before quite like it."

—Jeff Simon, Editor's Choice, *The Buffalo News*

"A mix of hymn and history, poem and prophecy, story and sermon."

—Jason DeRose, NPR, *Morning Edition*

"A mesmerizing platform for all the confusions, inconsistencies, and hard-boiled epiphanies concerning spiritual belief in 21st-century America."

—*Time Out New York*

"If there's one thing this pseudo-Christian nation needs, it's more deranged, slightly anarchic anecdotes of unique spiritual questing [like] *Killing the Buddha*."

—Mark Morford, SFGate.com

"An intelligent, challenging collection of essays and reflections that is a sharp addition to the body of spiritual journey memoirs. . . . [Manseau and Sharlet] see stories everywhere and nowhere, managing to maintain both healthy skepticism and rare hopefulness. An ambitious book in its scope and explicit desire not to find answers to the big questions, but to hone and shape the ways in which they are asked."

—*Forward*

"Fascinating, offbeat . . . religious practices you *don't* learn about in Bible school."

—*The Boston Globe*

"*Killing the Buddha* is not a book for those who like their beliefs unexamined, whether they're atheists, Buddhists or Southern Baptists. Rather, it makes a convincing case that faith is less about knowing all of life's answers and more about asking questions."

—*The Capital Times* (Madison, Wisconsin)

"A collection of writing that literally defies ideology, denomination, and creed . . . [*Killing the Buddha*] tackles the big spiritual issues of our day without the moral smugness and arrogance that taints most discussions of spirituality."

—*Baltimore City Paper*

"Marvelous, profoundly personal observations, as diverse as Randall Kenan's fictionalized gospel and Peter Trachtenberg's distillation of the story of Job in a Venn diagram."

—*Booklist*

"This book is a mystical souffle, a sensual, cosmic marinade. . . . It is book as quest and calling rather than text."

—*Pittsburgh Post-Gazette*

"Read it twice: the first time to savor the funny (sometimes heart-breaking) stories that Sharlet and Manseau collect on their tour; and a second time to savor the work of thirteen new apostles."

—Paul Zakrzewski, editor of *Lost Tribe: Jewish Fiction from the Edge*

"Some will denounce *Killing the Buddha* as heresy; others will dismiss it as reality-TV fancy. As the authors wryly note, 'There's a certain risk in making a book that involves America, a car and talk of the Buddha.' A brave book, indeed."

—*Shambala Sun*

"*Killing the Buddha* has much to say about the spiritual state of America. Thought-provoking and fascinating, the editors and authors remind humans that recognizing faith is more complicated than it seems. . . . *Killing the Buddha* is one of the best reads of the year."

—Pam Kingsbury, *Southern Scribe*

"*Killing the Buddha* gives us an America of mostly disorganized religion; a reassuring notion at a time when an Evangelical coalition seems to control our government and Islamic fundamentalism, like some agitated behemoth writhing beneath us, threatens to topple everything. . . . In a megacorporate, multinational, conspiracy-obsessed world, *Killing the Buddha* is a kind of antidote, rendering religion as a natural resource tapped by ordinary people in small, daily, idiosyncratic ways."

—Emily Votruba, *Brooklyn Rail*

"A weeping beauty of a book."

—Read Mercer Schuchardt, *The New Pantagruel*

KILLINGTHEBUDDHA

A HERETIC'S BIBLE

PETER MANSEAU & JEFF SHARLET

FREE PRESS
NEW YORK LONDON TORONTO SYDNEY

*f*P
FREE PRESS
A Division of Simon & Schuster, Inc.
1230 Avenue of the Americas
New York, NY 10020

First Free Press trade paperback edition 2004

FREE PRESS and colophon are trademarks of Simon & Schuster, Inc.

For information regarding special discounts for bulk purchases,
please contact Simon & Schuster Special Sales:
1-800-456-6798 or business@simonandschuster.com

Designed by Karolina Harris

Manufactured in the United States of America

10 9 8 7 6 5 4 3 2 1

Library of Congress Control Number: 2003064335

ISBN 0-7432-3276-3
ISBN 0-7432-3277-1 (Pbk)

דער גאָט פֿון מײַן אומגלויבן איז פּרעכטיק . . .

The God of my unbelief is magnificent . . .

—Yankev Glatshteyn, "My Brother Refugee,"
from the Yiddish, *Mayn vogl-bruder,* 1946

CONTENTS

THE BOOK OF PSALMS

BY PETER MANSEAU & JEFF SHARLET

MORTAL, EAT THIS SCROLL!

LATE morning, just before lunch, one of Lin Chi's monks comes up to him half-crazed, out of his mind with ecstasy, babbling about Buddha. Says he's seen him. Says he was just walking down the road when suddenly: Buddhamind. Enlightenment. Nirvana. The big payoff. The monk can't stop talking about it. Lin Chi strikes a match, lights his pipe, takes a long drag. Leaves the monk hanging, waiting for his reward. Instead, Lin Chi blows a cloud of smoke, reaches out, and smacks him.

"You meet the Buddha on the road," Lin Chi says, "kill him."

Imagine the monk's face. Better yet, imagine your own: You've been to church, you've gone to the zendo, you took your bat mitzvah money and ran. You're an atheist, or you're an agnostic, or you're an orthodox believer without a cause. Maybe you've tried not to think about it. You've opted for sex, drugs, and electronica, you've opted for a career; you're poor and you never had any options. You've run away from your family, you've started a family, you've given up on God, Family, and Nation. And *then*, when you were minding your own business, getting on with things, you stumbled upon—something. *Him*, Her, a Higher Power, Buddha, Jesus, the Shekhina, Shiva. The *mysterium tremendum*, the big white whale. And even though you're no seeker, you weren't looking and you didn't ask to find, you had to admit: God is Great. Allah Akbar! Holy Ghost Power.

To which Lin Chi says: Super. You found it. Now you can kill it. The Buddha you meet is not the true Buddha but an expression of your longing. If this Buddha is not killed, he will only stand in your way.

When Lin Chi contributed the idea of deicide to his godless religion a thousand years ago, he was talking not just about a long-dead teacher who had come to be known as Buddha but about the dominant ideologies of his day: One True Path, One True Story, One True Anything. The preachers and the gurus, the Christian Coalition and the secular masses, the heart that wants what it wants and the mind that always thinks better: These are the Buddhas we meet on the road, the Buddhas we know and love and listen to, the Buddhas we all are. Faced with modern-day atheists or fundamentalists or guys who thump thousand-year-old Zen aphorisms hard as any Bible, Lin Chi would probably say the same thing: Don't be a chump. A single story never explained anything.

What do you say about yourself, for example, to explain the things you do? Forget the hypothetical—let's start here, with this book. We had more reasons for making it than there are words between the covers. One of us is a Jew raised by a Pentecostal Hindu Buddhist, one is a son of a Catholic priest and a former nun. The priest kept the vestments in the front hallway and held mass in the dining room; the Hindu Buddhist asked Charismatic Christians to pray over her as she lay dying. Between us we've lived in monasteries, warehouses, hermit shacks, luxury condos. We've worked as truck drivers, casino hands, carpenters, court-martial reporters. We met when we both worked at a Yiddish library, for which we pulled books out of attics and Dumpsters, dragging artifacts of the old world into the new.

That's more or less what we had in mind when we began talking about killing the Buddha, and about what a Bible filled with heresy might look like, and about what Bibles and Buddhas, killings and heresies, had to do with each other. We had lost faith in the way faith gets talked about in America, the way it's seen as either innocuous spirituality or dangerous fanaticism, perfume or mustard gas. After years of writing about religion, for newspapers and magazines and in letters to each other, we'd come to think that it is almost always both: Show us the truth and we'll show you a lie, prove God is dead and we promise a resurrection.

Right after Lin Chi told the monk to kill Buddha, he said: "And burn all the sutras." He wasn't talking about bonfires and he wasn't the kind of guy to ban anything. He probably would have been thrilled had the monk torched the holy scrolls and then written them all over again, sentence for sentence, every mantra a revelation, the word made strange. All he'd have to do—all we did— was look around.

Like everyone else who knows how to read or count the stars, we've spent our whole lives studying scripture. When we were kids it was the story of

Apollo's chariot pulling the sun, and Bilbo Baggins with his ring, and Harriet the Spy writing her own Book of Revelation. Later, there was Marx on money, Darwin on your mother, Virginia Woolf on each minute passing. There were also the Batman comic books we read in the first grade, the *Challenger* explosion we watched a few years later, the *Penthouse* magazine we found down by the river in junior high. There was a billboard that read, "Jesus Christ, King of Newark"; a paperback copy of the Koran we stole from our high school library; a letter from Einstein we found pressed between Yiddish pages. Not to mention the texts we share with everyone: strange desert flowers and rain making streams in the gutters, headlines of nuclear threats and the most up-to-date mass murders; the lines that cross our palms, the creaking reports of our bones, everyone's X rays, interchangeable.

So many sutras. We made this book not to replace the Bible but to light it and its successors on fire; when you're done with it, you should burn this book, too. Or you could make like the prophet Ezekiel and eat it.

There's a certain risk in making a book that involves America, a car, and talk of the Buddha. All we can say is that had we owned a Cessna, we'd probably be wincing whenever someone mentioned Saint-Exupéry. The fact is that this book is about America because America has good roads, and we drove on those roads not because they're sacred veins of the land or paths into the mystic heart of the nation (three words to be wary of: *mystic, heart, nation*) but because they're paved. Such was our methodology: Drive south then west then north and back in search of homegrown heresy, belief in the raw. We had no itinerary, but that didn't matter, because nearly all the people we spoke to told us it was no coincidence we'd showed up in their church, their temple, their compound. America is a nation of experts in predestination. In comparison we're amateurs. Our criteria for forward motion were these: the leading of the Holy Spirit; nice weather; rumors and accusations. We were looking not so much for a sacred show-and-tell as for a holy-rolling striptease, revelation as an end in itself.

But getting naked isn't as simple as it sounds, and it's hard to say when an idea is really in the nude. The very word *heresy*, after all, hints at the belief it supposedly displaces. Strip off the heresy, and beneath there's orthodoxy, which turns out to be nothing but another heresy got up in drag. Kind of like one of those Russian dolls, the ones where you twist open a babushka only to find another one inside. The heresy of our title doesn't so much refute belief, in fact, as confirm its value, if not its current terms. Heresy is as old as it is new, the naughty secret and the fresh coat of paint. It's the pasties beneath the hair shirt as much as it is the new age robes thrown over it all. Put a tune to it and you get cacophony, not harmony, a song that's part punk, part country, part gospel, part death metal.

We wanted to hear it all played together, multiple turntables spinning at the same time. We knew where to find the sheet music—we'd take the Bible apart, scatter its pages in the wind, and put it back together again. Creation via apocalypse: translation with a dynamite pen. To light the fuse we needed new stories to scratch the flint of the old. We asked thirteen writers to provide them. We offered each one a solo, a single book of the Bible to be remade, revealed, replaced, inverted, perverted, or born again, however the spirit so led them. We gave them directions and waited for their improvisations; the stories we tell in this book are the questions we put to their answers. This book is not an anthology, it's a call-and-response. It's not so much a collage as it is a Franken-stein's monster—which is to say that despite the fact that it doesn't so much have seams as it has scars, it's some kind of scripture.

Why use the Bible as a blueprint for a project that takes its name from the Buddhist tradition? Because in America, the first nation founded on secular-ism, the Bible is always there, the book waiting for a sweaty-palmed ren-dezvous in every motel room. There's no refuge from the Bible's reach. It's there in the movies you like and the books you don't. It's on our money and in our courts and in our classrooms, everywhere at once, whether you want it or not. Consider its stories—Adam meets Eve, Jonah meets whale, Jesus meets a bad end—you've heard them all before. The Bible is in your bones before you crack its binding.

For our part—for this Bible's Book of Psalms—we traveled for most of a year. We rode the range, went to jail, called down the moon, ate dirt with a crowd, and generally inserted ourselves into the lives of complete strangers, who in turn treated us as confessors, or confidants, or possible notches in their I-saved-this-many-heathens bedposts.

People always figured one of us for a believer, one a skeptic; or imagined us as members of dueling doctrines, the Catholic and the Jew. We played the roles assigned us, mystic and cynic, good cop and bad cop, Laurel and Hardy; Ishmael and Ahab, Lenny and Squiggy, Tweedledee and Tweedledum and I'm the one in charge. Yeah, but who's the "I," smart guy? We became "we" be-cause it seemed like the only answer both of us could agree on. No matter how long we drove, neither of us by himself was able to get where he wanted to go, and the more we drove the further away we got from wherever that was. There were times when we drove in the wrong lane, times when we dodged drunk drivers, one time when in our rusty Ford we flew above the desert and beneath the moon; that time, we hollered. Two people, one voice, the "we" that is the author.

But One Voice is no more true than One God. Every day we argued over which stories to chase and which holy souls to believe and which of us was more of a charlatan and whether that was good or bad. In Tennessee we called each other liars, in Alabama we kept each other honest, in New Mexico we came to blows, in Colorado we loaned each other shoes. We're not sure, but we think that's how you make a Bible together.

Like the original, this Bible crosses freely between genres, between history and prophecy, confession and myth. Seven of the contributors responded to our call with nonfiction: Genesis, Exodus, and Ruth as personal investigations; Leviticus, Job, and Isaiah as critical riffs; Song of Songs as a love letter. Six responded with fiction: one book of biblical history is revised (Samuel), the rants of three prophets are translated and improved (Ezekiel, Daniel, Jonah), and books of the New Testament (the Gospels and Revelation) are entirely made up. Threaded through the chorus of our makeshift choir are our own counterharmonies, thirteen postcards from our trip across this strange, godless, pious land: not so much walking the Bible as stalking its shadow. Every one of these psalms is 110 percent true, pure American revelation.

Which is not to say that we vouch for the visions of the hermaphrodite angels, apocalypse ranchers, storm doctors, corporeal manifestations of the divine, or the electric chair gospel choir we encountered in our travels. They are all real human beings, and the names we call them in this book are the names they gave us. The miracles they describe, perform, and deny are just as real, the signs and wonders of people who want to know why they've been abandoned by God, people who think they've found God, people who swear they're going to wring His neck when they get ahold of Him. What follow, our contributors' chapters and the stories with which we knit them together, are songs sung by and to people reading tea leaves, people kissing crosses, people breaking windows, people wrapped in flags; people ducking for cover or looking to the skies, as if everyone was his or her own personal Moses and the whole world was one great burning bush, jumping with flames but not yet consumed.

Such was the world when we set out to find the source of the fire.

Then the eyes of both were opened, and they knew
they were naked . . .

GENESIS 3:7

GENESIS

BY A. L. KENNEDY

I N the beginning, it's simple, all very clear—you are and then know that you
are and that's enough. But not for long. Eventually, you need an explanation.

My explanation starts with certain facts: that I was conceived in Australia,
then born in Scotland at 3:57 A.M. on October 22, 1965 A.D. These are facts
that I take on faith—I can't remember anything about them.

Beginnings are particularly hungry for our faith. Our communal starting
point—too monumental to imagine and eternally out of reach—can seem the
hungriest of all. Without it, we lack definition, but it continually proves itself
impossible to define. We can't even fix a date for the opening of time. According to James Ussher, once archbishop of Armagh, God began to create our
heavens and our earth and everything herein on the evening before October
23, 4004 B.C. (Which would mean that my birthday perpetually commemo-
rates my ability to just miss key events.) The Eastern Orthodox Church didn't
specify a day but set the Year of Creation at 5508 B.C., while ancient Syrian
Christians were sure it was 5490 B.C. A variety of the faithful of many religions
have made a variety of other calculations, in cyclical and linear time, in order
to pinpoint the birth of everything. Modern physicists are less precise—they
propose a moment of singular significance, expanding from an infinite tem-

perature and into potential life somewhere between 20 and 10 billion years ago. With ourselves and our surroundings as our only tangible evidence, we assume that we and our world, our universe, have come to be: How this has happened we take on faith—we can't remember anything about it.

We are unsure of our inheritance, the traits we may find emerging in our blood: We need a cover story, an alibi, the consolations of a family tree. It's troubling, to be so rootless, to discover such uncertainty when we look for our ultimate home, to find echoes of this amnesia in our lives—we lose ourselves, after all, quite easily. The moment when we fall asleep, the one when we come back, fully awake—they both escape us. And the point when we first became aware that we were ourselves and other things were not, were separate— that slipped right by us, too. This is perhaps because awareness seeped in gradually, our knowledge nudged along by a particular burst of hunger, or an unusually pleasant touch: a sound, a movement, that we didn't make, couldn't make: something arising from somewhere beyond our will. Or perhaps it came in suddenly and complete—ourselves announced to ourselves, the earliest intimate visitors to our minds, erasing our first entrances, even as we arrived. Either way, it's impossible to recall. And when did we start to be knowingly dissatisfied, unhappy, or uncomfortable, wicked, good, afraid? Once again, we're not sure: There is only a muddle of incident, like a bundle of random family photographs: poignant, irrelevant, stilted, intense.

For me, there's the discomfort of chicken pox, my fear of the waiting spider in the fern beside the gate, a sad story about a green dress, my parents' shouting, the day when I cut my foot open, mumps—and that time when I slapped a comic book experimentally toward a fly and actually hit it. For a brief while, I was triumphant and then could do nothing but watch, stricken with guilt, as the fly lay where it dropped, apparently dead and my fault. Then, remarkably, a wing twitched, the legs next, and it recovered itself, filled up again with whatever constituted its tiny life, and flew away, resurrected, as if my wishing could have made it so.

Which is part of the story I'd tell you of me, the way I'd explain myself and how I came to be, even though I'm missing any knowledge of my first 3:57 A.M., of all those initial sunrises and nights. I tell my story, at least in part, to make up for this lack—and like any other piece of autobiography, it is a blend of memory and reported fact and the way that I feel I ought to have been and hope that I am and wish that I will be. It is an exercise of will. I make myself in my own image, what else do I have?

The knowledge of a Will above mine? I couldn't say when that particular awareness first announced itself—I only know He was there early, my God, a personality outside what people told me, beyond religion and the usual prayers.

At that age, of course, I had no need for anything beyond the usual prayers. Nothing about my personal life was large enough to bother God with in any official way: I pushed up the words I was told to use almost as if I were reciting a poem, something formal for a distant and habitually invisible relative. I knelt, as required, and asked that God should bless my mother and my father and my grandparents—both sets—no playing favorites, God should be told about everyone. I may also have mentioned unfortunate strangers, illnesses, that kind of thing.

And, in the beginning, I went to church, and that was simple, too. For a while it made sense that I should sit beside my mother in my least comfortable clothes while she made sure I stood and sang and sat, opened and closed my eyes at appropriate moments, and was put in the way of a gift I believe she had come to regard with some ambivalence. Trained as a Methodist lay preacher, she had studied the Bible enough to find its inconsistencies: the dubious spaces between words that were, in themselves, the products of translators and interpreters, political massage and cultural theft. Add this to the fact that my mother was often trapped by the bewilderment of a good person living an unreasonably painful life and you can understand that hers had become an, at least, unpredictable faith. Still, she put me through the motions of conventional worship, and together in the pew, we could look up and see my father— the evangelical atheist—perched high with his back to everyone and playing the church organ. Unbeliever or not, you'll end up in church if you want to play the organ with any kind of seriousness. He would operate its mystery of pedals and stops, glancing now and then into the carefully angled wing mirrors that made the instrument look like some huge moored vehicle, helplessly straining out music as it fought to race away with the building, drag us off to who knew where.

So there I was, a work in progress, with no way of knowing if I would ever be as frightened as my mother, or as violent as my father. What image would I be made in—the one of a woman who stayed in a marriage to give her child a father, or the one of a father who terrified his child? Of course, I didn't know, and for quite some time, this didn't concern me—my life was my life, without questions. I also thought very little about the contradictions of our family's religious observances. If I considered them at all, I simply assumed that God understood our situation and was entirely satisfied by our dressing oddly and then singing or speaking to Him. I assumed that He found the sermons as boring as I did. I assumed that He was He and not a She—I always have related better to men. I assumed He wouldn't be offended when I didn't think of Him as a Father. I assumed that He didn't mind when we moved house and no longer visited His church.

By the time I was five or six, our attendance, or rather lack of it, rarely occurred to me. I had the feeling that I was alone in wanting any more to do with God and made a little cross out of dry spaghetti bound up with green gardening tape—these being the only materials that came easily to hand. I used to bring out the cross when I prayed. And then my prayers became more personal and more plainly ineffective. And then I lost the cross. And then I didn't pray.

Until the next beginning—the one that means you're adult, fully responsible and powerless—until the sour, scared opening: "Please, God." In this beginning your requests are always personal and brought to God because you have nowhere else to go. Your pressing requests will vary: Let the sick not die, let the loved not leave, or the love, let the pain fade, the fear diminish, or let whatever mess I've made for myself be somehow lifted clear away. And because you've worked out that He isn't Father Christmas, isn't a Father with only you to love, then this is when the bargains start—when you promise you'll be good, or you'll be sorry, or you'll speak to Him more often, dress better, never do whatever you shouldn't have done again. But who are you talking to and how did you get here to be with Him, being you?

Which brings us back to our official beginning—Genesis—one of our species' more famous attempts at outlining its inheritance, its bloodline. This is the story we tell to each other, the way we explain ourselves and how we came to be, even though we're missing any knowledge of all those initial sunrises and nights. This is what and why we are, with those opening lines that are so quoted, so authoritative and so elegant, no matter in what version. With the lovely simplicity of poetry, physics, faith, here is the record of chaos being divided into forms. And we know this undoubtedly happened, one way or another, and here we are and why not cut and paste (rather badly) a number of slightly contradictory creation tales together and say this was, definitively, The Way? The best current guesses of science have the same simplicity and beauty, along with that prudent dash of justifiable awe.

Whatever the reader's level of orthodoxy, Genesis represents an attempt to catch the Almighty in letters. In the beginning is the word, because we justify our existence, our every action, in words, in stories, and why not do the same for our world, for God? In the beginning was the word, because it was natural to make our making in our own phrases, music, images, to recite it in the desert evenings like a spell. In the beginning was the word, because that's all that we could grasp.

It would be pointless to discuss here how literally you choose to take the Bible's word. Do you find God in gravity (unmentioned in Genesis) but refuse to see His hand in evolution—do you accept the workings of time but not of genetics—do you pick and choose amongst the rhythms of nature? What do you find in the word? Does it offer an Eden of the mind, a garden for the spirit, a beginning shared by Muslims and Christians and Jews, or the literal four rivers and Edin in Western Iran, or each one of these and more? Whatever the story and its origins, we needed to come from somewhere. Subject to grandiose hopes, to occasional feelings of loss, abandonment, we seem to have needed to feel our true home had once been Paradise. So we told ourselves we were the children of perfection, born in beauty—and, as what could have been a self-fulfilling prophecy, it had promise. We gave ourselves a bloodline touched by angels, the gift of everything, there and ready for us before we could ask.

But we can also be lost, even in Paradise, and the ambivalence of the gift is there in Genesis, too. Among the fruit trees and the fertility, the admiration of prose style and our elevated origins, the arguments over heresies and textual analysis, we can miss the terrible truth in the loveliness of the book's initial verses—a truth far more immediate than expulsion from a garden we never quite knew. Here we are told that chaos was shaped into matter by God. However this came about, our universe is, indeed, filled with separate objects, among them our earth, which is, in turn, busy with substances and shapes and various forms of life, among them *Homo sapiens*, female and male. Which means, delightful though the earth can be, that we are ourselves and other things are not. We live in a universe of numberless solids that can kill and injure us. Our bodies are subject to damage and decay. Our present home is a place of drowning, crushing, burning, earthquakes, lava, diseases, suffocation, and unexpected blows. Measured by the scale of Genesis, conjured out of its spell, we are less than tiny and fatally at risk. Even left in each other's care, we are shown to be frail, and—no matter how we act and how long we last—we do all die. Even in Paradise, we never had eternal life—each of the beauties around us would have an end. And, written for the descendants of the fallen, the expelled, this version of our origins makes it clear that we will be harmed and killed by the natural laws which rule us. Nature—God resting behind it, His job done—insists that we and all we love must be hurt and then cease to be. Genesis offers no alternative creation, no other choice.

Equally, it makes plain that we are condemned to a further, intimate separation of male from female, of lover from love, that other ghost of Paradise. It tells the tale of a time when there was only one pair: one love and one beloved: made for each other. Adam, the man named for red earth, and his wife, the woman of bone, have to be with each other, and they consider nothing else— that awkward other woman, Lilith, banished to other legends. They weather remarkable trials, unseparated: They love, make love, betray and blame, feel ashamed and hide from God together. However sexist the archaic spin, the world's first marriage is recognizable to any human who has ever loved. And, beyond this, there is no thought that Eve and Adam could be possible, or fully functional, alone. With or without the knowledge of good and evil, inside or outside the garden, Eve, her husband, and her children are never entirely solitary. The only pain absent from Genesis is that of loneliness. The whole book retains that particular mercy of Paradise, that flavor of nostalgia and loss unaltered by faith or doubt—the faint aftertaste of a home where we were never lonely.

But we're far from home now. Dwarfed by our surroundings, torn apart from all that is not us, we can hardly be surprised that we sometimes call out for a help that transcends us, that breaks and makes our rules. The beauties and, more often, the horrors of Creation can drive us toward the Creator and prayer. Genesis, after Eden, has its fair share of laments. Naturally, the human mind can't be expected to produce anything like a coherent or comprehensive picture of what a supreme being might actually be like. For the unbelievers this is obvious—a nonquantity cannot be described. For the believers (myself among them) it seems equally obvious that the finite will fail to grasp the infinite. The more literal-minded and devout will, of course, demand an omnipotent, omnipresent, omnicognizant God who can also be rendered easily in print by generations of variously qualified scribblers. I tend to find—no matter how divine the available inspirations—that the assumption this might ever be possible cannot be anything other than ludicrous, if not insulting, to the deity concerned. And, of course, the Kabbalists have (who knows quite

how) calculated the dimensions of God and are among those who are happy
to totemize each of the Bible's words—to say nothing of their numerological
values—in the sure and certain hope that God is literally in the details and ac-
cessible if only stared at hard enough.

Genesis does not show us God. But it does something very human in its attempts to approach Him. The book makes its own highly subversive summary
of our efforts toward shaping a something out of Everything, a focus we can
aim our prayers at, for fear of their going astray. We write that He makes us in
His image, but we have to make Him in ours before we can reach Him. This,
in turn, provides an intoxicating pattern we can judge ourselves against: the
touch of God in our flesh that excuses and justifies, that blesses and inspires.
But the pattern is changeable, treacherous: It can also appear to be a record of
God's separation of Himself into various, mystifying forms—a testament to
contradiction, uncertainty, fear, and peculiar tenderness. This is not God the
Father but the Self that defines Itself: terrible, incomprehensible, loving, and
absurd.

First, of course, there is the handyman God, the perfect craftsman, the
watchmaker who leaves us his finest watch. This is the God we thank for sunsets and healthy children and the touch of our lovers' hair. This is the God we
used to emulate in our cathedrals, raising ourselves to make the unseen orna-
ments of our masonry as highly finished as the pulpit, or the font. This is the
God we really do find in the details, whether we are monks who see His signature in the arithmetic of flowers or anatomists who open the body and find it
carefully packed with unnecessary beauties. This is a straightforward, practical God. Our lives have risks and inevitable endings, but that's only to do with
the Fall—even outside the garden things aren't all bad. God gives us a world
that can seem to fit almost as well as Paradise, and we can be grateful and dress
up and praise Him, sing those songs. Having made perfection, He does not
then put His feet up infinitely. He still appears to tinker, like an amiable, cardi-
ganed father. Or, at least, we do most often pray with the hope that He might
interfere if we ask Him. Genesis suggests prayers can be answered.

Equally comforting for us is the idea that God is the one who names the
more overwhelming elements: earth, seas, trees, and so forth: and that, once
he arrives, Adam can manage the categories from there, trotting about the garden like a schoolboy naturalist, naming the smaller bits and pieces of Creation, the ones on an appropriately human scale. To know the true name of
something is, naturally, to have power over it. It is entirely predictable that

human authors might emphasize the elements of a creation story that portray the world not just as our home and a massively elaborate gift entrusted to us but also as something which we have a manifest destiny to dominate. It could be argued that all civilizations can be divided into those whose creation myths lead them to be part of their environment and those (the Peoples of the Book among them) who are encouraged by scripture to expropriate responsibilities for which they are not suited—"And the fear of you and dread of you shall be upon every beast of the earth . . . into your hand are they delivered. Every moving thing that liveth shall be meat for you." Taking Genesis as their cue, more and more civilizations have eliminated many of the living things that some of us presume Adam took the time to name and then Noah to save. Our own description of an indulgent Maker has left us, like spoilt children, destroying out of greed, stupidity, and simple curiosity. Today the elements with names reserved for God alone—earth, seas, trees, and so forth—are all afflicted by mankind.

Not that Genesis really expects any better of us—the picture it paints of humanity, of key figures in three major world religions, would be attractive only to the highly perverse. Once mankind gets to work on it, life beyond the garden goes a long way toward confirming the Cathar heresy that Hell is on earth. It's perhaps significant that God declares His completed Creation "very good" and that Adam is an afterthought, his goodness unspecified. Abraham, Jacob, and the rest of his descendants are beset by enemies and used to war, but they're mainly at risk from their own families. Of the first two children in the world, one—rather famously—kills the other. In Genesis your brother is never your keeper and your family is not the solid, sunny unit idealized by the religious right. Jacob betrays his brother, Esau, and his own father; Jacob's children include Joseph, whose brothers consider killing him and then simply leave him naked in a pit; Joseph then torments both them and Jacob, civility only reigning when they act as if they are all strangers. Abraham comes a hair's breadth away from sacrificing Isaac, his own son. Lot's daughters get him drunk in order to fool him into impregnating them incestuously. Throughout the book, in fact, the irresistible drive toward coupling and fertility drags almost every couple into a variety of other desperate liaisons. Adam and Eve (of course) can produce the rest of humankind only by combining incest with adultery. Both Abraham and Isaac claim their wives are their sisters, in case they are murdered for them when they are abroad, and never mind the inevitable threat to both women's virtue and the rather more ghastly risk (usually run by poor Abimelech) of households being struck barren by God for un-wittingly dishonorable advances made to apparently single women.

This is a grubby, morally compromised, violent, scheming world—one that's not exactly hard to recognize. The customs, names, and life spans are unfamiliar—the unremitting lists of begats, the land deals and the livestock, may seem strange—but the atmosphere is not. As God says of man before un-leashing the flood, "Every imagination of the thoughts of his heart was only evil, continually." But if this is the nature of man, why did God make it so? If our troubles come from the knowledge of good and evil, why is it that we ate that fruit in the first place—why were we already likely to go so wrong? Weren't we perfect before then? To make a wrong choice, we must already have had free will—that's something we've never been able to deal with too well—and didn't God know we would fail? Couldn't He foresee the Fall? Can't He foresee everything? How can Original Sin be our fault? What game is He playing? Certainly nothing as straightforward as dice.

Genesis knows our nature—yours and mine—the one it implies God gave us. It predicts my lust, my envy, my insecurities, my desire to possess, and shows very little of what I might see as my redeeming qualities. When Joseph's wicked brothers cry out, "What is this that God hath done unto us?" we can find it amusing—after all, they are sinners and their sins have found them out. But if they have a nature that allows them to sin, which seems to predetermine the directions of free will, then whose fault is that? When I do what will harm me and others, when I long for what I should not have, surely I should be able to ask, What is this that God has done to me?

There's no point asking Him, of course. Genesis shows another familiar guise of God—the Absentee. God makes the snake "subtil" (and perhaps not recognizably a snake—he goes on his belly only later, remember) and yet does nothing to prevent the inevitable, and frankly rather rapid, application of ser-pentine subtlety. God is elsewhere when Eve and Adam eat the fateful apple, likewise when Cain kills Abel. God somehow loses sight of Sarah's maid Hagar when she is unjustly cast out and catches up with her only when she pauses by the well. This is the same God who has only heard of Sodom's evil and has to send angels out on reconnaissance. God is not there when the in-nocent Joseph is attacked and sold into slavery—He is only "with him" once he's unjustly imprisoned on the word of Potiphar's wife.

We recognize this God. At Wounded Knee and in Auschwitz, Kanpur, Soweto, Srebrenica, Sabra-Shatila, Belfast, in every other killing field—we find ourselves asking, Where was God? What is more frightening—that God could be withdrawn from a part of His Creation, or that He would actually be there, unseen but looking on—a voluntarily powerless voyeur, while Pol Pot and Stalin, Kissinger and Papa Doc, Eichmann and Idi Amin and the rest of the bloody regiment were both undeniably monstrous and unmistakably human? The torturers, the murderers, the rapists, the wife beaters, the child molesters, the extortionists, the tax-avoiding city gents and self-serving politicians who impoverish and mutilate by proxy, all the fathers who terrify—the Lord God made them all.

Why? Why make us so vicious? Why abandon us in such savage lives? We reach up with unanswered words, not knowing if God has hidden from us or if we have turned from Him. We see humankind and its Maker first part ways in Genesis. But not before we've learned that we're alike, that we're in His own image—an image that includes "the terror of God." This isn't God the Father, yet, but there seems to be a family resemblance. Genesis describes a little of man's terror, his small-scale misery, deceit, kidnapping, rape, and bloodshed. The epic havoc is left to the Destroyer God—the one we half admire and would wish more powerful yet, as long as He's on our side. Because it scares us when God appears to stand on the sidelines, but it can be even more terrifying when He does intervene. Acts of God, after all, are the precursors of insurance claims and closed-casket funerals.

It's that divine touch in our beginning, that bloodline—we see it in ruined cities, poisoned rivers, the ingenuity of bombs. We humans take after the Destroyer. It may not be what we want, but we can't seem to help it. In the same way, I see my parents' faults emerging in me—in my choice to try out my father's temper, or my mother's martyred love—that tendency toward brooding secrecy—and do I lie like my father, or only like myself? I can ask why it seems so difficult to emulate their finer qualities, their moments of nobility and dignity. I can ask why it seems so difficult to follow the gentler, more merciful God. Genesis offers a harsh answer—the path that mankind follows is frequently bloody, downward, dark: We find it difficult to create, we rarely recognize what is blessed. If this is meant as a warning, we have tended to use it as an alibi rather than take it to heart.

But there are degrees of wickedness. We don't all fall, all the time. And as long as we try to be good, we hope that we may be protected, that the Destroyer will be on our side—appalling, but ours. Sodom and Gomorrah are annihilated because both cities contain not even ten pure souls. The Tower of

Babel is never completed, because it is a sign of overweening arrogance, an attempt to touch Heaven punished by the removal of man's common language, the word that was with us and made us strong. And, of course, there's the ultimate intervention—the deluge. God looks out at the evil of men and simply decides to start again. It's the story that captivates schoolchildren, that has counterparts in Babylonian, Greek, and Indian myths, and may well reflect a communal memory of an actual, cataclysmic flood. Whatever its historical basis, Genesis uses the story of Noah to reassure. God could do this again at any time, but He says He chooses not to. He seems almost apologetic—"I will not again curse the ground any more for man's sake. . . . While the earth remaineth, seed-time and harvest, and cold and heat, and summer and winter, and day and night shall not cease." So we have that to rely on, at least. And from now on there will be the rainbow, reminding God (how can He forget?) of His promise not to kill us all. If God can be a monster, He can be with us, contained by His word.

And our goodness may be defended by our adherence to His word. The world of Genesis exists before the Commandments, but God is already commanding. He asks for flesh offerings, doesn't think much of vegetables and fruit. Some animals are classified as clean and some are not. Bloodshed should be answered with bloodshed. The ark must be built and be built just so, the animals collected according to divine instruction. God tells His favorites where and how to live. Disobey and you lose Paradise, are blasted with brimstone, exiled, turned to salt.

But God may be moved by words—those prayers may be worthwhile. Cain the murderer haggles a mark of protection out of the Almighty, and his blood is not spilled to answer Abel's slaughter. Abraham can bargain God down to a figure of only ten men to save Sodom—although there weren't even ten, which perhaps God knew all along. And Lot asks God to save Zoar for him to live in when Sodom and Gomorrah are destroyed. God even consents to a particularly convoluted selection process to pick out Rebecca, the future wife of Isaac—although He must have had all the time in the universe, so why not? And God makes promises, too. He selects Abraham when nothing in particular recommends him and promises him land in perpetuity and the right to found a people. He promises the former black sheep Jacob much the same. Abraham, of course, has to pay for his privilege by circumcising all the males in his care—and he also must consent to a change of names for him and his wife—God gives you a name to make you His. He'll do this again, turning

Jacob to Israel. This is the God of mercy. He makes coats of skins for naked Eve and Adam. He catches Himself in thorns, descends as an angel, sets a ram for Abraham to sacrifice instead of Isaac. Perhaps He does love us, after all.

Or perhaps we needed to write that He does. Certainly, some of His expressions of love can trouble us today. We all want to be chosen of God—the promise of land and dominion to His favorites in Genesis makes a simple, unequivocal bedrock for a number of fundamentalist claims. The Christian Crusades and the British Empire justified political agendas of massacre and theft with the help of declarations that God was with them. A story written by children of Israel, disingenuously promising them land in perpetuity, continues to bathe that land in blood. Even beyond the early political spin, Genesis shows that whatever God the Giver provides, the gift is ambivalent—the beautiful and fatal world, the tempting and condemning fruit—why would a promised land be any different? The ram in thorns God produces is necessary only because He has forced Abraham to the brink of killing the son he waited a hundred years to conceive—Isaac, his obsession and his future as a patriarch. The skin garments are handed over as the gates of Paradise are closing with Adam and Eve on the wrong side. Those clean and unclean animals aren't actually specified, and sometimes their classifications seem not to matter at all. Circumcision makes a covenant for Abraham, but when the Hivites are circumcised, their menfolk are still slaughtered for the sake of Jacob's daughter—even while Jacob's camp contains "strange gods." Cain gets away with murder.

In Genesis—as in the world—God can appear to make no sense. Sexual misconduct of all kinds seems to be accepted, unless it isn't. Murder is fine, unless it's not. Which is to say, God's favorites can commit adultery and kill, sleep with handmaidens and relatives and be either only moderately chastised or entirely unpunished. Even amongst God's chosen there is an arbitrary quality to God's decisions, which is terrifying when combined with omnipotence. Abel the hunter is loved, Esau the hunter is not. Noah gets drunk, passes out in a state of undress, and his son, Ham, sees him naked by accident—still, Ham and his offspring, the children of Canaan, are cursed forever. Esau is swindled out of his birthright and even his father's blessing by Jacob, who then goes on to steal an extra wife from Laban—a wife Jacob subsequently hates. Jacob's punishment for this is service to Laban that only makes Jacob rich. And God shows Jacob "the gate of Heaven" and then forms an angel to wrestle him and touch him to the bone—"I have seen God face to face," Jacob says, "and my life is preserved." The brothers who founded the Twelve Tribes have their good points—"Naphtali is a hind let loose: He giveth goodly words." And "Joseph is a fruitful bough." But this is the same Joseph so soured by his early trials that he inflicts emotional torture even on his own father. His eleven brothers were the men who left him to the pit and the slavers. Simeon and Levi are murderers with "instruments of cruelty . . . in their habitations," and Reuben has defiled his father's bed and is "unstable as water," while "Benjamin shall ravin as the wolf" and "Dan shall be a serpent by the way"—the book ending as it began, with the threat of a snake.

A believer could be forgiven for thinking that Calvin was right—that places in Heaven are reserved for the justified, however they transgress. God, it seems, commands but is not just. He kills my grandfather but not Pinochet. When I keep to His rules, I don't benefit: When I break them, things go wrong. I have the capacity to love children and yet I have no child. I pray for the relief of solitude and I am alone. I see the good suffer and the guilty prosper and I pray to God the first anesthetist, the One who made Adam sleep while he lost his rib and feel no pain. I pray for the relief of pain. Genesis brings us the wonder of acknowledging God but also its despair. The more its authors try to describe God, the more we fear, the less we understand.

So it is hardly a surprise that the book's only references to real companionship with God are elusive and brief. How Eve and Adam speak to God in the garden is a secret we have lost. And later, almost as an aside, we are told that Enoch "walked with God." There is no mention of rituals or bargaining between them, no commandments or promises, only perhaps the thought of an amiable stroll, of companions who go forward, side by side, no words needed. Perhaps God isn't so pleased by singing and praying, after all, perhaps it is silence He craves, the kind of relaxed stillness that grows between old companions. We are here, after all, and—should we choose to believe it—so is He and the world is as it is and we have free will to try to change what we don't like. Perhaps God allows His favorites to sin because He is not so very interested in sin, because it has its own penalties and rewards, morality operating like evolution—something that is unavoidable but takes time. This is emotionally unsatisfying and calls for the patience of saints, but it may also be true.

From Australia, to Scotland, to 3:57 A.M., and without explanation, there I am. And my parents were themselves and no one else for reasons they could not fully grasp: the shouting, the moments of violence, the silences and crying: I would have liked to understand them, but I never truly will. And my

own life: the love and fear of men I have from my father, the love and fear of
tenderness I have from my mother; too old still to be single, too old still to be
childless, an end to the bloodline; locked in a profession built of words—what
sense that really makes is beyond me. Perhaps it is intended to be meaningless,
or simply an encouragement to prayer, or to silence. I can't tell.

The God of Genesis, a God I recognize, is inexplicable. I try to be glad for
those dashes of unforeseen compromise and kindness—the times we don't get
what we deserve, but better. I never ask, for instance, why Mother Teresa is
dead and I'm alive, why my friend Paul was killed by brain cancer, and although I am much less good and useful, I was not. Above all Genesis, not to
mention reality, seems colored by the peculiar, magisterially dark sense of
humor which a remarkable number of religions agree is wholly characteristic
of God. He is, if not playing, then playful. Which, for example, allows me to
call Him Him. Never the Father for me, but I still think of Him as male, because my nature inclines to the physical love of men. It makes sense for me
that part of my longing for God would be flavored with the longing for a lover,
the other half to complete the pair—the precise love it would seem God refuses to grant me. Naturally, He must actually encompass every possible sexual identity and the absolute absence of sex. It is absurd to address my Creator
at all—we are too different—but if I must, I would rather do it with love, rather
have it as a kind of private joke with the Almighty.

This kind of God—incomprehensible, distant, ludic—leaves us with the
loneliness of adulthood and the responsibilities of a world where actions always bring reactions, often of an unforeseen kind. We can choose to pray, but
prayer may not bring the desired results. Many religions agree that prayer al-
ters the pray-er, if not the prayed-to, or the world. Prayer may, in fact, operate
according to natural laws, a closed system, God at one remove. Genesis offers
tantalizing suggestions that it does still constitute some kind of communication, however unpredictable, with a God we can't meet face-to-face but who is
still willing to appear in dreams, in words. This may not be what we want, but
it seems to be what we've got. Only Enoch, the quiet friend, gets a better deal,
living 365 years and then "he was not; for God took him"—the one human in
the whole of the Bible's first book who gets to go home.

More redemption than this is hard to find in Genesis. Still, its closing
verses do tell us to "fear not" and do attempt to explain that we are praying and
dying, loving and murdering, hurting and joking, living within a Creation we
are not made to understand. With every pain, every despair, we have to hope,

as Joseph says, that "God meant it unto good" because we have very little choice, beyond the possible relief of self-destruction. Our position is, in itself, not unamusing, the darkest of black jokes. Such a high level of absurdity—a beguiling, lifelong trap constructed of freedoms: torture and joy if you love it, torture and joy if you don't—this can really be bearable only if it's funny, unless you can arrange to go insane. Creation is funny if there's no God, no designer for the trap. And, naturally, it's funnier still if there is God, if He's been with us all along, since the beginning.

NEW YORK, NEW YORK

Peace be within your walls,
and security within your towers!

PSALM 122:6

THIS is how it started: We were under the city, moving from one side to another as if nothing had happened above. The hum and screech of metal wheels on metal tracks, the muted hiphop of other people's headphones, all the sounds that push a soul inside itself, that make the subway an accidental temple underground, they opened our eyes and woke us up on a Sunday morning even as the sway of the car rocked and lulled. The night before, we'd been kept awake by the noise of a city still making sense of disaster. There was a Puerto Rican Pentecostal church two stories below where we were staying in Brooklyn, and for days then weeks after the crash they had preached and sung and screamed every night, gospel jazz beginning at sunset, pounding on through evening until the glow of buildings that were no longer there lit up the horizon. There was an electric piano; there were drums; there were cymbals. There were grandmas quaking and stomping and wailing, and fat little boys sucked from the street into the sanctuary, into a rumble of prayer as constant as the train's. Next to the church stood a garage that was a nighttime refuge for an armada of ice cream trucks. There was no traffic, but had there been it would have been turned back because the trucks blocked the street, engines idling. Already October, the last days of ice cream, the season was ending badly. Some of the drivers moaned, some cursed, some polished prayer beads. All of them were men, many of them Pakistani, most of them Muslim. Bearded or clean-shaven, all were devout enough to decorate their trucks with the signs and symbols of folk religion: the double-thumbed gold hands of Fatima, and pairs of blue eyes crafted from glass to stare down the always-roaming Evil Eye. The trucks themselves were the most powerful totems of all: Mister Frostee, Mister Freeze, Mister Yum Yum!, decaled bumper to bell with red-white-and-blue bomb pops, glitter-studded green sparkle pops, dreamsicles in strawberry, chocolate, and orange. Their jingles never-ending so long as they idled, merry chimes and whistles rang over arguments in Urdu, Pashto, and English. The smoky sky was hurting business, but what could be done? It was not a time for sweet things. More and more ice cream trucks pulled up to join the debate, five, six, nine, each with its own treacly melody, loud enough to be heard in the farthest corners of housing projects, as the holy rolling jazz kept thumping into the night, tinny, surging, relentless.

The door at the far end of the subway car slid open and a man walked through with a plastic bag in one hand, a beat up Starbucks cup in the other. He said, "Ladies and gentlemen, may I have your attention please? I understand after all that's happening times are tough." He moved from face to face, holding any eye that would have him. "But the homeless still homeless, so anything you can give would be much appreciated. Thank you, God bless. Thank you, God bless." Then he began to sing, his voice thin and hard and aggressive, somewhere between supplication and threat. "What . . . a friend . . . we have in . . . Jesus . . ."

He stopped in front of us mid-song and said something, a mumble lost in the screech of the train pulling into a station. He reached into his plastic bag, digging deep for something he seemed to want to sell or give to us, but we each put a dollar in his cup before we could receive his offering. Then we went back to the surface, scene of the crime.

Manhattan: Even when the smoke cleared, the smell of it was everywhere, like something buried beneath the city, seeping up through the ground. It was a stink bad enough to make you fold up the paper on a Sunday morning, to force you from a good seat at a sidewalk café. Bad enough to make you look around for a place to escape the reek and to push you inside, even if the most convenient place was a church, a quaint little pile of red bricks shaded from the pale white sun by oak trees and surrounded by gardens, a chapel too far from the crater to be roped off by policemen but close enough for a northerly breeze to wrap it in the smell of everything still burning: plastic, concrete, ink, melted rivers of gold bullion, Pentium chips, bits of bone, scraps of leather, gabardine. The street was empty, the church was open. From within, the pipes of an organ promised distraction.

The procession had already begun. A young boy swinging a silver censer led a long line of priests and deacons, a dozen women and men in identical cassocks, equal in all ways but their accessories: glasses, beards, sandals, pearls. *Step. Swing. Step. Swing.* The altar boy focused on the floor's hardwood planks as the toes of his hightops peeked one at a time from under his robe. Careful not to trip and clang into the pews, the boy and his censer masked the stench sneaking in from the street, but incense thick as diesel exhaust doesn't make it any easier to breathe.

We slid into the only available seats, a few rows back from a gang of roly-poly leather men fresh from a night of clubbing, their heads shaved and their upper bodies hairy and bare but for their shiny black vests. More conservative, near-identical congregants lined every other pew, handsome men with torsos like V's wrapped tight in summer-weight cashmere, black, grey, one or two in beige, one hundred heads of close-cropped hair touched with silver. Behind us sat a tall blond woman wearing a designer cowboy hat and a matching white ventilator mask, like the haute couture sheriff of a toxic new frontier.

St. Luke in the Fields, one of New York's oldest Episcopalian churches, had once been a refuge from yellow fever, the diseased crowding its sanctuary even as they bled from their mouths and their eyes. A century and a half later the congregation found itself dying of a disease that didn't even have a name. When we asked a church worker the number of parishioners who had been killed by AIDS, he refused to hazard a guess. Dodging the question the way only a chronic survivor can, he told us, "Oh, I'd rather just pray," as if God was some kind of silver lining.

At the front of the church, a small man in white vestments stepped to a mahogany pulpit and gripped it as if he meant to pull it up by its roots. His hair was the color of steel wool, his beard darker but thin. When he spoke, he pursed his lips between phrases, looking at his congregation more than at his sermon notes. "Today is the Feast of All Saints," he said. "A day for remembering the dead."

The priest had just returned from a sabbatical in Rome. He had decided to dedicate his first sermon in months to the memory of the city he'd left and the future of the city to which he'd returned.

"The Feast of All Saints," he said, "marks a day long ago when Rome was made holy, like New York now, by ashes and bone." His voice didn't so much fill the sanctuary as settle like dry snow, erasing the colors that separate present from past. Like the cloud of incense, like the smoke of burning buildings, it seemed to stop time, opening the morning wide enough to contain an alternate creation myth, another tale of an unlikely beginning.

"When Romulus defeated his brother Remus for the land that would become the eternal city," said the priest, "he ordered his men to take up a plow and make a furrow in the shape of a circle. The city that was to grow within its circumference was to be itself a temple, a city devoted to life. Inside the circle would be holy ground, outside profane. Within the city's borders would walk the living, and beyond them the dead were cast."

A charge of recognition rippled through the church. The city. The dead. A circle like a hole in the world.

The story continued: Soon came the Christians with their resurrection dreams, lingering in the boneyards. They baptized each other by the graves, held feasts and celebrations at the doors of tombs. The tombs of the martyrs.

"At the tombs of the martyrs," the priest said, "power"—he paused—"began to emerge."

He breathed now into the microphone, scanning the room, letting his congregation catch up. To these battered believers, martyrs were not Christians eaten by lions, nor a generation of men devoured by disease. These days martyrs were men who flew airplanes into skyscrapers. The woman in the cowboy hat adjusted her mask. The leather men shifted uncomfortably, squeaking in their seats. The new martyrs seemed more frightening than the old. None of us needed to be reminded of their power. It was in the air.

And yet, the priest told the congregation, the ancient martyrs and the modern ones had something in common: They both brought death into the city. The terrorists with their airplanes; the Christians with their bones.

"Bones. Living Christians dug up the dead and carried their remains within the city walls. From outside the circle drawn by Romulus's men, into its center." Land reserved by old gods for the living was resanctified by a new god for the dead.

Imagine the shock of seeing corpses carried into the city. Something like a 747 screaming past your office window on a Tuesday morning. *What the fuck was that?* Soldiers run from their barracks, their swords drawn, too late to stop the martyrs. Law-abiding citizens recoil, hold lemons beneath their noses to ward off the stench, leave good seats at sidewalk cafés. At dinner parties and in pubs they say to one another, "Everything has changed," and they curse the name *martyr.* Those who claim *martyr* bring death from the margins to the center of our lives.

"I am haunted by that knowledge and that image," the priest said. "Here in a city where the *center* has become shunned and forbidden."

Which city, New York, or Rome? Both. Either. Take your pick. In the dirt of Italy, in the gray mud of Ground Zero, the living dug for the bones of those they had lost, sweating as they turned the earth, their hands pawing as they came closer. They dug until the last layer of dust was carted away, revealing the missing and the missed, wondering with each scrap found, How many times can the world end? How many times can it begin again? In Rome the bodies uncovered would later remake an empire: yellow bones, bits of skin like leather, wispy strands of hair, fingernails curved like claws. These are the ugly, far-back beginnings of all that has come of Christendom, even this elegant West Village church. In New York it will be no different. When the living dug here they found office equipment, smoldering chemicals, gold bricks, still more bones. If that long-ago Roman grave-robbing operation today is given the respectable name the Feast of All Saints, what will this awful new beginning be called?

The priest braced himself on the pulpit, deepened his voice, dropped his professorial tone.

"Names," he said, "are dangerous."

He nodded at the silent call-and-response that attends a high church sermon.

Names.

Yes.

Dangerous.

Amen.

"Names," he repeated, "are dangerous." The nature of the beginning we would make of this tragedy had everything to do with the name we would assign to those who had tried to make it an end.

"Martyrs?" No. Martyrs, he said, don't kill, they are killed. Martyrs don't storm the city, they are carried like kings across its borders. Martyrs don't desecrate the city, they sanctify it by their faith. And yet still the killers said the word *martyr,* and meant themselves.

"How can we reclaim it?" he asked. "How can we find a meaning in the word *martyr* that again makes it our own?"

He waited, and the congregation searched. Sunbeams the color of dried sunflowers filtered through the stained glass, drawing lines through the lingering smoke like a scaffold of light. Lines. Buildings. Circles. Yes. We remembered the priest's reference to the beginning of Rome.

"We go to the root of things," he called. We dig.

"Know that the word *martyr* means 'witness,' " he said. "Its meaning derives not from the violence that surrounds it but from the vision it requires. Let us reclaim the name *martyr,* then, as 'witness.' "

There was that Christian spin again—*reclaim*—making a sacrament of digging up bones when they fail to rise on their own.

But he wasn't speaking of that kind of martyr anymore; not victims or murderers but witnesses to the crime. Those who saw the story; those who tell it. The leather men. The gas-mask cowgirl. Us. You. Believers or not, history determines that we all bear witness. How many times can the world end? How many times can it begin again? As often as you survive. As often as you tell the story. The apocalypse is always now, but so is the creation.

After the sermon came the baptism of a little girl named Emma, a bundle of milk and roses in a white jumper. She was attended by two mothers—thin, striking, raven-haired women dressed in matching black pantsuits—and a grandmother just as slender and sharp, the three of them gathered around the baptismal font like Macbeth's witches at their caldron, won over by the occasion and their giggling baby girl.

Emma reached out and slapped the brass bowl. It was all a joy to her, even the water dribbled on her head from a silver pitcher. Imagine it through Emma—shiny shiny smooth warm mama man smile sparkle wet cold deep sounds: "Emma, receive the holy light." Emma squirmed in her mother's arms and stretched her little hands to grab for the candle. She wanted to get that holy light!

The pipes of the church's organ swelled—that weird, spiraling hysteria at the high end of the scale, raising the eyebrows of the music's bass foundations. Highs and lows wrenching us apart, making us all into Emma, nothing but sensation and reflection—hot and cold, bright and dark, hard metal and soft flesh, smoke rising and a building collapsing—as the pulse and melody of the music collided in the final phrases of the song.

The congregation stood, stretched, and shook off the hot sun that beamed through the windows. The priest took up his post by the door, patting backs and gripping hands, smiling and laughing. Emma's mothers received well-wishers, the deacons preened in their vestments. We slipped past and started walking down Hudson Street, into a cool breeze that stank of burning.

Burning for burning, wound for wound . . .

EXODUS 21:25

EXODUS

BY FRANCINE PROSE

I REMEMBER, with near perfect clarity. It is one of those sweet spring evenings that, in childhood, seem to last forever. My family has come to celebrate Passover at the home of my great-aunt and -uncle, in Brooklyn. Everything about it thrills me. The warmth of the brightly lit dining room, the long table set with the best dishes and a Seder plate, the exuberance and raucousness of the relatives, so much livelier and louder than my own well-behaved, scrupulously middle-class parents.

But what I love most—what is, for me, the highlight of the evening, more exciting than giddy conspiracies with my brother and cousins about how we will hide the ceremonial matzoh and ransom it back for money—are the plagues. Their recitation is by far my favorite part of the Passover Seder. As each plague is named aloud, we dip our fingers into our cups and transfer one drop of the delicious, sugary wine to our plates.

Blood.
Frogs.
Vermin.
Flies.
Murrain.
Boils.
Hail.

Locusts.

Darkness.

The killing of the firstborn.

It is the only time in my life when playing with my food is not only sanctioned but encouraged, and not just food but wine, which I and my cousins drink until we are fairly hammered. After the dipping is finished, I have to fight the impulse to lick my finger, resisting the temptation out of some cuckoo primitive fear that, if I do so, I might catch one of the plagues we have just so lovingly listed.

And what a glorious list it was! How mysterious and stirring! Some of the plagues—frogs, locusts, boils—were irresistibly easy to visualize. I was frightened of insects, and so instantly comprehended the horror of an infestation of vermin. Others presented more of a challenge. What was with the blood, exactly? Was it just in the rivers and the water supply? Or did it creep over the banks and run red in the streets of Cairo? "Murrain" made no sense at all. What could a livestock disease have meant to a city kid with basically no idea about the operation of the food chain?

Such mysteries were at once illuminated and further deepened by the woodcut illustrations in the Passover Haggadah. Each the size of a postage stamp, all ten were crowded onto one page. It was impossible to make out what was going on in the crowded images, though by looking really hard I could discern a few tantalizing clues. Frogs falling from the sky. Bony, moribund cows. Tiny figures covered with hideous splotches that could only have been boils. The indistinctness, the fact that the images seem to be communicating in an indecipherable code—along with the foreign, exotic, and ancient quality of the woodcuts themselves—only added to their creepy mystique. I could have stared at them forever. It was like watching certain horror films: forbidden and disturbing, therefore sexy and alluring.

Like sex, and like a horror film, the plagues built toward a climax, an orgasm of mayhem and blood. The slaying of the firstborn. In the final woodcut, a figure—was it an avenging angel?—held a scythe (or was it a sword?) poised and ready to do the maximum damage to the hapless, sleeping Egyptian households. The last-ditch special effect, the pulling out all the stops. The technique that worked, when nothing else had.

Never once, during all those years, during all those Seders, did I think—or was it pointed out to me—that those plagues had human victims, that the sufferers from boils and blood, the ones whose houses filled with frogs and locusts were human beings like myself. Around the Seder table, my parents and my relatives—deeply kind and compassionate people who would have been appalled to hear that a child was in pain or danger—never seemed to notice that the Egyptian firstborn had once been living human children. And it simply never crossed my mind that the firstborn whom the angel slaughtered could (except for a few particulars of place and time) just as easily have been me.

There are many reasons, I suppose, to enjoy and admire and be inspired by Exodus. Its themes could hardly be more stirring—or more beautiful, really. Oppression and liberation, courage, self-determination. Nothing less than the human spirit yearning to break free, then breaking free, screwing up, suffering, wandering, and painfully, slowly starting to learn how to live as a new, hopeful nation. It's the Founding Fathers, the Emancipation Proclamation, with highly cinematic hoodoo: The way that Moses and his brother, Aaron, make people listen to them is by magically changing their walking sticks into snakes. Exodus is also, as many—including, most notably, Cecil B. DeMille—have realized, action-packed. There's little in the Bible to equal, chapter for chapter, its roller coaster of incident, suspense, magic, hesitations, missteps, punishments and sufferings, renewals and redemptions.

And brutality. From the start, Exodus involves a series of bloodbaths—outbreaks of state-sponsored and divinely ordained carnage directed principally at children. It is a story of liberation in which whole populations are oppressed, enslaved, tormented, nearly wiped out. The victims, with the exception of the soldiers drowned in the Red Sea, are almost entirely civilians.

But what a fabulous spectacle! The burning bush! The parting of the Red Sea! Who would want to spoil the excitement and fun by sitting there and thinking that those Egyptian soldiers, flailing around in the churning waters, may have left behind in Cairo wives and children who would mourn them— minus, of course, the firstborn, who the soldiers themselves must have been mourning even as Pharaoh ordered them after the Hebrews, into the desert and into the sea.

Even children understand that Exodus is only a movie, that those are actors, not real people, movie deaths, not real ones. And as children, we learn from the movies that the deaths of our enemies are good deaths, to be celebrated and cheered.

• • •

Exodus begins by striking an ominous note of political anxiety that will echo until its last chapters: The Jews are prospering and multiplying, and their presence is a liability that makes the new Pharaoh nervous. He enslaves them, makes them carry impossible weights on their shoulders and break their backs sowing the fields, but still they continue to multiply and grow.

There is always trouble when one population begins to worry about the birth rate of another.

And so the book's first slaughter of children gets under way. Pharaoh directs the midwives to kill every Jewish male baby. But the women resist. Not only do they spare the babies but, when Pharaoh demands an explanation, they play with his head a little, claiming that the Hebrew women are so fertile that the midwives always arrive too late to assist at the births and murder the babies. So baby Moses survives, is found in the bulrushes and adopted by Pharaoh's daughter—who hands him back to his mother to nurse and raise him.

The rest—the burning bush, the staff into the serpent—is pure fairy tale, the sorts of signs and wonders that would separate a Greek hero from the crowd, or reveal a new Dalai Lama, or inspire a prophet. The twist, of course, is God, not just another character but an absolute. The voice that speaks to Moses from the burning bush is powerful and succinct. It's the voice of God introducing himself: I am that I am.

Moses speaks, Pharaoh listens. God hardens the Egyptian ruler's heart. And now comes the long, painful back-and-forth of let-my-people-go, a battle that God warns Moses He himself will make Moses lose. And it happens just as God says. Pharaoh orders the Jews to slave harder.

Warnings and threats. Promises and failures to keep them. Warnings, promises, threats, and lies. In other words, end-stage diplomacy.

And before you know it, blood.

The pools and rivers turn red. The fish die. There is nothing to drink. Recall your horror at drawing a bath and finding the water is dark. And that is only rust. Imagine if it were blood. Then it gets worse. Frogs in the beds and ovens, swarms of flies, locusts stripping the trees and blackening the earth, unprecedented and murderous hail. Darkness.

And all this is merely prelude to the grand finale, to the plague that succeeds where the others have not, the one that does the trick, that will cause Pharaoh, after all his stubbornness, not merely to let the Hebrews go but to expel them from Egypt. And that, of course, is the killing of the firstborn.

Unlike the massacre of the Hebrew baby boys, which Pharaoh arranges rather casually, almost capriciously, the massacre orchestrated by God is carefully prepared. "And all the firstborn in the land of Egypt shall die, from the firstborn of Pharaoh that sitteth upon his throne, even unto the firstborn of the maidservant that is behind the mill; and all the firstborn of beasts. And there shall be a great cry throughout the land of Egypt, such as there was none like it, nor shall be like it any more."

It is genocide without apology. And at the end of this dire prophecy comes the most important sentence of all, the real beginning of what the rest of Exodus will so ferociously and zealously continue: the demarcation of difference, the establishment of a separation between Israel and the other peoples and tribes, the forging of an identity, the birth of a nation, and all the exclusiveness that it will require: "But against any of the children of Israel shall not a dog move his tongue, against man or beast; that ye may know how the Lord doth put a difference between the Egyptians and Israel."

The killing of the firstborn is preceded by the first of the numerous series of almost obsessive, almost compulsively meticulous instructions that appear throughout Exodus—detailed protocols that, again, will form the identity, the tradition, and the history that will forever distinguish the Hebrews from their neighbors. The time and the manner of the animal sacrifice is ordained. It must be not just any beast but a lamb "without blemish," a year-old male. Present and future feasts—the celebration we now know as Passover—will be observed by eating unleavened bread, though, it should be noted, uncircumcised foreigners should not be permitted to partake of the ritual meal. And the blood of the lambs is to be used to mark the doors of the homes that the angel of death will spare in the otherwise merciless search for the children who die in order that God's chosen people can win their freedom.

And it came to pass exactly as the Lord predicted, or warned: "At midnight the Lord smote all the firstborn in the Land of Egypt, from the firstborn of Pharaoh that sat on his throne unto the firstborn of the captive that was in the dungeon: and all the firstborn of cattle. And Pharaoh rose up in the night, he and all his servants, and all the Egyptians; and there was a great cry in Egypt; for there was not a house where there was not one dead."

For there was not a house where there was not one dead.

Search "Ten Plagues" on the Internet. The first site that comes up contains a series of suggestions for "fun activities" connected with the plagues. For example, the plague of blood might be represented by putting red food coloring in the water glasses, the bathroom sinks, even the dog's water bowl. Cut out frogs from green construction paper ("bend the legs to make the frogs look as if they were jumping"), and put them everywhere—in the drawers, the cereal boxes, the shower. White dots punched from paper and Scotch-taped to the skin will eventually approximate the itching and irritation of lice. Do the same with red dots, and you've got your boils. Putting ice cubes around the house will remind you of hail. Cover the windows and turn out the lights and presto! the plague of darkness.

I'm hardly breathing as I scroll down to find out how we will reenact the killing of the firstborn. The answer, it seems, is obvious. Red ribbon tacked to the front door will warn the avenging angel to move past without stopping. "When the neighbors"—who doubtless will be curious by now—"ask what the ribbon is for, you can witness to them!"

One assumes that those most likely to engage in this fun activity are religious folk, people of faith. Yet nowhere is it suggested that they pray for the souls of the murdered Egyptian children. That would seem excessive, I suppose, and besides, it's not what religion does. In theory, perhaps, we're advised to love our enemies, but in practice faith has provided a host of reasons to hate those who don't believe in the same God we do.

To read Exodus is to watch the dawning of those rancors and divisions. God promises the Hebrews liberation and protection, but ultimately it's a setup. The actual consequences could hardly involve more strife, more danger and risk: thousands of years of warfare, of attack and defense, of suffering and bloodshed brought about by the way that belief so readily translates into the desire for the wealth and territory of those who practice another religion, into prayers that God will kill their children.

This was what I celebrated as I dipped my finger into my cup and watched the little puddle of wine in my saucer grow. How ironic that I, a child, should have rejoiced in this evidence that the lives and deaths of children meant nothing, that they were merely tools and pawns to be used or eliminated because of political exigencies. First the Hebrew children, then the Egyptian children. And thousands of years later, an American child dipped her finger in her wine and learned—without being told—that the suffering of the innocent, the murder of children, was not merely pardonable but a holy thing when the freedom of our group was at stake.

It all puts a peculiar slant on the Ten Commandments, which Moses receives a little later in the book. Is it just coincidence, just literary parallelism, that the number of commandments is the same as the number of the plagues?

Somehow, I think not. The rules of conduct, the rules of life, are meant to remind us of the tidy progression that brought death to the Egyptians. First we learn about the punishment, about God's ability to wreak havoc and mayhem on the transgressor; then we learn the ways by which that punishment can be avoided. And what exactly does "Thou Shalt Not Kill" mean in the context of all those slain children, those drowned Egyptian soldiers? The image of Charlton Heston coming down from the mountain proudly bearing the holy Commandments has become, for me, impossible to distinguish from that of the NRA spokesman brandishing a rifle in the air above his head and warning us that we will have to pry it from his cold, dead fingers.

What bothers me most about Exodus is what should make me admire it most—that is, it tells us a truth about how people behave, something I would rather not hear or know. Humans clump together in arbitrary, tightly knit groups that want to kill other groups and occupy their territory. Other people's children are merely bodies. Hebrew, Egyptian, Palestinian, Afghan, Tutsi, Kurd. It hardly matters who they are, as long as they are not our own.

This is as true now as it was when Moses was in Egypt. Though I am willing to admit it, I don't have to celebrate it, I don't have to dip my finger in my wineglass and extract sweet drops for the time when my group, my nation, triumphed at a terrible cost, when it was our turn to show another group who was boss. Nor do I have to thank God for making this point by killing the Egyptian children, just as God first presumably inspires the Egyptians to attempt to do to the Jews.

I no longer go to Passover Seders. I plead a prior engagement. Nor is my desire to attend rekindled when I hear, from time to time, about well-intentioned attempts to execute end runs around the problem of celebrating the killing of the firstborn. Years ago, someone told me about attending a Seder in which the names of Nazi concentration camps were substituted for the list of plagues. Dachau. *Drop.* Buchenwald. *Drop.* Auschwitz. A drop of wine for each camp. And somehow that seemed worse than the original, a betrayal of the text and of the true meaning of the Exodus, of even the hope of liberation.

I miss the warmth, the food, the ceremony, the comfort and fellowship of family. But I just can't do it. I can't sit at the table and dip my finger in the wine and celebrate—deify, in fact—this early, terrible instance of genocide without apology.

POOLESVILLE, MARYLAND

The steps of a good man are ordered by the Lord . . .

PSALM 37:23

WE were on the road less than a week when we learned a friend of ours had been killed in a car crash on his way home from a conference. He had been a seat-belt man, a family man, just days shy of a paternity leave to look after his second son. He used to say he owned three types of shoes—shoes for work, shoes for home, shoes for in between—and he never wore a pair for a task for which it wasn't intended. His life had been that ordered. He had been a conservative man—because, he would say, conservatives understand consequences—but after the 2000 election he had wandered around for days unshaven, his blond hair uncombed. He had been unable to reconcile his candidate's tactics with the principles he had thought they shared. Then the Supreme Court had handed down its decision, and our friend had suddenly seemed reborn. "There's a new sheriff in town," he would say. "There are rules. We must play by them."

After his memorial service in Washington, we drove through the night and woke up in one of those Appalachian mountain villages visited by the sun for just a short time after it creeps over the eastern hills, before it sinks behind the ridge on the other side of town.

"Where you headed?" the clerk asked us when we checked out of our motel.

We shrugged. The city shoes on our feet were caked in West Virginia mud; that's how ordered our lives were.

"Don't really know yet," we said.

"I know what you mean."

The clerk was a slight young man with a Caesar haircut, a silver loop ear-ring, and a rainbow of woven bracelets on his wrists. Perfectly respectable anywhere but there, where the kindest locals probably called him "artistic." He looked like he might have preferred "trapped." He wore a "Free Tibet" button pinned to his uniform and brown wooden *mala* beads tucked under his collar. He was a Buddhist, he said, though only a bit of one. To him, Tibet was not so much his adopted faith's promised land as it was an idea, and free-ing it was a catchall for fixing most of what was wrong with the world: Free those who mind their own business from those who don't. Free small-town queers like him from Bible thumpers and fence-post crucifixion. Free our friend David from drunk drivers and SUVs sliding on ice, crashing through highway dividers. Free everyone from the karma they don't deserve.

"Where did you get your button?" we asked.

"Well . . ." The clerk glanced behind him. "There's only one God around here," he said. "And despite all the talk, he's not always forgiving." The clerk had to travel if he wanted to find a religion that wanted him. Which was how he ended up at Kunzang Palyul Choling, "The Dharma Continent of Infinite Light"—a few hours east in Poolesville, Maryland. Kunzang, as he called it, was a Tibetan Buddhist monastery. More important, it was the first "church" he'd found that allowed him to pray or to sit or just to be without the usual de-mands and complications.

"I'd like to go back sometime," he said, leaning in on the counter so his manager wouldn't hear. "But I work days."

His hand skimmed across his shirt, brushing two fingers over his Free Tibet button the way a Catholic might touch his St. Christopher's medal. Maybe it was enough just to have a reminder of the place where he'd finally felt liber-ated. All he knew was that what Kunzang had, he wanted: a way out of suf-fering that didn't threaten suffering in return. "There's no hell in Buddhism," someone had told him—which isn't precisely true, but give him a few chants about compassion for all sentient beings and the clerk wasn't going to ask too many questions about doctrine.

"They've got this monument," he said. "They call it a *stupa*. It's like two stories high. And buried beneath it they put everything that, you know, op-presses people, guns and knives and things, they've even got AIDS down there. It's supposed to be this giant Buddha, and he's just sitting on all that negative energy, holding it down."

• • •

We followed the clerk's directions two hundred miles back east, through a town that was nothing more than a gas station and down a bumpy backwoods road, past a pig farm, over the Potomac River on a ferry named for Jubal A. Early, one of Lee's generals, to arrive at Kunzang just in time for the "Shower of Blessings," a ceremony revolving around a sacrifice. Behind the white pillars of the monastery's plantation-style mansion, burgundy-robed monks and nuns scuffed across cherry red carpets, bowing to 1,008 tiny blue-haired Buddhas sitting in perfect rows on nine long shelves. Other devotees, in khakis, in denim, in floral skirts, arrived from their day jobs and padded through the monastery in wool socks, their shoes neatly lined up at the door.

A woman in a cable-knit sweater checked the backlighting on two dozen hulking crystals that studded the prayer room like a giant necklace, glossy black crystals with edges like knives, lumpy yellow crystals that looked soft as velvet. They stood in a ring around the room, positioned to "accumulate" prayer and "radiate" it to the world. "Our crystals work like radios," the cable-knit woman told us. "They broadcast."

Within the circle two dozen practitioners sat before shin-high, fire engine red tables that stretched the length of the room like pews for five-year-olds. Many of the practitioners had not been working at their faith much longer than that. Lapsed Catholics, secular Jews, recovering addicts, computer programmers, whatever varieties of spiritual refugees they had been, they were all Buddhists now. Each one sat as close to full lotus as American joints would allow, grounded on two knees plus two cheeks like four noble truths, a foundation steady as a barstool or a Christmas tree stand.

In the center of the room a wiry, middle-aged nun called Ani Rinchen, born Janice Newmark, sat before a bright red drum that looked like it might have been stolen from a high school marching band. She wore her black hair shaved close to the skin, but her sharp widow's peak was still visible above her eyes. They were black and brilliant, like the eyes of a mare, and they seemed to fall naturally on the finest features, physical or otherwise, of whomever she spoke to. She lived in the monastery but worked in the world, leaving her robes behind and donning a hooded sweatshirt when she headed off in the evenings to area prisons, where she taught Buddhist principles— "Last week it was cause and effect; tonight it's karma"—to men serving life sentences.

She bopped the drum with a padded mallet, her thin wrist flexing in four-four time, faster and faster, chanting in Tibetan. Others traced the words in their prayer books, racing to keep up with Ani Rinchen's singsong: OM BEN ZAR SA TO SA MA YA. Rhythm in a strange tongue, a bebop-a-lula of prayer, numbing them and even us as it sped everyone along. The motel clerk had visited Kunzang only briefly but had still felt connected; maybe this was why. Ani Rinchen was like one of the crystals, beaming prayer into the cold winter night: SA MA YA MAN NU PA LA. From her mouth to the clerk's ear. Radio Free Tibet.

The Shower of Blessings was a *puja,* a weekly event offering prayers and a sacrifice to the Buddhas—plural. Forget the beatnik emptiness of Zen; Tibetan Buddhism is a cast-of-thousands production, a technically atheist religion that worships an infinity of Buddhas, deities, and not-far-from-divine teachers such as Guru Rinpoche. He was a holy man of the ninth century pictured throughout the monastery with wicked eyes and a curlicue mustachio, holding in one hand a skullcap filled with nectar, in the other a half-circle blade said to be convenient for obliterating enemies. That's Tibetan Buddhism in a nutshell: great bliss or great suffering. With every thought and action of this life and the countless lives you've lived before, you choose. The hope is to gather enough points through good deeds to be reborn as a karmic high roller, who can buy oneself free from *samsara,* the cycle of life and death, and retire to sunny Nirvana.

Around the prayer room Kunzang's members smiled at the apparent freshness of it all, the spiritual distance they had traveled, from their angry Jewish God and their hypocritical Christian one to this prayer room sweetened with incense and adorned with paintings of deities in the midst of sex ("very spiritual sex," a woman called Yesshe told us). They kept the beat of the prayer—BENZAR SATO TE NO PA—on their knees, and we joined in too, the rhythm pulling us like an undertow. Out to a sea of nectar, forget about the blade. Forget about suffering, too, forget an eye for an eye and good men dying for no apparent reason. Last week it was cause-and-effect, tonight it was karma; don't ask what anyone did to get there, to wind up in a prayer room or a prison, behind a check-in desk or on a coroner's table.

TISHTRA DRI DO ME BHA WA. Ani Rinchen's head nodded with the drumbeats from atop a long, thin neck it was hard to imagine had once been shrouded by wavy hair. She had been at the monastery since the beginning, some twenty years now, but before that she was Jewish and orthodox from Albany, New York. Her path to Poolesville had started there, walking home from temple one night with her father.

"It was a holiday, Sukkuth maybe," she told us later. "I asked him, 'If God made us in his image, why do we suffer?' He told me not to ask such questions, there were things in life we weren't meant to understand." Then he walked faster in front of her, like he was trying to get away.

Ani Rinchen rocked on her knees, still working the drum. She thumped out a beat for the rest of us to follow, and chanted louder as other voices grew tired and slow around her: MA HA SA MA YA SATO AH. She understood suffering now. There are rules, you break them, you pay. Karma. It wasn't what she'd expected when she'd first come to Buddhism, a disillusioned veteran of half a dozen enlightenment schemes, but at least it was an answer.

When she'd told her father that she was becoming a Buddhist nun, he'd acted as if she had died. And then he'd died, too, without a word passed between them from the time she'd first prayed in Tibetan, DRO WA DRAL WAR DAM CHA. *I commit myself to liberate all sentient beings.*

It was time for the sacrifice. A lean young man named Rodrigo rose from the floor and approached the offering, which was actually just a table weighed down with stale Fig Newtons, warm cold cuts, and chocolate oranges. He tied a pink bandanna around his face, Zapatista style, to make sure he didn't contaminate the food but also to protect himself from spiritual vapors. SA TO SA MA YA. He'd once heard about a yogi who retreated to a cave and tried to perform a Shower of Blessings sacrifice on his own, his concentration so complete that when it came time to offer the sacrifice, instead of presenting the fruit he'd laid out for the occasion, he took a knife and began carving chunks out of his thigh.

Following Rodrigo's lead, a dozen devotees rose on stiff legs and took up the plates of goodies; what they'd given to the gods they now returned to themselves. As they trotted up and down the rows of their fellow worshipers, air-dropping dried fruit and cheese cubes, they continued chanting. MA NU PA LA YA. One of the monks stumbled and spilled a whole plateful of the offering onto a sitting worshiper in a cardigan sweater. TO TE NO PA. A look of horror blossomed on the cardigan man's face as baloney, grapes, Chex mix, and cookie crumbs rained into his hair. Someone said, "How's that for a shower of blessings?" Cardigan tried to laugh.

Ani Rinchen carried a pitcher from which she poured red wine into our cupped palms. MA HA SA MA YA. When we failed to understand whether we were to anoint ourselves or have a drink, she mimed lapping at her hands like a dog at its bowl. And she kept praying, even as her fingers covered her face, HA HA HA HA HO.

It was late in the evening when the ritual ended, the sacrifice consumed, the cushions stacked neatly in the corner. The few who lived in the monastery with Ani Rinchen retired to the second floor. They all had jobs to get to in the morning; Ani Rinchen worked days as a secretary in a doctor's office, giving a portion of her paycheck to the monastery each week, putting the rest away so she could afford, in a few years, to go on a long retreat at a less public monastery in New York State. Three years of silence, back where she came from.

Those who didn't live in the small rooms above the prayer hall put their shoes on and climbed into their cars for the drive back to suburbs of Washington or Baltimore. Outside, one pair of headlights after another briefly brightened the night as engines hummed alive and tires spun on ice and gravel.

In the light of the beams, we finally saw the monument the motel clerk had told us about: the stupa, a twenty-five-foot-tall altar shaped like a space capsule with a window near the top, where a gold Buddha sat watch. All the strange things the clerk had claimed were buried beneath the stupa were really there, we'd learned, guns, knives, even electron microscopic images of Ebola and HIV.

Small offerings to the Buddha, red candles, blue bottles of water, yellow candy wrappers, shells, plastic whistles, coins and paper money dotted the flat surface of the base like stones at a Jewish grave. A blue plastic sign stood in front. THE THINGS YOU SEE AT THE STUPA ARE OFFERINGS TO THE BUDDHA, it read. PLEASE DO NOT TAKE THEM AND DO NOT HARM THE STUPAS.

IF YOU DO, YOU'LL EVENTUALLY EXPERIENCE THE TERRIBLE RESULT OF SUCH ACTION, INCLUDING FUTURE POVERTY, SEPARATION FROM ALL THINGS VIRTUOUS, PHYSICAL DEFORMITY, AND OTHER TERRIBLE FORMS OF SUFFERING.

Truth in advertising: There are rules, you break them, you pay. Keep your toes behind the line or Guru Rinpoche will chop them off for you.

We wondered if the clerk had seen the sign, or if it had been night when he'd been there too, the nectar and Fig Newtons offered inside, the blade waiting in the dark. Was this the price karma took in trade for liberation? Obedience to rules that pay you back ten times over if you break their rhythm, if you wear the wrong pair of shoes?

Our friend David wouldn't have bothered with the question. The precision that compelled him to maintain a distinct pair for each phase of the day would have led him to turn on his heels at the sight of such a melodramatic warning. "There are rules," he would say, "and we must play by them." Right: Take nothing, leave nothing, don't make offerings to a karma that maintains its order by the threat of a blade. David wouldn't have left anything. Neither did we. Not a penny or a candle or even a stone.

LEVITICUS

By Michael Lesy

I'M fifty-seven years old—well past the age when, according to Jewish tradition, someone should have taken me aside, stood me in some water, and whispered the secrets of the universe in my ear. Answers to the big questions: what came before; what comes after; what is above; what is below. No one told me anything. What happened, instead, was: I got private lessons from Blind Joe Death. First, my old aunt, the one who'd pawned everything to bring my father to America, died: Her apartment caught fire. Then my father: He lived so long, he lost his mind. Then my mother: She went blind, and stopped eating. Then my wife: She got Lou Gehrig's disease and died in her sleep. Every three or four years, someone in my family got sick and died and I buried them. No whispered secrets: just twelve years of death and dying.

As to my relatives: I've got no claim to fame, no inside track, no precious knowledge. On my mother's side, they were all scoundrels, fools, thieves, and adulterers. *Putzes, gonifs,* and *schnorers,* I believe, were the terms once used to describe such people. On my father's side, it was a little different: We were Levites, my father said. "The descendants of scribes" was the way he told it. One of my cousins even married a rabbi, but the rest of my family—one sharpened knives; one sold keys; one sold steel; one sold doors and windows. What can I tell you? They made a living. Their children went to college.

As for my father and me being descendants of scribes: It took me years to figure out when to stand up and when to sit down during services. I can count on two hands the number of times I've worn tefillin. Most of what I know about being a Jew, I learned from books. I bought them; I read them; I still read them. I taught myself.

For instance: I was fifty when I learned that, besides guarding the Temple and writing everything down, my ancestors, the Levites, also killed people. We were Israel's official executioners. Long before Egypt and the Exodus, Levi and his brother Simeon had rubbed out a whole city full of men related to a Hivite who'd raped their sister. "We'll live with you, peacefully," Levi had said to the rapist and his kin. "Just circumcise yourselves to make things right." The fools did; Levi and Simeon waited three days and then killed them all. A whole city of dead men with no foreskins.

That's why Moses knew who to call when he came down from Sinai and saw the Golden Calf, the false god made from jewelry. "Whoever is for God," Moses shouted, "join me." Moses was a Levite himself. We came running. "Go through the camp," Moses ordered us. "Gate to gate; no exceptions; brother, neighbor, kin; it doesn't matter. If they're guilty, kill them." We did as we were told. Brother, neighbor, kin. Three thousand people. That's how we earned the right to serve as the priests and keep the stories.

I tell you this now to warn you. My ancestors had a hand in writing Leviticus. If you're looking for stories of redemption, you need to look elsewhere. Purity and impurity; guilt, death, and being alive—"instructions for priests"—that's what Leviticus is about. According to tradition, Jewish boys were given Leviticus as their first study assignment. "Children are pure; therefore let them study the laws of purity."

Imagine: a book about purity written by people with bloody hands. Explained, now, by a man who knows only what he's read. A self-taught storyteller. If I were you, I'd be careful about what I believed. And what I didn't.

There are a lot of stories about how we—the Jewish people, I mean—got into so much trouble. Every one of the stories has to do with obeying and not obeying the Commandments—all 613 of them, the shalts, the shalt-nots, and especially, the consequences.

As I understand it, God didn't offer the Torah to us first. Instead, He went to the children of Esau. You remember Esau—the hairy one, the hunter—who'd been tricked out of his birthright by Jacob and his mother. "Will you accept the Torah?" God asked Esau's children. God was probably trying to make amends for what Jacob had done. Esau's children were wary. They asked to read the Torah before they agreed to anything. They got as far as the Sixth Commandment, the one about murder, before they stopped and looked at God. "That's a hard one," they said. "You must know: We live by the sword. That's who we are; that's what we do. Things happen. We can't agree to this."

God took the Torah to the children of Ammon and Moab next. You might have thought they would have accepted it—Ruth, the wife of Boaz, the great-grandmother of King David, was a Moabite. No, again. They read as far as the Seventh Commandment, the one that prohibited adultery. "Don't you re-member?" they asked God. "We're descended from Lot's daughters. How could you have forgotten? Lot slept with his own daughters in the cave. After you obliterated his home and turned his wife into salt. We can't even begin to agree to this."

God went to the children of Ishmael next. Once again, He was probably trying to make amends for the way their ancestor had been treated, thrown out to make room for Isaac. "Will you accept the Torah?" He asked. "Is there any-thing in there about stealing?" they said. God answered, "That's Command-ment Eight. Stealing is forbidden." They looked straight at Him and shook their heads. "That's how we make our living. We rob; we steal; we ambush people. How do you expect us to make money if we can't steal it? No deal."

According to what I've read, God went to every nation on the planet. They all had some sort of problem with the Torah. At last, then, He asked us. We didn't even have the sense to read the agreement. "We hear and we obey," we said. Such smart people.

Of course, like every story about every important event, this one has an al-ternate version. I can accept the first one. But the one I prefer—the one I be-lieve—is very different:

This time, we made it as far as Mount Sinai before we were asked to agree to anything. God drew us up outside a perimeter, twelve miles from Mount Sinai. "Don't cross the line or you'll die." Then it started: The whole moun-tain began to smoke as if it were a piece of coal in a furnace. Huge, shattering, shuddering shofar blasts trumpeted down on us. All of us were pure; the Golden Calf hadn't happened yet. God spoke to each and every one of us, in-side our minds, in a voice that was as different, person to person, as the soul of each and every one of us was different, one to another. Babies at their mothers' breasts heard and understood. God made the body of each pregnant woman "as transparent as glass," and as He spoke, the children in their wombs turned their heads and opened their eyes and saw. Supernatural sight was granted to us all: We could see the thunder, we could hear the lightning. We were, each of us assembled there, given the gift of prophecy. All the future and all the past flickered in front of us, in a glance.

That's when we panicked. "Please!" we begged. "Please stop!" We rushed to Moses. "You speak to us. That we can bear. But not God."

Which is when God lifted up Mount Sinai and held it over our heads like a basket. "Now," God said. "You must choose. Either accept the Torah and live. Or refuse it, here, now, in this place. And die."

"We hear and we will do," we cried. "We hear and we will obey."

Deals like that never have good outcomes. Leviticus ends with five sets of prophetic curses, seven curses in every set, each set more terrifying than the last, each curse more dreadful than the one before. All of the curses are retributions. When—not if—we break the promises we made at Sinai, God assures us: We will pay.

Every week, a portion of the Torah, accompanied by a passage from one of the prophets, is chanted aloud, during services, in every shul, every synagogue, on the earth. And every year, when we reach those final sets of curses in Leviticus, we chant them hurriedly, heads down, hunched and hushed, in an undertone, because we know: It's happened before, it'll happen again.

"If you do not obey Me and do not observe all these commandments, if you reject My laws and spurn My rules so that you do not observe all My commandments and you break My covenant, I, in turn, will do this to you."

First come panic and disease, fever, swelling, and lesions. The sky turns to copper and the earth to iron. Wild animals begin to starve, so they attack our livestock. When there are no cattle left, they hunt down our children. We flee to the cities, but plague breaks out. Then, when there is no food, we begin to behave like the beasts we fled. "You will eat the flesh of your sons and the flesh of your daughters."

Long ago, we made a deal we now know we couldn't keep. On the ninth day of the lunar month of Av, on the same day that the Babylonians destroyed the First Temple, the same day that five hundred years later the Romans destroyed the Second, on that day, in the very same year that Columbus made landfall in the Caribbean, the Spanish Inquisition exiled from Spain whatever Jews hadn't fled or been burnt or been converted or gone into hiding. We had been in Spain for more than a thousand years. We had been advisers to the Caliphate and to the Reconquista. We had served as court physicians, made fortunes trading spices and silks, composed books of gemstone clarity and other books of mystic splendor; we had worked as jewelers, pharmacists, textile makers, and metal fabricators. We had married and intermarried. Been assimilated. Until Ferdinand and Isabella expelled us. Later, the rabbis would explain this expulsion the same way they had explained all our other exiles: "Sometimes that is the only way to prevent us from becoming so assimilated that we disappear as a nation." Why were we expelled? According to the rabbis, God was trying to do us a favor. He was trying to keep us pure.

This, then, is how Leviticus begins and how it ends: Die now, or die later. These were—and are—our choices:

Refuse the Laws and die where we stand.
Accept the Laws and live only until we break them.
Be so dispersed that we disappear like water spilled into sand.
Prosper in our exile until our assimilation causes God to disperse us
    again.

The clearing where we stand is hemmed in on every side by darkness and foreboding. But: It's still a clearing. It's all we have. What do we do then— what can we do—in the only space that remains? We know what's come before. We suspect what will come after. How do we now behave?

Leviticus offers three answers. One is in the form of a story about two brothers; two are bound up, inside of, the code of Laws itself.

A story about two brothers. One was named Nadab, and the other Abihu. Nadab's name meant "willing"; Abihu's meant "God is my father." They were the eldest sons of Aaron, the High Priest, the brother of Moses, the one who'd stood with Moses before Pharaoh, the one who'd been left in charge while Moses was alone, on Sinai, listening to God.

Nadab and Abihu appear near the beginning of Leviticus. Something strange happened to them. It happened after a long series of ritual purifications, anointings, and immersions—all done to prepare Aaron and his sons for the priesthood.

Leviticus itself begins with seven long chapters that describe, in detail, not only the sacrifices the priests were to perform but the sins of omission and commission that the sacrifices were meant to rectify. For instance: The principal sacrifice, the "elevation offering," was not just a voluntary offering made by people who wanted to raise themselves to "a higher spiritual state." It was also required of anyone who (1) had failed to perform one of the 365 positive commandments; (2) had had sinful thoughts but had not acted on them; (3) had inadvertently broken a commandment, positive or negative, for which there was no prescribed punishment; (4) had just made one of the three required Festival Pilgrimages to the (yet to be built) Temple in Jerusalem.

Nearly every sacrifice the priests performed was an animal sacrifice. The blood of every bull, ox, ram, sheep, goat, calf, or turtledove that was sacrificed had to be ritually splashed, smeared, collected, and channeled. It was the blood itself—not the smoke of the flesh burnt on the altar—that linked the people, through the priests, to God.

Consider the description of the second of the sacrifices Moses made to prepare Aaron and his sons: "Aaron and his [four] sons leaned their hands upon the head of the ram. Moses slaughtered it and he took some of its blood and placed it upon the middle part of Aaron's right ear, upon the thumb by his right hand, and upon the big toe of his right foot. Moses brought the sons of Aaron forward and Moses put some of the blood upon the middle of their right ear, upon the thumb of their right hand, and upon the big toe of their right foot, and Moses threw the remaining blood upon the altar, all around." Eight days after this sacrifice, Moses ordered Aaron and his sons to begin their duties. First, the priests made a "sin offering," then an elevation offering, then a "peace offering," and finally a "meal offering." A bull, a ram, a goat, and a calf were ritually slaughtered; their flesh, fat, livers, and kidneys, their heads, breasts, feet, and tails were piled on the altar. Aaron raised his hands and blessed the people. Then he and Moses went into the Holy of Holies. When they came out, they blessed the people again.

That's when something remarkable happened: A line of fire, "like a pillar," came down from Heaven and ignited the elevation offering on the altar.

The rabbis, in their commentaries, have traced the path of this heavenly fire. First, the rabbis say, the fire went into the Holy of Holies, the sanctuary where the Ark rested. Moses and Aaron had just been there, but their presence had been exceptional: The Tabernacle was a place that no one but Aaron was permitted to enter, and even he was not permitted to enter it except on Yom Kippur, the Day of Atonement.

From the Holy of Holies, the rabbis say, the fire flew to the Golden Altar and lit the incense on it. From the Golden Altar, the heavenly fire flashed to the Copper Altar. "The people saw and sang glad song and fell on their faces." And that's when Nadab and Abihu did the things that killed them: "Each took his fire pan; they put fire on them, and placed incense upon it, and they brought before God an alien fire that he had not commanded them."

The rabbis have been trying to describe and explain what happened next—when and where and why it happened—since it occurred. It appears—as far as I can tell—that the brothers acted spontaneously, and, although they acted separately, they seem to have acted at the same time. They lit sacred incense in their own censers, then walked straight into the Holy of Holies with it. They acted without thinking, without planning. They seem to have been overcome with emotion. They died as soon as they came out of the Tabernacle.

Two threads of flame came out of the Holy of Holies. The threads divided into four strands. Two strands of fire entered Nadab's nostrils; two entered Abihu's. According to the rabbis, "their souls were burnt, although no external injury was visible." Moses ordered two of Aaron's cousins to drag the dead men out of the camp by their tunics.

Different rabbis give different reasons for the brothers' deaths. Some say they were drunk; some say they hadn't even washed. Some say they were so haughty, they'd refused to marry any woman in the camp. Others say that the brothers died because they were impatient and presumptuous: Neither son had even asked their elders' permission to do what they'd done.

Presumptuousness, impatience, haughtiness, uncleanliness, drunkenness. All plausible. But their deaths were extraordinary. Too extraordinary to be explained away by gossip.

The sages answer: The brothers died as they did because, as priests, they'd been held to the highest standard. In fact, say the rabbis, the brothers had done one of the worst things any priest could do: They'd entered the Holy of Holies unauthorized. Equivalent to someone, now, walking unprotected and unauthorized into the containment vessel of a nuclear reactor, then diving into the coolant pool. Would anyone who did that come out alive?

As with the two stories about how we came to accept the Torah at Sinai, there are other explanations besides the usual ones offered by the rabbis.

Consider: The sages all agree that the brothers were extraordinary men. They did what they did out of an excess of religious devotion. Overwhelming piety caused them momentarily to forget the laws. Some rabbis even say that their deaths were sacrifices that expiated the sins of all Jews, past, present, and future.

So: If Nadab and Abihu were neither villains nor the worst sort of fools, what were they?

Rabbis who lived long after the destruction of the Second Temple tell a story about four sages who went into "the garden." The garden in the story is called Pardes. Pardes may be the Garden of Eden; it may also be Paradise. It may also be the very center of all the great secrets, the core cosmology, the place where the "what comes before, what comes after" questions are answered.

The rabbis taught: "Four sages entered *Pardes*, and they are: Ben Azzai, Ben Zoma, Aher, and Rabbi Akiba. Rabbi Akiba said to them, 'When you arrive at the stones of pure marble, do not say, "Water, water." ' Ben Azzai looked and died. Ben Zoma looked and lost his mind. Aher cut the shoots [of the plants that grew in Pardes]. Only Rabbi Akiba entered in peace and left in peace." There is always a price for entering the Holy of Holies. Jewish mystics—Kabbalists—interpret Ben Azzai's death as a metaphor for a transcendent experience. Azzai's soul left his body at the moment of his revelation. His soul left him, but it did not return. As for Ben Zoma: He simply went crazy. Aher, the one who "cut the shoots" of the plants (that is, Aher tried to destroy the ideas inherent in the revelations), the commentators say became a heretic. Only Akiba—the great Talmudist, the great scholar and teacher, the great interpreter of the Law, written and oral—only he is said to have survived both the hallucinations ("pure marble" is not "water") and the revelations.

Back to Nadab and his brother: What if they were like Ben Azzai? What if they were ecstatics whose souls left their bodies and didn't return? In all of Leviticus, Nadab and Abihu are the only great ones who didn't follow the rules. In fact, they are the only ones who acted with the kind of intense religious spontaneity and devotion that we, here, now, in this century, consider the authentic mark of true, deep religious feeling.

Leviticus is an ancient text. Its present is not ours. But what if Nadab and Abihu had lived in our present? What if they were as modern as we are? They paid a price, but did they deserve it?

Leviticus doesn't care. They died because they broke the rules. They died because God killed them.

• • •

If spontaneous gestures are forbidden, even to priests, how are the rest of us supposed to behave? "Know the rules and obey them" is the only answer Leviticus gives. Inside a palisade of laws, surrounded by a tangle of rules — that is the only clear, safe space that Leviticus offers us.

Leviticus divides the world into the clean and the dirty. "Live outside in the filth," Leviticus says, "and you'll surely die." All things animate and inanimate are separated into the pure and the impure. All things physical are linked to all things spiritual. The laws of kashrut separate flesh edible from flesh inedible: Clean animals are distinguished from dirty ones; permitted fish from forbidden ones; loathsome birds from lawful ones. "Eat filth and you will become filth."

Chapter after chapter, verse after verse are devoted to a skin disease called *tzaraas*. It's a disease that no one now can identify any better than they can identify some of the birds, reptiles, and insects that Leviticus classifies as forbidden. One hundred years ago, rationalists and empiricists tried — and failed — to prove that *tzaraas* was a form of leprosy. But the sages have always known better:

The blemishes of *tzaraas* reveal a disease of the soul. Slander and selfishness, promiscuity and thievery, false oaths and pride — these produce a white spot the size of a large bean. That spot can grow. "And the person with *tzaraas* . . . his garments shall be rent, the hair of his head shall be unshorn, and he shall cloak himself up to his lips; he is to call out, 'Contaminated, contaminated!' . . . He shall dwell in contamination; his dwelling shall be outside the camp." Chapter and verse describe dozens of procedures to identify *tzaraas*, track its progression, and then cleanse anything and everything, anyone and everyone that may have been touched by it. After the contamination and cleansings of *tzaraas*, Leviticus begins a new list of filthy things — all human, all reproductive: menstrual blood and discharges, ejaculations and oozings.

I spent days and then weeks reading and rereading all the rules and laws and decrees of Leviticus. Rules about forbidden relationships that outlaw incest as well as homosexuality; rules that forbid the eating of blood and fat from even kosher animals but also include prohibitions against wearing clothes that combine wool and linen. "We hear and we will obey." But as I read those rules, one after the other, I began to feel as if I were falling into a tangled morass.

• • •

Almost as soon as Aaron's cousins had finished dragging the bodies of Nadab and Abihu out of the camp, Moses ordered Aaron and his two remaining sons to complete the cycle of sacrifices they had begun. Aaron and his sons complied, but Moses noticed something amiss. God had already ended two lives because of a mistake. Moses wanted no more errors. He reproached the priests; they answered him. Moses immediately understood he had been wrong to scold them. The priests finished their sacrifices.

In the text, the words used to describe Moses' reproach are "Moses inquired insistently." His scolding was wrong, but his questioning was the right thing to do; you have to pay attention, or you'll die.

The rabbis say that those words occur exactly at the middle of the text of the whole Torah. "Insistent inquiry" is at the center of the Torah. "This teaches us," says the sage Degel Machaneh Ephraim, "that the entire Torah revolves around constant inquiry; one must never stop studying and seeking an ever broader understanding."

If this is so, then permit me my own "insistent inquiry." It won't take long.

In Leviticus, the way in which nearly every rule, law, and decree was taught to us was from the top down: God told Moses; Moses told Aaron. Once Moses instructed Aaron, he would summon Aaron's sons and then repeat—to Aaron and his sons—what he had just explained to Aaron alone. After this, Moses would summon the elders. To them—and to Aaron and Aaron's sons—he would repeat what he'd just taught the priests alone. Which was itself a repetition of what he'd just taught Aaron face-to-face. Finally, Moses would summon all the people and teach them in the presence of all the great men what he'd taught everyone else. We were almost always the last to know.

Again and again, throughout Leviticus, that's how we learned the laws. Except, say the sages, in Chapter 19: "God spoke to Moses, saying: Speak to the entire assembly of the Children of Israel and say to them . . ." Only in Chapter 19 did God tell Moses to teach us all—every one of us—at once.

What did God tell Moses to teach us? "Say to them: You shall be holy, for I, the Lord your God, am holy." How, then, did God tell us to be holy? These were his instructions—in order:

Honor your father and mother. Observe the Sabbath. Don't worship idols. Conduct every sacrifice—in particular the peace sacrifice, the one you make to express love and thankfulness—with great presence of mind.

Leave a portion of every harvest, a corner of every field, for the poor. Don't steal. Don't deny something that's true. Don't lie about anything. Don't cheat anyone. Don't rob anyone. If a man works for you, pay him what you owe him as soon as he's done.

Don't insult the deaf. Don't trip up the blind. Do justice: Don't favor the poor just because they're poor; don't favor important people just because they're important.

Don't gossip. Don't stand aside when you see someone in danger. Try to save him. Don't hate your own brother. Don't take revenge on people. Don't bear grudges against people close to you.

After all this, God told Moses to tell us: "You shall love your fellow as your-self—I am God."

Moses told all this to us at the same time. After being the last to know the other rules, these rules we learned, every one of us, standing together, as we'd once stood, all of us, assembled at Sinai.

The question remains: How do we live? Alone, in a clearing, with exile on one side and obliteration on the other, caught between two kinds of law, how do we conduct ourselves?

Nadab and Abihu represent an answer. But they didn't survive, any better than Ben Azzai survived in the story about Pardes. You remember: In that story, only the great sage and scholar Akiba lived to tell the tale. Knowledge and clear-mindedness saved him. But the rest of us are not sages. Not even close. My ancestors may have helped write Leviticus, but I can barely remember, let alone live within the bounds of, all the laws.

What choices do we have left?

Listen to this story: Two rabbis were approached by a man who said he wanted to be a Jew. The man spoke with each of the rabbis separately. "I'm going to stand on one leg," said the man. "Teach me the Law before I fall down."

The first rabbi was a very smart man with a very precise mind. In fact, he'd been trained as an engineer. He happened to be carrying a yardstick with him when the man approached him. That's what he used to beat the man before he could even get his balance.

The other rabbi was just as smart as the first one. The man made his offer, then hoisted himself up on one leg. He wobbled a bit; the rabbi did nothing but look at him. After a bit, the rabbi said, "Whatever you hate, don't inflict it on anyone else. That's the whole of the law. All the rest is commentary. Now—go study."

• • •

Sound familiar? Jesus, good Jew that he was, said much the same thing. Two thousand years later, it's become a smiley-faced cliché. Reread what Hillel said, though. "All the rest is commentary. Now—go study." "Go study." That's what Akiba did. That's why, in the story about Pardes, he lived and Ben Azzai died. Mind. Clarity. "Insistent inquiry." Along with empathic knowledge. Akiba was a tree with branches and roots; he reached down into tradition and up, into the sky. Of course, in the end, even Akiba didn't know enough: He backed a final, fatal revolt against the Romans. He even believed the leader of the revolt—a man named Bar Kokhba—was the true Messiah. The Romans liquidated all the rebels. Akiba, they tortured to death—with "iron combs."

"A degenerate with the permission of the Torah" is what the sages call a man who is careful to obey every one of the laws. The choice, though, is not between scrupulous obedience and ecstatic abandon. The choice runs right down the middle. If you really want to know how to fly, you need to know how to walk.

As for me: The lessons I learned from Blind Joe Death made me a kinder person. But only for a little while. My father died; my mother died; my wife died: After each death, I became a more decent person. But it never lasted. After a while, I'd forget how close death really is, how vulnerable we all are, how short a time we have to breathe the air and stand in the light. How foolish it is, under the circumstances, to treat people cruelly or callously, or inattentively.

I keep trying to remind myself.

HENDERSON,
NORTH CAROLINA

Destroy, O Lord, and divide their tongues . . .

PSALM 55:9

THERE was a man waiting for us in the parking lot of the only store off exit 229, I-85, just north of Henderson, North Carolina. How he knew we were coming we can't guess; he must have had some kind of trip-wire strung to the hand-painted sign out on the highway that read, "MiRAcle this Exit," because he was standing there as we rolled into the lot, and when we opened the car doors he said, "You here to see it?"

"We are," we said, and he pointed. His hand was a curled claw of melted fingers and scabby stumps. We followed his direction and saw a little white shack with words scrawled all over it in the same unsteady hand that had lured us off the highway: "Its here its here Its here." He told us that once on this spot a hitchhiker had looked up into the sky and seen four clouds in the shape of letters: *E-S-U-S.*

"Well shit that ain't nuthin," he said. "*ESUS* isn't even a word." Then sure enough the wind picked up and a fifth cloud blew across the sky, making it a proper miracle, spelling the name.

He moved his mangled fist through the air like that *J* floating into place, a hook to hang the story on now that the clouds were gone. The advertised "miracle" was actually just photographs of that divine skywriting, on sale in the white shack for three hundred dollars each. We couldn't see them just then. The shack was padlocked, and Mr. Miracle didn't have the key. When he insisted we buy something else to make the stop worthwhile, we asked for the local paper. The letters of the headline were deep black and even: "GUN-MAN TERRORIZES CHURCH: She-Male Intruder Reportedly Calls Americans 'Killers.' " There was no picture.

Reverend W. F. Buddy Faucette had been a preacher for forty years when the devil came into his church, said a prayer, drew a .38, and pulled the trigger.

Buddy heard later from the police that the devil wasn't a man at all, and not really a woman either. "He got all the parts, y'see," Buddy told us one afternoon in the print shop he owned on the main street of town. The devil had even tried to show Buddy his bosom. Reached in and tried to draw up a breast full and soft as a woman's.

No one in the church had ever seen anything like it, but Buddy wasn't surprised. "This kind of thing been prophesied," he said. "Look it up, it's in the Book."

That's how we'd found him. With a list of names gathered from the Henderson *Daily Dispatch* we'd bought from the miracle man, we'd rifled through the Vance County directory looking for the number of anyone involved in an incident local reporters were calling the country's "latest act of terrorism."

"This is spiritual war," Buddy told us. He'd been fighting it since he got the call to preach in 1959. Back then he told the Lord he couldn't do it; he didn't have that kind of voice.

"You hear me quiet, now," he said to us, deep and low. "That's how I was then."

The Lord told him to read the Book of Joshua; He would do the rest. Buddy did so and slipped into the back of a church to see what would happen. But the devil came in after him. Whispered in his ear, "Buddy, you can't do it. You don't got the voice."

"Well," Buddy replied, slowly, "get thee behind me, anyhow."

"Okay," the devil said. "I will—if you can tell me just two words you're a-gonna preach."

"Well," Buddy said, and that used up the only one he had.

So he marched up to the pulpit, put the devil in front of him, and opened his mouth. Out came the story of Joshua: he who won the Promised Land by killing everyone in it.

When Buddy was done the devil was nowhere to be seen, but Buddy had found the message that would build Trinity Full Gospel Church.

"Battle's heatin' up," Buddy told us, the print shop behind him quiet and still, his voice gentle as it always was except when the spirit spoke through him, as it seemed to be doing more often. His silver hair swooped up like a torch, his ruddy cheeks drooped to his chin, he didn't feel old. The visitor with too many parts had been a sure sign that the devil could still hear Buddy preaching.

The next evening we visited the church—a steepleless white pine box, striped by narrow windows glowing blue. One of Buddy's deacons, Billy Joe, pointed to two colorful pictures on either side of the altar, an empty stage. "You just look right up there," he said.

Billy Joe had come with Buddy and a few other men to meet us in case we'd been sent by the devil ourselves. Buddy looked to be a powerful man, but of the bunch Billy Joe seemed readiest to handle any fighting that had to be done, spiritual or otherwise. A plumber by trade, he kept his shoulders pulled to his neck and his short-fingered hands flexing between fists and stretched-open palms. He wore tight blue jeans spotted with paint, white leather cross trainers, and a T-shirt depicting the crucifixion in lifelike detail, Jesus' chest on the front, Jesus' back on the back, "Dying to Meet You" dripping across the top in red bloody letters.

"Take a *good* look," Billy Joe said. "I want you to go ahead and study on what you see."

Behind the pulpit, the two identical images stared down like the eyes of the church itself, filled with fire and rapture and souls pulled into the sky. On a road that stretches to the horizon, cars drive into ditches, into telephone poles, into each other. In the foreground a tractor-trailer jackknifes and bursts into flames; in the upper left a jetliner crashes into a high-rise. The bodies of the worldly burn everywhere. But the souls of the saved unman taxis and graves and float through office windows, flying up toward Jesus, who shines above it all like the sun at high noon.

"That's what going to happen and that's where we're going," Billy Joe declared, only he said "gone." "Not a doubt about that. Rapture's gone come and we will be called to His presence. We are gone to meet our Heavenly Father. In Heaven."

He breathed through his nose and stared for a long minute, his pupils a bit too close together. He'd recently gone through a bad separation from his wife, but he claimed it'd opened his eyes. Maybe it had; they seemed to stay moist without blinking. He nodded, and kept nodding until he was sure we understood and agreed, until we nodded, too, just to stop him from nodding. He seemed to take that as a victory.

"We going up!" Billy Joe shouted, and his arms shot toward the ceiling as if someone had kicked a field goal.

Buddy nodded, too, his quiet agreement like a blanket thrown on Billy Joe's fever. Yes, he said, the war is raging, and the signs did indeed suggest that one day soon the difference between this side and that will be as clear as it is between fire and wind.

Billy Joe paced in front of the pulpit, speaking in time with his steps. "Not. A. Doubt. About. That." He stopped in front of a gold-toned cross, the only one in the church, stretched his arms out to his sides like he was playing airplane, and locked us into a close-eyed stare. "He fought for us," he said. "So. Now. We. Fight. For. Him. We are fighting the devil every day of our lives!"

Buddy felt the need to make a distinction. The "intruder," he said, was not the devil himself. "No, sir, just some poor soul the devil used to his own ends. Man is man and woman is woman, and the devil got that poor intruder trapped in between."

"Yes," murmured another deacon named Wesley, a smooth-skinned Jacob to Billy Joe's hairy Esau. College-educated and well-traveled, Wesley had married into Buddy's church and emerged as its resident theologian. He wore black shoes, black slacks, and glasses, and although there's no uniform for a Holiness preacher, Wesley just looked like one. He seemed aimed for a pulpit; probably Buddy's, probably soon.

"When that person walked in here this Sunday last," Wesley said, "I knew it was the Enemy at work. Billy Joe told me later when he saw that intruder's yellow raincoat, he thought it was the gas company checking on a leak. Isn't that right, Billy Joe?"

Billy Joe sat in a pew next to Wesley and glared at his watch.

"But I knew it," continued Wesley. "And you know what? There was no fear in me." He put his hands together, pressed his fingers to his lips, then opened them like a flower, lowering and spreading his arms to take in the whole room. "There was no fear in this church. The devil at our door, but why should we be afraid? We know the power." The word came out shortened: "The powa of our Lord, Jesus Christ."

Wesley stopped, content to leave it at that. He and the other men, Buddy, Billy Joe, and Billy Joe's daddy, Billy, stared at us from across the aisle, all of us sitting sideways in pews meant to keep you looking straight ahead. Wesley had played the trump card. When they talked about and around Jesus, they leaned forward, as if about to pounce. But when His name came out in the open, they sat back satisfied, like they'd just sealed the deal, like they'd just pressed a button to drop the A-bomb. Once the wick is lit, why bother saying anything else?

Earlier that day, we'd gone to the Vance County lockup to meet the intruder they thought was sent by the devil. We sat across from her, separated by unbreakable glass, and listened while she spoke with her hands and breathed into a telephone receiver connected to the wall. She had the jaw of a man and the lips of a woman, skin the color of coffee with lots of cream and, we'd noticed when a male and female escort of guards had brought her in to meet us, toenails painted purple. It looked like her nose had been broken in several places and had healed in a zigzag, and she had a mole beneath her right eye she was given to tapping. She wasn't trying to pass. The longer you looked at her the more uncertain you were, as if her skin was loose clothing she kept rearranging.

The Vance County sheriff, Thomas Breedlove, didn't think she was dangerous, but while we spoke to her he paced in the corridor, his hand propped on his hip just above the handle of his weapon. Sheriff Breedlove himself had driven us to the jail in his silver Lincoln Continental, warning us all the way that the "terrorist" was "mental," a condition he thought sad but irreconcilable. "It won't tell you nothing," he'd predicted.

He called the intruder "it" not because he was uncomfortable with her ambiguous gender but because she was. When she had walked into Buddy's church the week before, on a cold, clear winter morning, called to pray out of the surrounding scrub forest from which she emerged on a dirt path, she was a man in a hard hat and a yellow slicker. But when she sang, her voice was high and clear. "Ladies said it sounded like an angel," recalled Buddy, who at first simply took her for an opportunity to share God with a black man. They were welcome, of course, but none ever came.

When Buddy shouted, "Let all who will, come!" she prayed at the front of the church on her knees, right next to the women in their flower-print dresses, joining their chorus of Holiness voices. Only, when everyone else had had enough, she remained at the altar.

Buddy knelt down beside her. "Why, there was a tear coming down there from its eye," he told us, so he'd asked her, whispering in her ear, "Are you praying for something special?"

"For the war to end," she answered in the voice of a man.

"Well, I'd like that, too," Buddy said.

She was silent for a moment, then added, "Americans are killers."

"No, no," Buddy assured her, "we are not a bloodthirsty nation. We do what we have to do."

She seemed to ignore him but kept praying. She prayed as the church folks just had—out loud, full-voiced, in a language no one spoke to anyone but God—praying until Buddy grabbed her by the collar of her raincoat. He tugged her away from the altar rail, clear off the ground.

"I am not afraid of you," Buddy said once he had her outside. "Do you understand?"

"Then it went calm on me," Buddy recalled when he told us the story. "Tilted its head back-like to get a fuller view. And it said, just as clear as me to you, 'I live in fear every day of my life.' "

Buddy shook his head. "Imagine that," he said. He wished he could've comforted her, but at the time he said nothing. "My voice failed me."

Next thing Buddy knew, as soon as he'd returned to his pulpit that morning, the devil had come in after him. "He's got a gun!" one of the women shouted. Buddy swung around to see. His eyes stopped on his grandson. The boy had just come up from the basement Sunday school; he stood in front of the apocalypse paintings at which the devil was aiming.

Click, click, click.

No bullets.

"Poor thing," Buddy said later. "I didn't say it then, but I'm saying it now. You tell it if you see it I'm a-gonna pray for its salvation."

Back in the jailhouse we told her, "Reverend Buddy gave us a message. He says he's praying for you."

She put a finger over her lips—shhh—and rolled her eyes upward, and with her other hand she pointed above. When we'd entered the room she had picked up the phone through which we were to speak, but the only thing she would say out loud was her name. She'd told the arresting officer it was Christy but demanded as a man that he be put down on the police report as "Isshizean Zean," along with the facts that he was Jewish and from New Jersey. In the few words we heard, her accent shifted as effortlessly as the depth and tone of her voice; she could have been from anywhere. Her fingerprints revealed nothing and the gun was untraceable.

She told us she was "MIKAEL DourenT," the first name to be all capitals, and also the final letter, behind which she said her true name was hiding. Then she went silent, but she didn't stop talking. Our conversation proceeded by gesture and emotion. She laughed, and when we laughed, too, she started to cry. She kissed the phone receiver, into which she did nothing but breathe. She made a fist with her left hand.

There was a tattoo at the crook of the thumb. Deep black, blurry at the edges, but the shape of it was clear: a heart. Not a valentine but the real thing, a four-chambered organ, the aorta poking from the top like a horn.

She propped her head on the tattooed hand. Slowly, her tongue began to extend from between her lips; longer and longer, its tip narrowing until it was like a finger about to tap the glass. Then it turned, hooking back on itself. It moved toward the tattoo, quivered and licked the black heart with a swirl. Her teeth held her tongue like a small animal, a trapped rabbit or a squirrel. Bit by bit, she pulled it back in until it was gone.

She pointed above again, then brought the pointed finger down and aimed it at us like a gun, smiling; her teeth, we noticed, were white and well cared for. Then, the gun still cocked, she pursed her lips and leaned forward, as if hiding from her own hand. Her eyes sagged, tears rolled, her lips began to move as if she was looking for words. No sounds came through the receiver.

"I'll tell you what," Wesley said, "prayer is so powerful we don't even need to see that person to force the devil outta her. We can go ahead and do it right here. Isn't that so, Buddy?"

"Well, I don't see why not," Buddy answered.

"That's right," Wesley cheered. "We can pray the devil off her from clear cross town."

Billy Joe clapped his hands and rubbed them together. "Whew!" He couldn't wait to get started. He began marching between the pews, praying like a fire hydrant cranked open. "We thank you Heavenly Father for the opportunity you are about to give us to welcome you among us and fill us with the most Holy Spirit of your only Son as it is in Heaven and shall be on earth forever and ever in your everlasting glory! Father! Thank you! Amen!"

Wesley interrupted him. "Pastor Buddy, would you lead us this evening in a prayer for the troubled person who brought a firearm into God's house?"

"I would surely like to."

Buddy reached behind the pulpit and retrieved a glass bottle with a half-torn olive oil label.

"Who is willing?" he called out.

Billy Joe stood at attention. "I am, Buddy."

"I am willing, Pastor Buddy," Wesley said.

Buddy ignored the two younger men, turning instead to Billy Sr., who had been sitting quietly, his hands folded in his lap.

"I am if you need me, Buddy," he said and shuffled toward the center of the room, lifting his arms as if surrendering. Buddy plugged the bottle with his thumb and turned it over, then dabbed oil on Billy's hands and temples.

"Let all who will, come!" Buddy shouted. "Let all be blessed who pray in Jesus' name!"

He turned the bottle again and blessed himself, then passed it around to Wesley, to Billy Joe, then to us. We dipped the bottle into our palms, and with Buddy, Billy Joe, and Wesley, formed a circle around Billy Sr., gripping his flannel-covered shoulders with our oiled hands.

"Lord!" called Buddy. "We're praying to you now in the name of your most holy son Jesus!"

"Glooooory!" Wesley hollered. "Hallelujah!"

"Lord!" shouted Buddy. "We know you're in that prison cell with that soul who brought a weapon into your house and we know the devil's there too!"

Billy Joe began mumbling his prayer like an engine revving at a stoplight, waiting for the signal to change. "Heavenly Father we pray that you come before us this night we pray for your presence and your blessing your mercy Heavenly Father."

Buddy rolled on. "Lord! We ask in your most holy name to expel those demons from that lost person, to wash him or her in your loving mercy, to make free his soul of demonic possession!"

Billy Sr. stood dead still in the center, his arms up, his fingers fluttering like a dainty good-bye. His prayer was a steady beat under the others': "C'mon down Jesus. C'mon down Jesus. C'mon down Jesus."

"LORD!" Buddy called. All heads jerked back, the volume of his praise was so great. The air in the church changed, charged with all voices at once.

"LORD!"

"C'mon down Jesus!"

Billy Joe clenched his fists and started raving like an Appalachian jihadi, his voice popping and ringing. Recognizable words fell away, replaced by rolling exultations in a language that sounded like a cross between Aramaic and Klingon:

"Shanaza palamniaz rapuptanah! Shana zarni pakling ostababajar!"

Across the circle the spirit came simultaneously to Wesley and caused him to chant in Latinate so crisp it might have come straight from the Vatican:

"Paliate rotinatur opiscopicopum! Adjerminate oliosphate copulum horarum!"

"IN JESUS' NAME!"

"C'mon down Jesus! C'mon down Jesus!"

"Sha na ba ta ba rabbadada ostapakanar!"

We began to shout, ourselves.

"Help!"

Help? Who? The hermaphrodite gunman? Sure. Buddy and co.? Absolutely. Us? Hell, yes. We were scared of Christy-Isshizean-Zean-MIKAEL-DourenT-and-more-hidden, and we were fucking terrified of Billy Joe and his holy war. Even Sheriff Breedlove had given us a fright, drawing a phony revolver on us when we'd first met him. To see if we'd jump, he'd said, and to teach us a lesson about how things that aren't real can still hurt you. "See now," he'd said, holding up the cap gun, "you'd pulled that on me, I woulda shot you."

"God! Help! Help, God!"

We stuck to English, but we began praying like Billy Joe and Wesley, our shouting unheeded in the spirit-filled circle of powa: God-help-us-Jesus-or-whatever-save-us-from-Hell-save-Isshizean-Zean-too-get-the-devil-outta-her-and-this-place-too-while-you're-at-it—Breath—Help! Help! Help!

"LORD!" Buddy roared, his head thrown back and his lips distended, stretching to let out the mighty word. We could hear Billy Joe's and Wesley's tongues weakening, but they each strained to muster a few more spirit-filled syllables, until they came to a shared, ululating climax. Billy Sr. let his arms fall, and Wesley faded us out, wringing his hands together in a prayer grip, his voice murmuring as all others fell quiet: "Glooory ... glooory ... glooory ..."

The prayer circle joined hands: Billy Joe linked to Reverend Buddy, Buddy linked to Billy Sr., Billy Sr. linked to Wesley. We took the hands offered to us, completing the circuit between Wesley and Billy Joe, who still was shaking with the spirit, convulsing every few seconds as though receiving an electric charge. His grip tightened with every jolt, and we could feel it—sure as we'd felt the cold outside and, inside, the erratic heat of the church's clanging radiator—surging through Billy Joe's fingers into ours, a charge like a knife in an outlet, shooting up our arms until it became a ringing in our ears. We felt it as sure as we'd felt the strange unsettling power glaring through the bulletproof window at the Vance County lockup. Sure as we'd jumped when Sheriff Breedlove had pulled his toy gun.

When the circle broke apart, Wesley cradled his arms and rocked them back and forth, whispering. "I just feel the Lord holding me like a little baby." Then we all just stood there, the silence so great it felt like we were separated by glass, until Wesley said, "And I know you boys felt something, too."

> Where you die, I will die, and there I will be buried.
>
> Ruth 1:17

RUTH

By Lê Thi Diem Thúy

ONE

Last night I dreamed that my mother's death was a lie, one she told, one she staged, in order to "get out of something." As in life, she did not elaborate. I was confused, amazed. I told her I thought it excessive to stage one's own death. I also thought it was the best lie she'd ever told.

In the dream, I saw her as I had never seen her in life: naked, admiring herself before a mirror. She was standing. She raised her arms over her head. She glanced vaguely toward the ceiling and, smiling, said something like "Oh yes, I was over there the whole time."

I knew I was dreaming because she had a full head of hair, and the bones in her chest were no longer visible, and the flesh on her arms, when she raised them, was full, and there were small, silken threads there that caught the light.

In the dream, I was the age I am now but my body was small as a child's; as I sat listening to her, I saw that my feet didn't touch the ground; they dangled. I didn't like seeing them like that. What age was I?

My mother's body lies between her father's and her brother's, in the rambling cemetery overlooking the sea in Phan Thiet.

After the funeral, my younger sister and I swam in the sea. It was raining

and we were the only people in the water. Our cousins sat under beach um-
brellas and watched us. Their mothers, our aunts, told me that, as the oldest
child, I would know three years of mourning, "Nothing but mourning!" and
then, after the third year, "Happiness. Like you have never known." I didn't
believe them.

I was happy then and there, floating on the water.

I boarded a plane and flew back to the States, alone. Whereupon I sat down
and began a note to the doctors and nurses who had taken care of my mother:
My name is thúy lê, my mother was My Nguyen. You may remember her—

I pushed the note aside. I wasn't asking if they remembered her. I was saying, I
grant you permission to remember her. I was saying, Will you remember her with
me? I was saying, Read her name aloud, next to my name, and remember us.

I continued—I am writing to let you know that she passed away on March
23, at 11:05 A.M., surrounded by family and friends, in her childhood home in
Vietnam. Thank you for the kindness and the care you gave to her.

The phone call came in early December: My mother had been admitted to
the emergency room. A tumor the size of a lemon. Advanced stage of colon
cancer. Spread to the liver. What can be done? Painkillers. At this late stage,
when the cancer is so far advanced. She's young, only forty-eight years old.
However at this late stage, I have to tell you. There are very effective
painkillers.

I listened closely and carefully. I opened my notebook, and turning past the
pages where I'd copied out a recipe for "Pear and cherry tart, serves 8" and a
recipe for "Mussel and tomato soup, serves 4," I made the following notes:

CAT scan—cancer
biopsy tomorrow
cancer in uterus
spread to liver

and then I did my laundry and packed some things

ink cartridges
letter box
atlas

denim dress
striped T-shirt
tank tops

and washed my hair.

I went to bed, woke, and boarded a plane to San Diego.

I pulled the hospital curtain aside and there she was, thinner than I had ever seen her. She sat up, and I leaned in to hug her. As I held her in my arms, all I could feel was my own panicked heart, racing.

Her doctor came by and as he spoke to me, she listened, unblinking. Whenever he looked at her, she smiled. As soon as he left, she turned to me. "What is it? What did he say?" "I'm not sure," I said. "I'm trying to understand."

On the plane to Singapore, en route to Vietnam, I sat beside a man from New York City. He was part of a group of people who were headed to Bali for a vacation. "Scuba diving," he said. "Ever been?" "No," I said, "though I've always wanted to." Outside the window: clouds and night. "What's in Vietnam? Are you from there?" "Yes. My mother."

Flying back from Vietnam, there was a long layover in Singapore. I floated in the swimming pool of the airport hotel. It was night and plane after plane took off over me, while a three-quarters moon hung high above, looking down as I looked up, neither of us blinking.

It is close to two years now, but I seem to smell again the choke of bouquets slowly filling the house in Vietnam. I remember the chill of the blocks of ice delivered one at a time and placed underneath her coffin. Twenty-six blocks in all, before we took her from the house.

The bus carrying the coffin overheated and stopped in the middle of the narrow dirt road, blocking the two buses carrying the mourners from continuing any further. The pallbearers pulled the coffin from the back of the bus and heaved it onto their shoulders. Aunts and uncles, siblings and lovers, children and childhood friends stepped off the buses and followed my mother's body. We made our way up the hill, toward the cemetery. "She's unhappy." "No, she's acting up, exactly the way she used to." "She wants to be carried all the way up." "Of course, she does. It's gentler this way."

When we got to the cemetery, I stood at the head of the grave and looked out across the staggered gravestones, past the valley of small wooden houses, to the hills in the distance. It was 6:30 in the morning. We had been up since 4:00. The sky before us was pale blue and gold. But off to our right, there were dense gray clouds and the sound of thunder. Our party gathered around the grave, the young priest opened his mouth to intone about my mother, and it rained.

Not a hard rain, nothing to run from, but rain nonetheless; yet another reminder that nothing was going as planned. My cousin turned to me and whispered, "Your mother wasn't ready to go." I thought about the conversation I'd overheard the night before, between my younger sister and her boyfriend, who had phoned from Bangkok. He must've asked her how she was doing. Either she said, "I am fine." Or she said, "I am not fine."

One evening, shortly after I returned to the States, I accidentally knocked over a small water glass. Though there was time to catch it, I felt unable to do so. I watched as it rolled off the table; it seemed to roll very slowly. I thought, It will break. It will break. It will break. And then I thought, No, it won't. It will roll like that forever. When it landed in broken bits at my feet, I burst into tears, surprised. Then I went on to break a yellow vase, and a beautiful blue dish. I would have gone on to break everything in the house, except that something in me said: Don't play the fool.

Time was like a muscle, expanding and contracting. Whatever had been storming inside of me came to a momentary halt. I sat on the floor and listened as the radiators stirred to life; they made strange, gurgling sounds that struck me as infantile, searching. Outside, the wind shook the trees and beat against the building. My two cats were hiding under the bed. The hyacinth on the windowsill gave off a mournful scent. I lay down on the floor, exhausted beyond reason.

TWO

I envy the girl who seems to step forward from nowhere and becomes steadfastened to the woman's side. The girl has lost a family, a husband, gods, but she doesn't seem to care. So long as she is beside the woman, all is right. No harm comes to her.

She is content to walk the length of any road the woman takes her on.

She'll lie at the foot of a stranger's bed and feel secure, because the woman directs her to do so.

She is better than seven sons and will give birth to a boy from whom a great and mighty king will descend.

Who is this girl, who does not waver; who, from the moment we meet her, is resolute; who cries once, but never again?

Ruth's first conversation with Mahlon. They are both twelve. His family has just moved to Moab from Bethlehem. He runs from the house and hides behind a tree that she is sitting in. She calls down to him:

"What's wrong?" she asks.

"Nothing."

"What happened?"

"Who are you?"

"Saw you running."

"Go away. I don't want to be here."

Ruth and Mahlon, teenagers.

"Who were you before I knew you, before I found you to love you like this?" she asks, pressing her palms flat against his chest. Mahlon says, "I was a boy, lying in a field, trying to get away from God, who, as my father kept saying, is king. Your hair smells good." "Was God not in the field?" "Is. He is everywhere and in all things, Ruth." "That's your father's voice." "It's God's voice speaking through my father speaking through me." "I like your voice by itself. Tell me about the field."

What Ruth sees while standing in the gleaners' field: That the gleaners were women whose bodies looked, in the evening light, like so many needles, rising and falling, mending the field with a darkening thread.

Naomi gathers the girls to her:

This happens three times. The first time was when Ruth and Orpah married her sons, Mahlon and Chilion. As she embraced the girls, she saw how her sons stood close by, proudly looking on. Shame her husband was not alive to see this, Naomi thought.

The second time was ten years later, on the day of the funeral. As Mahlon and Chilion were lowered into the ground, Ruth and Orpah both leaned into her.

The third time was when Naomi set out for Bethlehem. Ruth and Orpah set out with her. She stopped in the middle of the road and turning to them said, Go back. They were all three widows, but she counted herself the only widow, because the girls were young—they were crying now exactly like children—and would one day remarry. She embraced them. She kissed them. Then she insisted that they go back.

For a moment, they both remained in her arms, then Orpah, crying, slowly turned away. Ruth held fast to Naomi. The girl seemed barely able to stand. And yet, she made such declarations! Where you go, I will go. Where you sleep, I will sleep. Where you die, I will die.

An unsent postcard, addressed to Orpah:

> These are the gates Naomi and I walked through. Naomi seems well, but I don't know what I am doing here. Every now and then I'll see two boys walking together and I'll think Mahlon and Chilion, age seven and nine; or on my way to the gleaners' field, I'll pass by a group of old men sitting at these very gates, and I'll think Mahlon and Chilion, now sixty and sixty-two; a man walks toward me on the street, tall and thin and somewhat sickly and I'll think: Mahlon at forty, Mahlon at fifty.
> He is not there and he is not here, either. What did I expect?
> There is a man here named Boaz. ~~Naomi believes that he~~
> ~~Naomi thinks that I~~

How Naomi might characterize Boaz:
Strong. Perfect.

How Ruth might characterize Boaz:
Not unkind.

While Boaz sleeps on the threshing floor, Ruth lies at his feet, and practices whispering what she will say to him when he wakes: I am Ruth. Take me into your hands. Throw the cover over me. Cover me. Draw me nearer to you.

Ruth remembers a shape she saw:
After Naomi had lost all her men—first her husband, then her sons—she lay down on her bed and, curling her head to her knees, cried, "I have no one."

Ruth thinks of Mahlon and practices speaking of him in the past tense:
He was. He was. He was.

• • •

Ruth, Orpah, and the sun:

As Orpah was walking away, the sun shone brightly upon her. It struck the clasp of the necklace that Chilion had given to her. A blinding spot of light. Whenever Ruth pictured Orpah now, it wasn't her face or even her body that came to mind, but the back of her neck, with its burning center.

THREE

We are approaching the second year. Then there will be a third year. When the third year passes, the happiness my aunts predicted, the happiness of the sort I have never known, may arrive. It may be something like the sadness of these years, sadness of a sort I have never known.

In the late afternoon of this great day that my aunts speak of, I will be standing here, at the window, watching a woman with a red umbrella cross the empty parking lot below. The phone will ring and someone I have not seen or heard from in many years, let's say ten, will be on the other end of the line. If I were Ruth, I would listen to his breath and think of Mahlon.

The man is not unkind. He will ask, How are you? But before I can answer, he will tell me how he came across my name in the paper. How he looked at my name for a long time, how he ran his finger across the letters as if to tie them together. How he lifted his finger and there was my name. How he said my name aloud to himself, slowly sounding out the syllables, as if he was learning to read for the first time.

I will wonder: What name is he talking about?

If I am myself when the man calls, and if the rain continues to fall, I will take the rain as a good sign and say, This is wonderful! It's as if the rain brought you. I may open the window and tell him, Listen, holding the phone to the sky.

If I am Ruth, and I continue talking with this man, all the while thinking, Perhaps he is Mahlon, but he doesn't know how to tell me, I may boldly tell him that I feel restless and wish that he could somehow come to me.

An awkward silence will follow.

As myself, in the silence, I will look at the sky, focusing on a string of clouds.

To salvage the conversation I will say, The rain has stopped. The sun is going to set soon. It's begun to turn the sky to rose. He will tell me about the weather in his part of the country. Maybe he is in Montana and they haven't seen rain for months.

As Ruth, I will imagine my fist against his chest or the flat of my hand—of both my hands—pushing against him, pushing him away while at the same time feeling the pressure of his leaning into me, the fact of his body nearer to me, and his eyes, his face, everything about him closer now. As Ruth, I will press my forehead against the windowpane and, studying the shape of my feet in the darkening light, ask the man if he is afraid.

The man will tell me that he is not afraid; he is not a farmer; the drought doesn't affect him as much as it does the others; imagine hundreds of acres of dry— And here the man will make what sounds like a strange inhalation of breath.

Are you all right? I will ask.

Oh, I've been lying on the floor this whole time and I just sat up to get a cig-arette, the man will explain.

You smoke now? This will be Ruth asking, incredulous, concerned. She will drop her gaze to a car passing by on the street below. With her eyes, she will follow the car as far down the road as possible.

As myself, I will step away from the window and—cradling the phone against my ear—I will walk through the living room into the kitchen, open the refrigerator, and pour a glass of water. The man will listen to the sound of my footsteps. He will guess—correctly—that my feet are bare. He will feel embar-rassed, as if by thinking about my bare feet, he has crossed some line.

As Ruth and as myself, I will not know what the man is thinking about. As Ruth and as myself, I will suddenly feel I have no idea who this man is. I will take a sip of water, put the glass down on the kitchen counter, and I will say to him, It's strange that you should call today, of all days.

He will say, Why is that?

He will say, You know, you haven't answered my question. How are you?

And then, regardless of whether or not this person is at all connected to some happiness of the sort I have never known, as Ruth and as myself, I will look at the glass of water I've just poured and say, I've been swimming. And something I've noticed is that when I am doing the crawl, and I turn to look at people swimming beside me, they often appear to be swimming in place, es-pecially if they are doing the breaststroke. It's a wonder we get anywhere, let alone to the other side.

• • •

A day to the year, two years, three years, four years, five years since my mother died. All day yesterday, as if in anticipation of today, I felt an intense pain at the very center of my back. It was as if I had been kicked there.

But when I woke this morning, something in the air smelled like early spring. Grateful for this strange sweetness, and for the intactness of my own body, I looked at the ceiling and whispered to no one, "Here we are."

It is raining, but not hard and not cold.

Just now, the wind blew, and each of those bushes lining the edge of the parking lot across the street seemed to shudder.

Night. The heater by the window is whistling. A car passes, rain spinning off its tires. A man is standing in the empty parking lot, calling to a dog. The dog bounds toward him, its collar rattling as it runs. Closing time at the restaurant below; someone is emptying the night's wine bottles into the recycling bin; glass shattering. Two women walking by. One says to the other, "Oh, I know." And now they are both laughing. On this desk: a jar filled with sand collected from the cemetery in Phan Thiet; a small lamp illuminating a glass of water; and a box of matches I picked up from a café my cousin took me to the day my mother died.

Outside, the rain falls at a slant from right to left, softly and almost without sound. Here I sit. Thrown across the wall before me: the twitching shadow of my hand as I move the pen across the page, from left to right.

Let the words hold brightly, like a sunstruck clasp.

Let the words splinter, as I imagine Ruth's mind splintering after she has lifted sheaf after sheaf of wheat from the gleaners' field and, drawing them to her, finds no trace of Mahlon.

Let the words keen, as I refused to do during my mother's funeral.

Let the words lie so that when someone asks, "Where is your mother now?" I can say, "She is probably in her kitchen in San Diego, banging pots and pans around." Or "She is on her way to the casino to lose money she doesn't have." Or "She is driving, without a license, to her favorite Vietnamese restaurant, in Orange County."

Let the words be humble, let them know the world did not begin with words, but with two bodies pressed close, one crying, and one singing.

MYRTLE BEACH, SOUTH CAROLINA

Our mouths were filled with laughter,

our tongues with songs of joy . . .

PSALM 126:2

As we left the church in Henderson, Billy Joe jogged after us into the parking lot. "Stop right there, boys!" he shouted. We did, even though we knew that should have been our cue to run. Charging toward us, his plumber's fists pumping, just when we thought, He's really going to hit us, he burst between us and past, knocking us aside like bowling pins. "I got something in the truck you boys are gonna need," he said and stopped short before a spotless metallic beige Dodge Ram with a king-size cab. He rummaged in the pickup's glove box, then spun around with a postcard in each hand, pointing them like six-shooters. "You boys put these on your dashboard," he said, "and you'll never get lost." We each took a card: miniature reproductions of the apocalypse paintings behind the church's pulpit, everything from the crumpled cars and the twisted bodies to the tractor-trailer in flames, the airplane crashing into the skyscraper, and Jesus above it all like a sunspot on a Polaraid of the end times.

"Thanks," we said.

We weren't fifteen minutes back on the highway before we opened our windows and let the postcards fly into the wind.

• • •

Dick's Last Resort in North Myrtle Beach, South Carolina was the last place we expected to hear folks talking about God; it was the kind of place where you were likely to find yourself seated under a bra stapled to the ceiling. Pastel stalactites of lingerie hung down in a semicircle around the bar, dangling evidence that real people had sat on barstools and unhooked themselves there; that lady golfers had said, "Can you help me with this, honey?" and then like magicians pulled cups and straps through their sleeves.

Dick's was also the kind the place where if you looked quickly at the crowd you might mistake them for hungry Klansmen at a KKK luncheon. A full half of Dick's patrons, men and women, grandmothers and children, dug into their buckets of coleslaw and barbecue wearing three-foot-tall cones of white butcher paper on their heads, each cone's pointed top rolled into a ball that resembled the reservoir tip of a condom. The waitstaff would routinely scribble on hats an embarrassing sexual factoid in black Magic Marker: "I shave my crotch"; "2.5""; "I'd rather be eating *her.*"

"Don't mind them," the bouncer shouted when we stopped in for a much-needed drink in the least spiritual place we could find. "They're just the Dick-heads. They come for the atmosphere but stay for the abuse!"

The Dickheads whoop-whooped in their pointy hats; there was nothing they loved more than for the waitstaff to be rude and sarcastic with them. It was the theme of the place, in fact. Apparently, it was fun.

We'd pulled into town a few days before to check in for a week's stay at the Meher Spiritual Center, the "home in the West" of the late Indian guru Meher Baba, believed by many to be the "Avatar of the Age," the latest in an endless parade of "corporeal manifestations of the divine." Baba "dropped his body" in 1969, but as seen in the videos frequently shown at the center, he'd been a manifestation with a kind, almost silly manner; one of his most popular teachings consisted of pulling a hard candy from his pocket and winging it at one of his followers. He tut-tutted around with a jolly gait that seemed to forget the heft of his barrel-wide body, and this, combined with his oversized eyes and long, sloping nose, gave him a resemblance to both Charlie Chaplin and the Hindu elephant-god, Ganesh. He heightened his mystique by communicating through a Ouija board–like slate, which he twirled and bobbled as smoothly as a Harlem Globetrotter and on which his long fingers could spell words nearly as fast as they could be spoken. In response to questions about his spiritual identity, Baba tap-tapped things like "I am God in human form. Of course many people say they are God-incarnate, but they are hypocrites." To which a Dick's employee might have replied, "Thanks for clearing that up, Baba."

There were at one time as many as a million devotees of Baba in India and thousands in the United States. Their numbers had dwindled, but several hundred still lived right there in Myrtle Beach, by day running alligator tours and sea captain carving emporiums, by evening walking the winding paths of the compound, an exquisite piece of land with oceanfront, woods, and a freshwater lake, given to Baba by a wealthy follower decades ago and now valued at $50 million. Baba had been fond of tooling around the lake in a Venetian gondola donated by another fan, but besides boating and strolling there's not much to do there, and very little ritual to partake in. Devotees make do by trading Baba stories, modeling Baba scenes in clay, and making Baba pictures, in oil or charcoal or colored macaroni. Baba Lovers, as they call themselves, believe with the sincerity if not the fervor of first-century Christians. Bereft of the teacher but still enthralled by his memory, they are touched as deeply by his image as they are by the words he left behind. A portrait of Baba hangs on every wall of every building at the Meher Center. Baba's eyes don't need to follow you as you walk across a room; there are so many pairs of them that he never misses a thing.

One generation removed from their master's physical presence, the loose community built around the Meher Center is now engaged in a tricky negotiation between its desire to spread Baba's message and his directive that his teachings not be used to start a religion. How do they do it? Easy, they act like nothing's wrong. Baba saw all this coming, after all, so they just keep hoping he will work it out. In the meantime they sing Baba songs, do Baba dances, sit in Baba rooms filled with Baba chairs and think Baba thoughts. Like any religion that doesn't want to be seen as "merely" a religion, they start teaching Baba early on, so the word and the man will be bred in the bones.

In the Meher Center library there's a children's book called *Baba, Baba Everywhere,* the first page of which shows a kid's drawing of a brightly colored cup of alphabet soup. "Baba, Baba in my soup," the book begins. On the facing page, Baba's features float in a dark broth: two intense black eyes, a great big nose, and a mustache that would have been equally enjoyed by Frank Zappa or Joseph Stalin, all surrounded by little yellow B's and A's. The next page reads: "Baba, Baba, on my stoop." Here's Baba on concrete stairs

watching two girls play hopscotch. "Baba, Baba in my hair." There's Baba
peeking out from a forest of wild brown and blond strands. "Baba, Baba
Everywhere!" Baba as wide eyes on a wildflower, as a hooked nose on a
water bug, as a smiling sun, as a whistling cloud, as a mustache on a breaking
wave.

The Baba world looks like the world the rest of us see, with a slight but significant difference: If it's all Baba, it's all good. Baba Lovers don't want the
world, they just want the world to be more than it seems. More meaningful.
More intentional. Just plain *more*. Keep turning pages in *Baba, Baba Everywhere* and you'll find Baba as the air you breathe, Baba as the ground beneath your feet. Look down and he's looking up: eyes, nose, mustache, and
an impish grin on a globe shaped like his head. It would be scary if it wasn't
so cute. Or maybe it's the other way around.

Which brings us back to Dick's. When we asked for a seat in the "No Dickheads" section, the bouncer pointed us toward the bar. We were less than a
mile from the Meher Center's gate, and we couldn't resist asking the locals
what they thought of having the sometime home of God just down the road.

"Weirdest thing," the bartender said. "Never heard of it until yesterday."
His name was Frazier, a thickset guy in his late thirties, wearing a goatee, a
blue Hawaiian shirt, and denim shorts to his knees. He liked to put his leg up
on a case of beer and lean in while he talked. "Live here thirty years and don't
know a thing about the place. Then yesterday I find out there's a girl here who
knows all about it. Hold on just a minute—"

Frazier came out from behind the bar and disappeared into a forest of
Dickheads. Two stools down, a chubby girl in black jeans stubbed out her
cigarette and blew smoke in the air. She turned to us and said she'd heard us
talking about religion. She was raised Southern Baptist, she confided, but
now she was a witch.

"Oh, really?" we said. "Is there a Wiccan community around here?"

"Nope."

"You're it?"

"Yep."

A few minutes later a red-bearded, red-eyed giant appeared behind us. He
sized us up, looking us over with eyes as big as our heads. "You the guys asking folks about religion?" he demanded.

We both nodded, starting to rise and puff out our chests—it's an instinct,
you know—even as we eyed the door.

"My name's Barry and I live on up near Bolivia, North Carolina. We got some Buddhist fellers up there now and they're just the nicest bunch a guys you'll ever meet. They got a crew that go out weekends, clean up litter and roadkill on the roadsides."

Barry swayed a little as he spoke, left to right, forward and back. Maybe he was just excited to be talking about the Buddhists of Bolivia, but he looked like he was going to fall on us.

Just then Frazier came back with a pretty young blonde in tow. Close-cropped hair and a dimple in her chin, she was holding a waitress's apron; her shift had just ended. Tattooed on her right arm were purple grapes so carefully drawn they suggested a Greek statue; it was hard to imagine her making the crass remarks Dick's was known for. She knew all about the Buddhists of Bolivia, though.

"I brought them some donuts once, and listened to their prayers for a while," she said. "Because they only eat what you bring them."

Frazier put a beer in front of her and made the introductions. Her name was Liz Wilcocks, and though she was no longer an everyday Baba Lover, her parents had been among those who'd moved to Myrtle Beach to be near Baba.

"So how did it feel to grow up at God's summer home?" we asked.

"Who? Baba? Oh, it was no big deal. I mean, people thought he was God and all, but it wasn't so important. Some of the Baptist kids in town said it was devil worship, but the worst they did was make fun of us on the bus. I never thought Baba was God, but being there made me curious about those kinds of things.

"Like once I tried astral projection. I had to stop, though. I was pregnant with my daughter, and I was afraid what would happen if I left my body and couldn't get back. I didn't want her in there alone."

The next day Liz visited us at the Meher Center, where we were staying in a cabin on the lake. She brought her two-year-old daughter, Zoë, a daffodil blonde with chubby cheeks and a dimpled chin just like her mother's. Liz took Zoë everywhere but Dick's; she was a single mom. At the center, she pushed Zoë through the woods in a stroller, guiding us through scenes from her childhood—Ping-Pong in the Baba rec room, hide-and-seek behind Baba trees, stalking alligators in the Baba gator pond—as she rolled Zoë to Baba's playground. There Zoë slid, swung, and scooped up fistfuls of sand, but what interested her most was the screen door of the gazebo at the heart of the playground. She leaned the whole of her weight into it, pushing with muscles she was just learning she had. "Come on, Farthead, you can do it," Liz coaxed. When the door budged open a few inches, Zoë giggled and clapped her hands against the weathered wood, letting go just long enough for the door to swing back toward her, bumping her down to the gazebo's floor. "Oh, Zoë, you're fine," Liz said. "Can you try again?" Zoë scrambled up, small pink hands pounding at the wooden door like it was a drum. "Push it, don't hit it, Zoë," Liz said. "You can get through."

Liz didn't know yet what she'd tell Zoë about Baba. "It's true," she said, stretching to catch the door with her hand as Zoë ambled onto the porch of the gazebo. "Baba *is* everywhere. I just don't know why we have to talk about him so much. Okay, maybe people think he's God; great; move on, you know? The world's bigger than the Meher Center, and it's sure as hell bigger than Myrtle Beach."

She glanced over at Zoë, who had turned around to be sure her mother had seen what she had accomplished. "I just love looking in her eyes," Liz said. "I love looking at what's ahead for her." Then she stopped talking long enough to catch Zoë from falling down a shallow step outside the gazebo.

"What I was saying last night," she said, taking us back to Dick's. "I'm going to try it again. Astral projection."

"Why?"

"I don't know. It seemed close to what I'm hoping to experience."

"What's that?"

Liz smiled and looked across the lake at the dunes separating it from the ocean. "Not Dick's . . . ," she said, and we thought of the hanging bras, the condom-capped patrons, the neon beer signs in the window. "Not all my nights in a bar . . ." She had been working there for five years.

Finally she answered: "More."

Baba; more—not different names for God but different names for longing. More, more everywhere. But only because it was nowhere to be found. "Baba, what is life?" a follower once asked him. "Life is a mighty joke," he answered. We could hear the Dickheads laughing.

Here is the king walking before you.

1 SAMUEL 12:2

SAMUEL

BY APRIL REYNOLDS

RHETORICALLY pregnant, yet without predicate noun or adjective, *I AM* . . . rang out, but no one acknowledged the sound. *I AM*. . . . The beginnings of an emaciated, ancient hope battled cranky refrigerators and petite wives afflicted with adenoiditis, and lost. *I AM*. . . . Twelve men woke coughing away morning phlegm, unclear in which direction lay the path to glory. For a moment the voice subsided, only to reappear within their dreams, in their place of worship, ruthlessly turning to terror. *HE* knew no other way. Nightly, these men were pursued by flaming cherubs, a machete-wielding Christ—wooden statues from their church come to life with deadly aim. *I AM* . . . *I AM* . . . *I AM* . . .

None of the twelve deacons rose from bed in a cold sweat, but like women, they woke covered in perspicuous moisture, embarrassed as they reached for Kleenexes to pat themselves dry. There was no need to tell each other about the nightmares. For the deacons, each man's experience was felt collectively. Each donned his Sunday gloves in the same fashion, all shared an identical aversion to peanuts. Each fucked his wife in the missionary position, each politely demanded that his wife demurely cross her ankles behind his back, as if waiting in a dentist's office. Each knew the culprit behind his nightmares. No, not themselves—the decisions to put on a production of *West Side Story* and to hold a canned prune drive were good ones. Who could have foreseen that no one would come to either function? The fault did not lie with them, not these God-fearing men. No, it was the church. The wooden structure in which they worshiped was to blame. There was no mistaking their collective shudder when they stepped through its doors, the revulsion they felt when they walked past the wooden artichoke cornices perched at the edges of each pew. The walls, the partitions, the floors, the sloping double hammer-beamed roof, all made of oak, birch, and pine, were thwarting grander ambitions. Something had to be done.

The Ethiopian United Federated Church of Christ had been founded and built by a group of black lumber foremen, who had not only been woodcarvers by trade but idolized English woodwork. They had dreamed of Devonshire paneling in walnut, but their reverence had been tempered by constant financial constraints, forcing them to use compressed pine shavings for decorative wainscoting. Sprinkled throughout the church were ornament pieces carved from birch, when the thirty foremen would have preferred oak. The Ethiopian was a potpourri of wood, cleverly disguised with shellac. They had used lacquer, penciling the Ascension in high relief along the side paneling to hide the cheapness of some of the wood. The congregation never knew which was which.

Since 1916, the EUFCC had had a constant population of the not-yet-bourgeois. Most parishioners were accountants and secretaries, though none of them could afford to travel during vacation. By the time the last founder died in 1968, the deacons were left with a mahogany pulpit worn glass-smooth at the edges, and eighty-three congregants. Under their tenure the Ethiopian United Federated Church of Christ's congregation had dwindled to thirty. So it wasn't just the nightmares filled with statues made of varnished pine, elm, and alder. Visions were something these men could endure. Between the twelve of them, they had served in three American wars, witnessed a score of urban riots, and walked with King—all braved with nary a cry of discomfort. A greater fear loomed. Young mothers now decided to have their children baptized elsewhere; no one darkened their offices for counseling; there hadn't been a wedding at the Ethiopian in almost six years. Moreover, their small congregation was aging. Most of the collection money was spent on WD-40 for wheelchairs. Two parishioners had died in the past year, and three others were on their last legs. In a few years, there would be no one to attend Sunday services.

So they started looking for a new pastor, a man who might lead new souls to their church. Traveling by train, they tore a wide swath into the South: Washington, D.C., Richmond, Raleigh, and it took until Charleston, South Carolina, for the twelve men to figure out that they should sidestep the larger southern cities altogether. Most of them had as many denominations as New York. Even the towns caused problems. Macon, Georgia, alone had more than three hundred places of worship. Churches like the African Methodist Episcopal Zion, Associated Gospel Churches of Macon, and the Baptist Bible Fellowship had more than five services on Sunday, and each turned away would-be congregants because of lack of space. But the deacons persevered — Sweet Briar, Southern Pines, Bishopville — until they found not quite what they were looking for in a small town inside Lafayette County, Arkansas.

The deacons encountered, preaching to a congregation of 150, one black-as-tar Charlemagne Zephaniah Harpon, known to his parishioners and neighbors as Reverend Carl, conducting church like an emcee at an R & B concert. Slim as a ballet dancer, he mocked gravity, jumping and twirling in front of the pulpit, hovering in the air for what seemed an impossible amount of time. When his feet finally made contact with the ground beneath him, Reverend Carl took off, racing back and forth along the stage, pausing every now and again to deliver percussive footwork — brush, flap, shuffle, cramp, roll. Without a microphone, those not in the front pews could hear only one call, "Jeeeeeeeeeee . . ."

And then the almost desperate response, "Come on, baby. Give me the rest!"

"Suuuuuuuuuus. . . ."

"Sock it to me!!!" The twelve stood at the back of the church unable to make out the particulars of the pastor's sermon because of the cacophonous roar. A seven-year-old boy, shaking a tambourine, leapt into the aisle. Young women and children huddled around the stage, gasping at the pastor's verticality. It wasn't just his antics that disturbed the deacons. In their own suppressed fashion, they could appreciate the pastor's toe dancing. There was something quite beautiful in the way he moved into a ballerina's first and fourth positions. No, what they found most troublesome was that, without the benefit of language (no one beyond the front three pews could hear a thing), the entire congregation seemed involved in a bacchanalia. Where was the reverence? Why didn't one soul have a Bible open to read the Scriptures along with the pastor? Not one sleeping child lay hunched over his mother's lap.

Women who had obviously spent the entire previous night in curlers and under hair dryers needlessly ruined their hairdos, sweating their straightened coiffures back into nappiness. Men they assumed to be as old as themselves were also infected, laughing and crying openly as they slapped their knees. Joy and sorrow, the deacons believed, should not be on such wanton display. From the back of the church the twelve men took it all in, becoming less and less impressed with the soot-colored preacher. But concessions had to be made. They just couldn't face another night battling a knife-wielding Mary, and time was not on their side.

Up close, they were tempted to call off the entire thing. To begin with, he was short. Really short. As tall as a child just before puberty. With his processed hair, plated gold rings on the thumbs and pinkie fingers, he perched on the edge of his desk, swabbing himself dry with a powder blue towel, dressed in a purple-and-green-plaid polyester suit that not only was a size too small but looked as if someone had lightly dusted the lapels with silver glitter. Twelve men bottled a collective sigh when the Reverend's tentative smile revealed a gold lateral incisor.

"Hello, Reverend," said one of the twelve. "My name is Deacon Dan Shannon, and these are my colleagues: Deacon Rueben, Deacon Simon, Deacon Levi, Deacon Judah, Deacon Zebulon, Deacon Issachar, Deacon Gad, Deacon Asher, Deacon Naphtali, Deacon Joseph, and Deacon Benjamin. We are all deacons for the Ethiopian United Federated Church of Christ in New York City."

"What can I do you for?" Carl couldn't help but be impressed as the deacons filed into his office and stood against the wall.

"That was quite a service, Reverend."

"You should see me at Easter."

"Yes, well, I'm sure that would be quite a sight." Deacon Dan lapsed into lengthy silence, suddenly unsure where to begin with their proposal. Because of the glitter, the conked hair, the jewelry, they had all failed to recognize the most important aspect of the pastor before them. Carl Harpon was a true believer. His thought and purpose clear: *There is none as holy as the Lord: For there is none beside thee: Neither is there any rock like our Lord.* All donations were used for the church. He was as poor as most of his congregation and was proud of it. There was a reason why most of his parishioners behaved like zealots. He helped them file their taxes, filled out forms for Section Eight housing and food stamps. Every Sunday, 150 people gathered to pay homage to a man who not only sat down with them for dinner but helped them paint their houses and could unclog a toilet.

"Okay, fellas. I don't mean to rush you, but I got to pop my head in the Sunday school class. The kids get a real kick out of me coming in with my towel." But that was said because of his rising unease with the silence, the indistinguishable suits and bow ties. Sons of guns sizing me up, he thought.

"Oh, yes, and we wouldn't want to keep you," Deacon Dan said, clearing his throat. "Are you married, Reverend?"

"No. No, the Lord—"

"Yes, well, that could be taken care of in short order, couldn't it?" And before Carl had a chance to answer, Deacon Dan delivered the pitch. The other deacons, on cue, belched out small bouts of laughter around the performance. "We don't have frescoes, you understand, but we do have a relief or two that we are quite fond, dare I say, proud of." But it was the presence of twelve mocha brothers in the same suit that swayed him in a way no other argument they gave could. Twelve. His congregation of 150 had only three deacons and two ushers. Twelve? Their idea of modest was something else in Harlem, he thought as he heard their offer. Least three hundred, I bet. He pressed and pressed, but the deacons wouldn't give him an exact number, saying only, "We have a modest congregation in Harlem. But we do have great expectations. With your help, of course." And Carl leapt at the chance. The deacons were running out of time, but Carl had his own private desires, too.

And yet he should have known something was amiss when he could never tell the deacons apart and thus never got their names right. Every conversation he initiated had to be stopped and corrected before it had a chance to leave the ground. Their eighteenth-century smiles, able to quell even the most suspicious, convinced him to get on the train and settle into the small one-bedroom apartment next to their church. The living room window had been knocked in, the sink ran brown water, but he loved it. A delight he had never experienced overcame him when he realized he could buy lightbulbs, a stick of gum, and a mousetrap all from the same corner store. And more than anything he loved that the Ethiopian United Federated Church of Christ was an all-wooden church in the middle of concrete Harlem. The effort and skill, all in brown hues, inspired him. Some etchings weren't deep enough to withstand time, a wooden carving of the Last Supper had worn away into an unrecognizable lump, but the engraved, double hammer-beamed roof, along with the mahogany pulpit, hinted at greatness. He sat in the pews at sunset and noticed that from the lone window in the church, sunlight refracted in such a way that in the large wooden relief of the Virgin and Child, Mary's praying hands shaded baby Jesus' face. None of the deacons had observed this carpenter's feat.

"Bunch of black guys got together and did this?"

Their contemptuous smiles weren't directed at Carl. "Yes, Reverend."

"I can't wait to see the folks who praise the Lord here. Can't wait."

During his first Sunday service Carl realized they had lied. A congregation of sixty was modest, not twenty-seven (three congregants had died while they searched for the new pastor), fifteen of whom who would be dead in less than three years from old age. Twenty-seven people, including the twelve deacons, and a six-hundred-dollar church endowment. From the vantage point of the pulpit, there didn't seem to be a cousin, out-of-town guest, or even a wayward teenager who needed to be punished for being caught with a joint among them. Just a recent widow and octogenarian couples who shared oxygen tanks. Afterward, when Carl asked if any of the flock had grandchildren, the deacons shrugged with embarrassment and admitted they didn't know.

Carl set to work, bringing southern savvy to the Ethiopian and performing the Herculean task of leading the sheep back into the EUFCC fold. "Put your pride in your pocket," he told the deacons. "I want each and every one of us to go and sign up for food stamps." They were scandalized when Carl used the vouchers to buy breakfast muffins and coffee for the morning commuters who walked by the church. "Let me fill your stomach now, and come by on Sunday so I can fill your soul." For four months while pouring coffee, Carl learned who had a hard time keeping up with their rent, how many women had children out of wedlock, and who was able to keep a steady job. And they liked him, not simply because he showed an interest in their lives and remembered their squabbles but also because he seemed to be as poor as they were. Every day he stood behind his long cardboard table in some outlandish suit, in dire need of a shave, without shame.

Still the community resisted. Each Sunday, Reverend Carl preached to the same twenty-seven members. The mild pleasure the neighborhood experienced when morning after morning this new pastor remembered how each of them took their coffee didn't scour away what they felt about the deacons. Cold men, cold, uppity men whose sole purpose seemed to be making them all ashamed of their predicaments. "Reverend Carl's out there giving away breakfast, but where the fuck are those twelve motherfuckers?"

What was needed, he decided, was a show. A kind of production the entire neighborhood would know in advance would be guaranteed entertainment. "Who's the crazy in the neighborhood?" Carl asked one Wednesday.

"Excuse me, Reverend?"

"You know. You telling me ain't not one soul in ten blocks of here ain't crazy as a peach orchard boar?"

"One of those southern sayings again, Reverend?"

"Yeah. But we got one, don't we, Deacon Dan?"

"I'm Deacon Rueben, Reverend. Her name is Matilda Johnson. She's four blocks down."

"All right, then." Carl walked to the door, grabbing his hat.

"You know, we deacons try not to attract that sort of element to the church." Carl struggled into his coat and opened the door.

Deacon Rueben called Carl back. "People in the community call her Twin, Reverend. And be careful."

He found her squatting on the steps of a failing brownstone with a long, heavy stick on her right side and more than a dozen empty Tab cola cans on her left. Twin was the size of two people, hence the nickname, and took up more than half of the step she sat on. She had lived on one of the ten blocks surrounding the Ethiopian longer than anyone could remember, and most called her crazy because her meanness often made itself manifest without reason. In the neighborhood she was known to be deadly, able to spit on a child three doors down if she had the inclination. And despite her size, this woman could chase down a smart-aleck teenage boy for more than six blocks, hurtling empty Tab cans with amazing accuracy.

Without introduction, he said, "You mean old bitch, come on to church."

Though she had never come by the Ethiopian for breakfast, she knew about the new pastor who seemed to be handing out goodwill as if it were free. "I got bad habits," she said. "Been kicked out of six churches."

Carl rocked on his heels, then spit between his feet.

"Well, it's never too late to get religion."

"That's what you say now." She smirked at him, and without being told he realized she had heard this very statement before. In all likelihood, a score of previous reverends full of ambition had in turn stood just where he was standing now, asking would she come and grace their church in order to increase attendance. And when her mischief became too much to bear, when the very congregation her presence had helped build couldn't tolerate the humiliation, they had cast her aside. It shamed him. She was the local freak show simply because her antics mirrored the God she knew. Galling though it was to realize that his very original idea was in fact an imitation of what every brand-new pastor had done, still he knew he had to have her. So he lied. "We got a soup kitchen on Tuesdays and Wednesdays and eggs, bacon, and grits for breakfast on Saturdays, Sundays, and Mondays."

"Where this place at?"

"Church, Twin." He reached out and shook her hand, promising himself that if she showed up he would never ask her to leave. "It's not a place; it's a church. And I welcome you to it, Sister Twin."

The next morning Carl made sure to inform those on the way to the subway that Sister Matilda "Twin" Johnson would be attending Sunday services. The news reached the entire community before the end of the morning rush hour. As tempted as they were to see just what would Twin pull, only thirty-three teenagers dared to enter the Ethiopian that Sunday. Shoulder to shoulder, they filled the back three pews, while Twin sat alone in the middle of the church. His regular congregation took up the two front rows. "Morning, beloved." Those who had come to see Twin giggled into their hands. "I can't hear you. I said, Morning, beloved."

"Morning, Reverend Harpon."

"Just call me Reverend Carl. I see this Sunday we got new faces. Now just stand on up one by one and introduce yourselves." He scribbled their last names in the margins of his Bible. "I got a message for you today, brothers and sisters. I know some of you have come out today not for the Lord but for a show." They settled into an embarrassed silence. "I know it. What will she do today? y'all are thinking. So I got a message for you today."

"Tell it to us."

"I want each and every one of you to pick up your Bible. That's right, pick it up from your lap and hold it close to your heart." The sound of rustling paper and purse zippers creeping open filled the church. "All of God's ways right between these covers, beloved."

"Amen."

"Now I want you to close your eyes while I give you the rest of this message today. I see some of you in the back. I said close them eyes." He waited until the few who hadn't did what he instructed. "There is the destruction of the wicked found in this good book. And the righteous being tried."

"Yes, Lord."

"And with all that: the love of the Lord and our Savior, the praises to His name . . ."

"Yes, Jesus."

"His sometimes harsh judgments and yet the glory found therein . . ."

"You tell it."

"But I got a hard message for you today, beloved." He paused for a moment. "Sometimes you got to put down the book."

"Ooh." Every eye opened, baffled. Even to the untrained ear, Reverend Carl's command smacked of blasphemy.

"Oh, yes. I said it. Sometimes you got to put it down. Can't take the good word to work with you. And we all know there some things between man and wife . . ."

"I know that's right."

"Sometimes we get so big, so full of ourselves, that we all walk around thinking, I don't need no book. Not that book no ways."

"Make it plain."

"I know that there are those of us who think, This book here can't help me get no job, can't help me with my Section Eight housing. So I want you to do this for me. Put it down." Both those in the front and those in the back pews continued to stall, waiting for him to take back what he just said. "You heard me, beloved. This beautiful book and all its stories and all its goodness and all its wisdom . . ."

"Amen."

"Put it down. Take it away from your hands, like you trying to take it away from your life. I want you to put down the book right now. Stand up, beloved. Take a step back. You feel it now, don't you? Right now, right here, you longing to get that book back in your hands. Hold that feeling, beloved."

And then the moment they had been waiting for arrived. Sister Twin, sitting in a sea of empty pews, jumped up and hurled her Bible at Pastor's head. Carl, too, had been expecting that moment and calmly ducked behind the pulpit. The Bible flew past his ear and landed with a thud upon the stage. Except for Twin's heavy breathing, the church went silent. Carl stood up and straightened his tie. "And sometimes you got to pick the Good Book up. Let's all turn to First Samuel, chapter two, verses one through ten." He began to read. "My heart exults in the Lord, my strength is ex-*alted* in my God!" He stopped, looked down into the pews. "Sister Twin, look like you got to come up here and get yours."

• • •

So they came back. Sunday after Sunday they returned, their numbers growing exponentially as they waited to see how and when Twin would cut the fool
or knock loose someone's teeth. The same spell Reverend Carl had cast in
Lafayette County, Arkansas, he wove in Harlem. Carl's brand of religion
called for an almost overwhelming love of the Lord, tempered by practicality.
Simply put, it was in the community's best interest that they attend regular services at the Ethiopian United Federated Church of Christ. Capable of fixing
the very worst of their problems, he found affordable yet competent lawyers to
represent their sons, helped them out of countless problems with their land-
lords. He had even helped one family buy a brownstone. During the first nine
years the Ethiopian grew tenfold. Now they had 275 regular congregants, and
that number swelled to 350 on Easter Sunday and the midnight service on
Christmas Eve. The church could now sustain both a regular and a youth
choir. Carl opened a homeless outreach program. For those willing to be baptized in the kiddie pool, graciously donated by Brother Elijah, breakfast or
lunch was available directly after the religious rite was performed.

Reverend Carl was busy. From dawn till night, some aspect of church business concerned him. But the deacons, too, were hard at work. As best they
could, they changed him. Dark gray or navy suits were bought and given to
him as nonholiday presents. The deacons offered to take his bright green and
pale yellow suits to the dry cleaners and then paid the owner to lose them. The
twelve even managed to have him married in less than two years. In 1976,
Carl married Regina Taylor, a woman thirteen years his senior, widowed with
three young boys, seven, nine, and twelve. Her pedigree and genealogy, however, suited the deacons. Like all their wives, she was an Alpha Kappa Alpha,
and her family claimed to be able to trace their ancestry back to Columbus,
though they didn't like to discuss their family history before 1809.

Just before they married, the deacons had asked her to perform only one
task. "Obviously, Reverend Carl is a full grown man. We can't ask that he grow
taller, but perhaps you could try to put a little weight on him. Some girth on a
man connotes power and respect. I'm sure you're well aware of that, Regina.
There are wonderful protein shakes available that we've heard are quite effective." She never bought the dietary supplement, choosing instead to dive into
southern cookbooks. Fried chicken wings smothered in gravy with grits for
breakfast. Shit on a shingle and dirty rice for dinner. It took her five years to

perfect fried pickles, but she did it gladly. The deacons had arranged the marriage, but in her own queer way Regina loved her husband. In her circle of friends and family, he was the only person darker than she was. Called burnt toast all of her life, she was more than grateful she wouldn't have to fight the color battle in her own home. Her first husband had been high yellow, and he had never let her forget the reason they'd been allowed to rent a summer home in Myrtle Beach was because he was the only member in the family in need of a tan. And as much as she loved her new husband's blackness, she adored that the attention Carl bestowed on his congregation he gave to her without prompting.

Carl knew Regina's favorite color and flower, smacked his lips when she called him to the table for dinner. He didn't love his wife, but he treasured her matronly ways, and her children, now his children, were tolerable. King had been married with four children, and because Carl married a widow with three sons, he only had to worry about getting her pregnant once more. Each night he went to bed with the feeling that it was all coming together.

The Ethiopian thrived under his direction. The only exceptions were the deacons. Secretive, manipulative, they seemed constantly to try to undermine him. He insisted Kwanzaa was a holiday worth embracing, but to no avail. They wouldn't budge on the issue. Lately, he lamented being so engrossed with the numerous programs he had started at the Ethiopian, since they gave him little time to investigate what the deacons were doing with a portion of the church donations.

The changes they made were gradual. Though the excuse was always the same. Woodworm. "We are being ravaged by woodworms, Reverend. Something should be done quickly." Church funds were now being used internally, and bit by bit, the deacons replaced as much wood planking as they could afford with either limestone or treated brick. The baptismal pool, that bright blue plastic children's pool bejeweled with teddy bear stickers that for years Reverend Carl had tried to convince the congregation were in fact a certain kind of cherub, was quietly given back to Brother Elijah and replaced with an Italian marble natatorium. The deacons had even turned to fashion. Sunday hats once so lavish they were almost impossible to understand were replaced by demure counterparts. Small black skullcaps with a touch of netting began to dot the pews. Their appearance was duly noted. "Oh, girl, have you seen Miz Sister Christian over there? Look like somebody's trying to go white on us." But the deacons were everywhere. They quelled censure and rumor before it had the chance to reach three people. Their admonishments were always firm yet polite, "Sister, please." Well-placed Scripture kept wagging tongues in place.

But the transformation everyone noticed most was what the deacons did to Sister Twin. That mad bitch of a woman, who despite being a regular attendant at the Ethiopian United Federated Church of Christ never put a cent into the collection plate, not even when it was passed around twice, was changed just like everything else at the church, only this time the congregation noticed. For the last eleven years Sister Twin had shown up for both the morning and evening services and thrown a holy fit in the third row of pews from the front.

Always midway in the service, Twin would begin to mew, and then it was on. She'd tear her clothes, hop on top of the pews, and march back and forth while bellowing the lyrics to "Oh, Happy Day." She'd hurl extra songbooks and her Bible at the congregation, and her aim was deadly. And if the spirit so moved her, she'd dive headfirst, fists flying, into the deacons' pit. So every month some poor church officer had a swollen jaw. But the deacons fixed her. And despite the regular congregants noticing, their relief was so heady, the solution so simple, that no one questioned just what the deacons were up to. Sister Twin, at the request of the church, became an usher. No more jumping and carrying on. Instead, her malice was channeled into making newcomers sit at the very back, making sure none of them had a direct line of vision of the pulpit. Some took Twin's promotion as the last straw, jealous that their own mothers had been overlooked for the position, but others saw it as the deacons did. "At least she can't carry on the way she does if she has to keep busy. You know?"

Microphones were brought in. Suddenly there was no need for Reverend Carl to scream from the pulpit; his praises to God could be whispered. The microphone hurt Carl in a way no other change had. Its introduction stripped the yearning that had surrounded Wednesday and Sunday services. Come early and often had been the mantra, since those in the middle pews could only guess at what sort of salvation he uttered. Now, without mystery, he stood before them vocally naked, unable to stop his voice from becoming a feminine screech when he caught the spirit. It was as if the microphone had exposed him as a fraud. As hard as he tried, he couldn't understand the amplifier's frequency response, directionality, and sensitivity. Even to his own ears his sermon sounded unpracticed. The all-wooden church he loved had become an enemy, swallowing the very best of his words. A stringy sound, as wobbly as a young boy's, echoed throughout the church. Every Sunday he strained and crackled, unable to find a deep pitch that suited him. And both he and his congregation suffered.

With its preacher forced to whisper his sermon, the Ethiopian's reaction decreased in volume. The call-and-response stuck and stopped at odd places. Instead of responding to Carl's voice, the parishioners answered his echo. Seconds of silence would eat away at his sermon while the congregation waded through white noise. With Twin busy as usher and Carl scared to lift his voice beyond a murmur, the congregation wavered, unsure when and how to react to the service.

For the first time, those who attended the Ethiopian came out of obligation. Brothers and sisters gathered as if preparing to be chastened. It had changed into a place where children could take midday naps. And when Carl brought the problem to the deacons' attention, he was unable to refute their ready answer. "There are those in the back who are incapable of hearing you, Reverend. We had thought a microphone was the best way for those who aren't able to sit in front to hear your wonderful sermons." A few began to fall away, unwilling to endure the pastor's jarring voice, but they were quickly replaced by associates of the deacons; nothing stood in the way of certain ambitions. A bourgeois mocha-colored set looked up at the Reverend from the front pews with closed mouths and arched brows. It took everything Carl had not to jump down from the pulpit to stop their polite clapping.

"You're out." Ralph, the pastor's assistant, blurted the news before he closed the door to Carl's office.

"What?" Carl looked up from his latest sermon, bleary-eyed. He had been working on the First Book of Kings for days and come up with nothing. Woefully blank of any real strife. Solomon was wise. The baby and the prostitutes. Who hadn't already heard that one? Solomon wasn't a three-hour sermon; he was an aside, an architect's delight.

Closing the door, Ralph stood in front of the pastor, breathless, though he hadn't run from anywhere. It wasn't an act, he had panted himself into a state of nervousness outside of Carl's door. "Look, I don't know what's going on," he said, but that was a lie. The deacons had been quite explicit as to what they wanted Ralph to say. "Tell him he is being replaced. And that the decision is final."

Carl stood up from his desk and stretched. "All right now, breathe."

"The deacons found somebody else. A new—"

"What?"

"The deacons, they got a new pastor for the church."

"I been head reverend at this place for almost eleven years. They can't just—" Carl dropped back into his chair but then stood up again to pace around his tiny office. Sons-of-guns.

"Look, the deacons have come up this new cat. Right out of seminary. They tell me that's where it's at—"

"You think the sheep are going to take this? Who did everything but jump into a ditch to get that new drum set?"

"This guy they got, 'spose to be a real dynamo."

"Eleven years, almost twelve long years, I put my love and heart into that pulpit and now you want to take it away? And you got the nerve to come to me and tell me, 'You're out'? I'm out, Ralph?"

"Look, are you even listening to me?"

" 'Fore I came, you couldn't even get fifty dollars out of the collection plate, and now—"

"I know. But this new cat the deacons cooked up—"

"I heard you: a real dynamo."

"He is, man. You gotta see him."

"Where are they now?"

"They waiting for you in the conference room."

Carl walked in, noting they all sat on the same side of the long conference table. On the other side a single chair had been placed in the middle of the floor. Someone had a provided a glass of water, half-filled.

"What is it? I can take it. Come on, you got the nerve to try to sic Ralph on me, so out with it."

"Have a seat, Reverend. And please lower your voice."

"Can't tell me what—" But he checked himself, knowing that they were capable of waiting until he broke down and did exactly as they demanded. "Okay. Okay."

"It's, it's . . ." As one, they all mouthed the same stutter. Carl was suddenly frightened. In the eleven years he had known them, they had never been at a loss for words. Light enough to garner respect, dark enough to quell suspicion, the deacons of the Ethiopian United Federated Church of Christ, Carl realized, had decided to use their absolute power. The youth choir had recently begun calling them the Holy Men, a title they neither rejected nor affirmed.

Cabbies may have passed them by, but they slowed down before their fear got the better of them. These twelve men sat before him without mirth or music. "Reverend Carl, thank you for coming to see us today." Carl moved to the edge of his chair. "Let's begin, shall we?

"The Ethiopian has had its door open to tend its flock for sixty-seven—no, sixty-eight—years. And I will tell you a strange fact, Reverend. Since our inception we have never had a white, or should I say, European-American, as a parishioner. Yes, yes, I am shocked as well. Perhaps the closest we've come is that young man about seven years back. Please help me with the name, Brother Dan."

"I believe his name was Timothy."

"Yes, Brother Timothy. He was one of those mulatto fellows, but he fell away from the fold." Deacon Gad paused to sip his glass of water. "In all those years, one lone young man. His wife was black, so she doesn't count. I find that fact odd. Don't you, Reverend?"

"We're smack in the middle of Harlem . . . Brother Rueben?"

"I'm Deacon Gad."

"We're in the middle of Harlem, Brother Gad."

"Yes, well, that can't be helped." Tapping the edge of the conference table, he signaled the switch of conversation. "What we mean to say is, we want change. And after long, thoughtful discussions amongst ourselves, you understand, we've come to the conclusion that you, Reverend Carl, cannot usher forth that change."

"Now wait a minute—"

"Really, Reverend Charlemagne, don't interrupt. The drum set was a . . . What is the word I'm thinking of, Brother Levi?"

"Lovely."

"Yes, it was a lovely idea. But we have moved beyond that now. The Ethiopian should be about inclusion. We should open our arms and embrace the greater metropolitan area."

"And quite frankly, we have all wondered about your . . . How can I say this? Indecision."

"My indecision?"

"Yes, Reverend, your indecision. There is the problem you seem to be having with the microphone. Have you noticed the look of horror on some of the parishioners' faces when you begin to speak? Tut, tut. Please, let me finish. And of course, we all know that Twin should have been made into an usher, well, years ago. Brother Issachar and his swollen jaw can attest to that." A low murmur of affirmation rose in the room.

"And that's why you want to let me go, 'cause Sister Twin can't help but to sock one you guys when the Lord overcomes her?"

"Reverend, I erred in giving particular examples. The problems are greater than that. We feel you have lost the Ethiopian's flock. And over the past few years, all of us have taken note that your calling doesn't seem as strong as it used to be. Of course it saddens us to come to this end. We are not heartless men."

"To be sure," Deacon Judah added.

It was their inflection, its slow rise and fall, that cornered him. While in his office, he had thought for once the deacons would fight with heat, shrilly, they would tell him to get out, but without a crackle of anger he wasn't sure how to respond to their accusations. Didn't the numbers say it all? Close to four hundred folks came for Easter. He had poured every goodness he possessed into the church and now these twelve men gathered in judgment and said it wasn't quite enough. Perhaps he should have prayed, right then and there. Requested from the deacons a moment of silence in order to ask the Lord for guidance. But the long conference table, their demure expressions stopped him.

Now was the time to turn to King. He searched his memory for an appropriate line. He lifted his small hands, folding left over right. Unwittingly mimicking their cadence, his next words sounded as if he should swallow. "Who is it that is supposed to articulate the longings and aspirations of the people more than the preacher?"

But the deacons knew the Reverend better than he thought they did. Sooner or later, they knew, he would rip a sentence from the great one, and they were prepared with more than one of their own. "Yes, Reverend, but King also said, 'This is no day for the rabble-rouser. There is no place for misguided emotionalism.'

"And of course the sermon we love best, contains the advice 'The church is not an entertainment center. Monkeys are to entertain, not preachers.'

"One last question: Have you been taking the protein shakes we suggested?"

Carl pursed his lips. "Deacons, my wife is a fine cook . . ."

"Yes, yes, we thought so." Brother Dan clapped his hand lightly on the table and then drank a sip of water. "We're done here, don't you think?" They all stood up, unnecessarily straightening their ties in unison. Deacon Dan quickly moved from behind the long length of table to give fluttering, consolatory pats that never actually touched Carl's shoulder.

"I want to give next week's sermon to say good-bye."

"No, no, that won't be necessary."

"But I think—"

"Yes, we're sure you do; but we all believe the transition would be that much easier if your leaving was not only immediate but absolute. There's no looking back. And a final sermon of good-byes would suggest regret in some way. We can't have that now, can we? Come, come, Carl. We want you to meet the new Reverend." Ralph walked over to the side door and ushered him in.

Excuse me, Lord, but goddamn he's big, Carl thought as he watched a young black man, the color of creamed coffee, tuck his head in as he moved through the door. Like most people, Carl didn't notice the space between the top of the preacher's head and the top of the doorframe because he couldn't take his eyes off of the man's curled neck. At six foot six, at least two hundred fifty pounds, dressed in a dark gray wool gabardine suit, the man was more than impressive. Yet it was the tuck into the chin that connoted bridled power. Never mind that the new pastor's head was a full foot and a half away from the top of the doorframe. The gesture did its job. Carl couldn't help but gasp as the new guy walked into the conference room.

"Hello." His voice was as big as he was. "Jasper Hass. The *H* is silent; the *a* is soft." An enormous paw lifted out of his pants pocket and swallowed Carl's small hand. "You have a beautiful church, Reverend. Perhaps a touch too much wood, but the deacons assured me they are trying to rectify the problem."

He couldn't remember how he got home. Packing up his office, how many hands he had shook on his way out, whether or not he had eaten dinner, all had been blasted from his memory. That night he talked his wife into a state of confusion. "I mean, 'To be sure.' Who says that?"

"Obviously the deacons, Carl."

"All right now, don't you start. 'To be sure.' You should have seen him. As big as a goddamn bull."

"Language . . . ," his wife gently reprimanded him.

"Shit, I'm no reverend now. It don't matter."

"Carl . . ."

"As big as a building and the color of cream. Couldn't get through the door. Had to tuck his head in."

"Well."

"Could you just let me finish? Could you do that for me?" Regina answered her husband with silence, though she wanted to ask him practical questions. What were they going to do for money? Though her eldest son had graduated from college in May, the middle child would start in the coming fall, and their youngest needed new shoes every six months. She hadn't held a job since they first married, and did the deacons expect them to give up their apartment?

"Are you paying me any attention?"

"Of course, Carl."

"All right, then." Carl readjusted the sheets. "It's not just that I'm bony. You know. I don't think that's it. Deacon Levi made that the last word, like me not being able to put any weight on was the last straw, but that ain't it. It's politics. That's what it all comes down to. They think I'm too black to run it right. Wouldn't even let me put on a show for Kwanzaa. You know that ain't right, Regina. Plucked me out of Arkansas like they was doing me a favor, but I tell you what, it was the other way around. When I first got there, they didn't have a window to piss out of."

"Carl . . ."

"Can you just let me be mad for a minute? What man in they right mind lets himself walk around in a pair of socks just like eleven other niggers? Just tell me that much. That's right, nobody." He stopped, suddenly disgusted that he wasn't able to clamp away his anger. It wasn't just the deacons, Carl realized; the clamor from the pews had gradually been subsiding. He should have pulled a Twin, hurled the microphone with its long tail into the air, and refused to ever use it again. That's what he should have done. He should've, he should've . . .

For thirty days, Carl's dreams were tortured.

Then, on the last Thursday of the month, Twin rang his buzzer.

She began before he could close the door. The deacons had moved out of the pews and were now sitting on the stage, just behind the pulpit. "It's no secret they're pulling the strings. That big-ass nigger Jasper is just a puppet. You should hear him. He's got a good voice, I'm not going to say he doesn't. Like he just got over a cold, but nicer. But he talks to the congregation like he's conducting a business meeting. Half of us don't even know what the fuck he's saying, but don't nobody wants to stand up and admit it." Carl winced as she told him the choirs had been given new choral music. "My Rock" and "Precious Lord" had been replaced with Armenian medieval liturgical chants and "Ride la primavera" by Schütz. The youth choir had been told they were allowed to perform only three times a year, because their voices weren't mature enough to handle the intricacies of the new music.

Three weeks ago, the deacons had issued a statement saying there was to be no more carrying on ("Their words, Reverend, their words") during Sunday services. Those that Carl had originally brought to the church were being ostracized, separated into a smaller midday service. "That fucker Jasper doesn't even bother to show up, and parishioners are forced to conduct themselves. Pitiful." And, and, and . . . And some Sundays there were more white people than regular parishioners. Somehow the deacons had managed to get the Ethiopian United Federated Church of Christ on several tour guide lists, and now buses lined up, full of German and English tourists, every Sunday morning. It was only because the regular congregation had threatened to revolt that the tourists had to stand in a separate line in order to attend service. They had been arriving earlier than the congregation and had begun taking the best seats.

The taste of bile filled his mouth while he listened. "Anything else, Sister Twin?" She hadn't expected such calm from him.

"And they told me to get the fuck out. Yesterday."

"Twin—"

"I been going there since 'seventy-four. Even when I was sick, I made sure to go in the morning and in the evening. They got no right to cut me loose. I got a taste now for it."

"I'm not running the church anymore, Twin."

"You think I'm talking for my health? You got to do something."

"What?"

"Shit, man, I don't know, you're the preacher." Twin grabbed her jacket and struggled into it. Carl showed her to the door. "So what, now?"

"I don't know yet." He desperately wanted her out of his apartment, if for nothing else but to rinse his mouth out. She left, and Carl ran to the bathroom, collapsing over the toilet, only to heave and heave for naught. After an hour, the only thing his stomach could produce was bright green bile. He had done too much, he thought. Given and given, neglected his own sons, and still they had forsaken him. He slid to his knees and reached for the towel on the sink. Tourists? Germans are in the church? He tried to stand up and found that he couldn't. And Jasper, that fucking Jasper was shaming the profession by letting the deacons take control. What in the devil was a medieval liturgical chant, anyway? Twin was right, I am the preacher. "But without my church," he said aloud, sarcastically.

He had told them not to cast him aside. Not in those words, of course, he had used King, but then . . . he couldn't allow himself to finish the thought. Laying full length on the bathroom floor, Carl saw the Scriptures rolled out before him, a parchment of sin and bitterness: *This new king will take your first sons, your best daughters . . . and take . . . and take . . . And ye shall cry out in that day because of your king, whom ye shall have chosen for yourself; and the Lord will not hear you in that day.*

Carl spent the better part of the afternoon in the bathroom.

"Carl, dinner's on." He struggled to his feet and sat at the head of the dinner table, pale gray. Regina had made catfish dipped in buttermilk and cornmeal and hush puppies, dirty rice, warm green bean salad, and watched it all grow cold on her husband's plate. His sons, Pepin, Jackson, and Daemon, squirmed in their seats, uncomfortable because of their father's clenched fists resting on the table. "I was chosen, yet shamed."

"Excuse me, Carl?"

"Never mind, Regina."

He dreamt again that night, except this time instead of torment, it filled him with solace. God was real, and His Scripture a living thing. *I said indeed that thy house and the house of thy father should walk before me forever, but now be it far from me and they that despise me. . . . Behold, the days come, that I will cut off thine arm, and the arm of thy father's house. The Lord kill and maketh alive. He will keep the feet of his saints and the wicked shall be silent in darkness. The adversaries of the Lord shall be broken to pieces; out of heaven shall he thunder upon them: The Lord shall judge the ends of the earth; and he shall give strength unto his king, and exalt the horn of his anointed.*

Carl woke the next morning with the words *And this shall be a sign . . .* echoing in his mind.

Gasoline is an unstoppable perfume. Sickly sweet, it permeated through its containers and into Carl's clothes before he unscrewed the caps. He wondered what to do with them afterward. Regina and her meticulous nature would miss them as soon as she laundered. Goodwill, he thought.

Slipping inside the back the door, he headed for the deacons' offices. On a Thursday night, the church was barren. Carl had decided long ago that everything needed a day of rest, even the Ethiopian, so no programs were ever planned for that day. At least they let me do that. When he reached their offices he twisted off the top, ready. The twelve men shared two offices, six cubicles in each room. The carpet soaked up the gas, and he danced out, leaving the door ajar, spilling a trail around the corner, down the hallway, and repeated the process in the choir, conference, and Sunday school rooms. When he reached his office, he barely recognized it. The walls were covered with honorary degrees from various universities, citations of honor, doctorates for programs whose names Carl was unable to pronounce. A large bronze bust of Booker T. Washington filled a corner of the office, and the desk was littered with photos of Hass and the deacons shaking hands with Ed Koch and Jesse Jackson. Sons-of-guns managed all that in thirty days, he thought as he poured the lighter liquid over Booker T.'s head. The smell was almost overpowering as Carl staggered into the Ethiopian's sanctuary.

He created intricate paths along the side aisles, pausing as he rained gas over the pews and almost weeping as he drenched the relief of the Last Supper. The only thing left was the pulpit. Standing behind it, he suddenly doubted his convictions; maybe if he had given them more time, the deacons would have come to their senses and asked him to return. He put the can of gas down beside him and prayed. "I'll stay my hand, Lord. Give me a sign and I'll walk away. Open every door and window on my way out."

There was nothing but the soft patter of gas dripping off the pews.

"It's mine to do with whatever I see fit. Mine to run. Mine to lead, Lord. And they forgot to ask me for the keys." The "they" grew arms and multiplied. They, the deacons, they, the officers, they, the very parishioners who had thrown holy fits until they deciphered the sound of his voice and cast him aside. Swayed by clever photo ops, they didn't deserve to receive solace in his wooden sanctuary. Where were the couples he had married and counseled? Or those whom he had baptized? They should have clamored at his door, risen against the deacons, something. He had led them to a promised land, but then they turned, and with their silence said they could manage the rest alone.

As he left by the back door, he dropped a lit match.

• • •

The fire was a pyrologist's dream. The secrets of a patchwork wooden church were revealed in an uncontrollable blaze. The fire split into two, making quick work of the side panels that weren't solid but compressed wood shavings. Exxon unleaded behaved as paint thinner would in some places, eating away at cheap shellac and exposing the pine pews to the flames. Following Carl's path, fire blistered down the aisles, leaping into every pew. The floors began to groan. Shouts of discordant music rang out as the organ surrendered to the flames. The blaze in the back offices was mundane by comparison. With nothing hardy to munch through, the fire melted the deacons' cubicles down into black plastic bubbles.

There should have been nothing left, nothing able to escape as the Ethiopian's supporting beams buckled and the entire structure crashed into a smoldering heap. But even godly bitterness couldn't maim what had been recently purchased. The deacons would pick up their skeleton and start anew, anoint what remained blemish-free and send what Reverend Carl had loved best to the junkyard.

The Italian marble baptismal pool remained in the middle of the ruins, unscarred. It rose from the rubble, clean as bones.

BROWARD COUNTY, FLORIDA

Who knows the power of your anger?

PSALM 90:11

MY daughter was a virgin!" Dawnia Da Costa's mother told us. It wasn't an assertion, it was an accusation. How could the Lord take an innocent? How could the Lord take one who'd not yet been blessed by love? God's will. She spat the words out and ground them into the floor.

We sat silent, staring at them. We'd come to the southern tip of Florida looking for Santeria, the Cuban religion of African gods doubling as Catholic saints, of chicken bones and love candles and goat blood on the streets outside the INS building every morning, prayers to the Virgin Mary and her Yoruba alter ego, Ochun, to let a brother or a sister, or a daughter, come to the promised land. Instead we'd found Dawnia's mother. She didn't need candles, she didn't need chicken bones; all she wanted was blood.

"A virgin!" Dawnia's mother said. "Lord, how she felt!" She spoke of the last time she'd seen her daughter alive, before Dawnia left for church one Friday night three years ago.

"Are you a preacher?" Dawnia might have asked that night, the lilt of Jamaica in her voice as much of an enticement as the curves of her hips and her breasts. And Lucious Boyd would have smiled. In his reply, she would have noted the erudition of his tone, his long American vowels. "Yes, I am a preacher," he might have answered; and from what the witnesses tell us about the dark-skinned girl who climbed into a church van with the light-skinned black man, how she wavered before getting in as if on the edge of faith, we know she was excited, and afraid.

Faith is dangerous. Friday night, 2:00 A.M.: Dawnia just now coming home from church, Faith Tabernacle Pentecostal United, a church of Caribbean exiles making good in America. She's a big girl, handsome, known for her bright laughter and her powerful lungs. She loves Jesus, she loves her church. Friday night, nowhere else she'd rather be. She's twenty-one, going to be a nurse, so God-fearing she won't even wear slacks; but she loves to party, loves to pray, loves to sing. She's an alto. She sings solos.

Friday night, her throat is itching. She wants to let it loose; she wants to pray; she wants to sing; she has the solo. "There is power, power, wonder-working power, power in the blood of the lamb!" It's a song, it's a prayer, it's a vibration in her bones.

The clock creeps into the morning. The choir decamps to a Denny's, where they drink coffee and laugh about life back on the islands; then they shift to the parking lot, short bursts of song escaping their lips between good-byes like hiccups of gospel. Dawnia gets behind the wheel, alone with her solo. She cruises through the warm dark Florida morning, her windows down while she sings. There is power in the blood. Her voice shakes the car so hard she doesn't notice it sputtering. Then it rolls to a stop. She's run out of gas.

Faith is dangerous. Dawnia walks down the highway in the dark, cars whiz by, nobody stops, just as well. She keeps company with the Lord. She sings to keep herself safe. "There is power in the blood, power, power, wonder-working power!" She comes to a ramp, exits the highway on foot, walks out of the dark, into the white light of a gas station. She sees a turquoise van. A church van, "Generation of Hope" written on its side. In it is a man with broad shoulders and dark eyes; they spot her wandering and he rolls up beside her. His eyebrows are raised, his lips are set in a careless smile.

"Are you a preacher?" Dawnia might ask. The man would laugh. No, not really; but he does give sermons at the funeral home he runs with his family. He's a businessman, but solace is his trade. Isn't that about the same thing? Dawnia gets in the van.

Faith is dangerous. Three A.M. Dawnia's gone. Her mama's awake. She wants her daughter. Dawnia, her eldest, Dawnia, her strongest.

"She is physically *strong*," her mother told us, sitting in her beauty parlor between a pawnshop and a gun store, making a fist out of her daughter's strength. "She is always with me," she said. Three years later, she still saw Dawnia nodding to Lucious Boyd's pious words; felt her daughter's shoulders tensing as he drove past her car without slowing down; heard her praying—Oh my God help me!—as his hands pushed her down to the floor of the church van—Jesus help me!—as his face came from above like the maw of an animal—God—as he tore into her like the Beast himself—Please!

"I pray for him to suffer," Dawnia's mother said. "May the Lord make *that* so."

Dawnia's church prayed with her: "Let him suffer," they prayed, a chorus of hate so deep it didn't so much stain their faith as transform it. Even before they knew his name, the day the police found Dawnia's body, naked, raped, stabbed, run over, and oddly, tenderly, wrapped in a shroud of bedsheets, they prayed for him. The day the police caught him they prayed for him, every day of his trial they sat in the back of the courtroom and prayed for him, the day the jury said guilty they prayed for him, and now, the Sunday after the verdict, a new holiday they called Victory Day, they prayed for him. Let him suffer, thank you, Jesus; give him the chair, thank you, Jesus; make him bleed, thank you, Jesus. They were a prayer in a red dress, a red suit, red suspenders. "It's the color of Jesus' blood," said the Reverend of Faith Tabernacle, as if that explained why he and his church had chosen it as the special color of their celebration. "Today we're celebrating Jesus," a congregant said. "Today we're wearing red for justice."

Red is the color of their prayer. Red is the color of blood. And there is power in the blood, that's what they sang. A choir forty-five strong at the front of the church, the band bursting out of its corner, the women in the pews sizzling in their seats until like popcorn they hopped into the air. Thank you, Jesus! That's an *s* like a *z*, Jee-zus! That's a red bloody Jesus; say it again! A boy in a black suit over a red shirt put his hands in the air and let his fingers flutter like butterflies until the spirit filled them and they turned into talons. There is power in the blood! The soloist wore a red skirt suit and a red hat shaped like that of a pilgrim. "There is power!" she sang. "Power! Power! Power!"

From somewhere in the choir loft tambourines rose up and rippled across the singers like a school of silver fish. The drummer banged his way past the Plexiglas shield designed to contain him; the piano player, a teenage boy, splashed across the keys as if skipping stones on water. Two rows ahead a tall man with the heavy jaw and thin frame of an undertaker rocked back and forth, his arms glued to his sides, his hands like paddles.

Then the bass simmered. The choir quieted. The Reverend preached. "She has been *justified*!" He was the biggest man in the church, his legs alone taller than the full height of a boy, his head as wide and thick as the dark mouth of a cannon, his words shaped like an Englishman's. "My God," he said. "We can *rejoice*!"

Later, we'd sit with him in his office, lost in deep leather chairs, straining to see him behind the bronze eagle that swooped from a pedestal over his neatly piled sermons. His God, he said, was a loving one, and His love was like a lion, like a fighter plane. The Reverend loved fighter planes, he loved his new country's F-16s. "Do you understand," he asked us, one hand in a fist pressed against the black marble of his desk, the other stroking its sheen, "what this nation, under God, can do to God's enemies?" If we hadn't before, we did then, under the anger of the Reverend's glare.

In the pulpit, the Reverend roared his adopted American creed: "You can run, but you can't—"

"*Hide!*" his congregation shouted.

"Let us sing!" the Reverend commanded.

The soloist shook her head hard and her red pilgrim hat punched the air. In her hand there was suddenly a red handkerchief like a splash of blood. "We won!" she sang. Red scarves burst into the air around the church like so many gunshots. "We won! We won! We won!"

In the front row, a half dozen white men, detectives and a prosecutor, special guests for Victory Day, nodded their heads; they knew this song. The lead singer pumped her hands: "We won the war! We won the war! We won the war!"

"Yes," said the Reverend. "Yes!" The choir subsided, folded up into twitching quiet like wings behind his shoulders. "Did we not know it would be so?" The guitar player twanged, warned, played a blues. "The wise man Solomon says in Ecclesiastes, 'But it shall not be well with the wicked, neither shall he prolong his days!' "

"Yes!" The congregation shouted with joy.

"St. Paul tells us in Romans, chapter twelve"—"Tell us!" screamed a woman in the back pew—"St. Paul tells us in Romans chapter twelve, verse nineteen, 'It is written, Vengeance is mine, I will repay, sayeth the *Lord*!' "

The congregation roared. "Jesus!"

"And does it not say, in Galatians chapter six, verse seven"—"Oh yes," the congregation said, women crying and men dancing—" 'God is not mocked!

For whatsoever a man soweth! For whatsoever a man soweth, that he shall also reap!' " A flurry of keyboard and a burst of rumbling bass followed the words. The Reverend waited. He looked at the pews, his congregation of exiles and immigrants, Jamaicans and Antiguans, their skin so dark, their souls washed white in the blood of the Lamb. The Reverend did not know what it meant to be "black" until he came to this country. He wished not to know. He was not black, he was a man. Just like, he'd told us—especially like—the white men who filled the first pew. The detectives. The prosecutor. These powerful men, who had listened to the power of the Lord, heard the power of Faith Tabernacle. The Reverend stared at the white men. "I am well pleased," he said, "with what God has done. With what God is about to do."

"Isaiah!" a man in the back shouted his prophet's name.

The Reverend ignored him. "I will say now that we have the blessing of dignitaries among us." The white men shifted in their seats. "These men," said the Reverend, "who have done"—he paused—"so much. I have not seen one flaw in these men. If it exists, I am not looking. I have not seen one such flaw—such as racism." The prosecutor nodded.

The man in the back again shouted his prophet's name, like a bullet fired at the altar. What did he mean? Nobody cared. Why did people say the sheriffs shot black people as if they were dogs? Nobody knew. Why didn't they put Lucious Boyd away when they thought he'd killed a black whore? That didn't matter. What mattered was power. The power of prayer, the power in the blood, the power of Faith Tabernacle to make white men do their will.

The guitar thrummed and the red handkerchiefs waved. At the Reverend's invitation, the prosecutor stepped up to the pulpit. He was nearly as big as the Reverend, with dark hair going silver, boyish cheeks, narrow-set eyes that beamed concern. And teeth. Bright white teeth.

"I'm seeing a whole lotta red out there!" he shouted. The guitar leapt up behind him. "Can you hear me?" he called. *"Yes!"* "Can you hear me?" *"Yes!"*

He reminded them he'd been there before, campaigning. Two years ago, didn't even know what church he was in, when the Reverend had pointed a finger at him and demanded, "What are you going to do?"

"Only then did I realize that I was in Dawnia DaCosta's church. And when I knew that, I came up—you remember?—I came up to the pulpit and I said, 'I will do everything in my power to make sure justice is done!' "

"Thank you, Jesus!"

"Yes! And in return, I asked for one thing—what was that?"

"Oh, Lord! Justice!"

The prosecutor, who would not comment on his plans to run for higher office, who was a lector in his Catholic church, the racial mix of which he told us he had never noticed, who loved hockey and his two children and his wife, none of whom he had brought that morning to Faith Tabernacle, who said there were no bad parts of *his* town, the prosecutor had asked for one thing.

Votes? No, no.

"Your thoughts and your prayers!"

"Power in the Blood" resumed, the red-hatted woman belting, "We got it! We got it! We got it!" A woman in the second row of the choir let her long hair fly as she slammed her torso backward and forward like a wet rag snapping. The detectives danced, hips and shoulders this way, then that. Despite ourselves, we did too, even though it made us feel like accomplices, two more lightning rods for the power Faith Tabernacle meant to draw down from the sky and up from the grave. We got it whether we wanted it or not, though what it was we couldn't say. They'd already had deliverance, that was how they'd come to America. And they were certain each and every one of them was saved. What did they want? Not chicken bones, not candles, and not a creamy white Christ bleating "Forgive!" They wanted blood. To get it they needed power. "We got it! We got it!" They needed the D.A. who stacked their young men up in jails like piles of sugarcane. "We got it!" They had it, and now the D.A. felt it, the power they had. We could see it in the way his bones seemed to shake free from their joints and the way his bright white teeth sparked electric, as Faith Tabernacle anointed him—old women running to him, young men seizing him, the choir singing for him, the pastor smiling at him. He gave his smile back to the pastor. It was as though, both would later claim, there was no more black and white between them. Just red. A wave of it that could take Lucious Boyd to the chair, the prosecutor to the judge's bench, and the Reverend to a brand-new marble pulpit.

Lucious Boyd didn't say a word at his sentencing hearing a few days later. "Nice to see you, Mr. Boyd," the judge said; Lucious Boyd simply nodded. We sat in the visitors' gallery, ten feet away. He had sleepy eyes and a broad jaw, a face that spread out like an alluvial plain, handsome but tired; his skin was as gray as it was brown. Every day of the trial he'd worn a new suit, but now he wore a prison-issue coverall, beige. It rounded his shoulders and made his chest look hollow, but still he smiled, even for the prosecutor, just as he had smiled at the Reverend when the Reverend had sat in the gallery, praying for justice and power and blood. Why not? They'd won the war, to them went the spoils. Lucious was a preacher himself. He knew the cost of a covenant. He knew a deal had been struck on the foundation of his body. Over his bones the Reverend and the prosecutor would not just shake hands but bind themselves together in order to build a bright red temple.

Sentenced to death, Lucious Boyd would never hear the temple's choir. Nor would Dawnia's mother. "I don't need that church no more," she told us when we went to her beauty parlor and sat in an empty room behind the styling chairs, lit by cold blue fluorescent bulbs. She had hated Victory Day. As far as she was concerned, "Power in the Blood" belonged to Dawnia. And she had hated the things people had said to her there. "People say God use Dawnia as a sacrifice. People say God use her to kill Lucious." She paused, for a moment too angry to speak. "But people use God in a wrong way."

Where were you when I laid the foundations
of the earth?

JOB 38:4

JOB

By Peter Trachtenberg

ONE

What's the difference between a Jew and a pizza?
What do you call an Ethiopian with two dogs?
How can you tell a cancer patient from a bowling ball?

One of the most persistent problems in Western theology concerns the relation between God and suffering. Why does God allow the innocent to suffer,
or conversely, why does He spare the wicked? The attempt to solve this problem is called theodicy. Here one ought to add that suffering is problematic
only in the monotheistic religions, e.g., Judaism, Christianity, and Islam,
since only they posit a Creator who is both infinitely powerful and infinitely
good. We might represent such an entity by a Venn diagram (named for the
English cleric and logician John Venn), a group of circles, each representing
a logical set, the intersection of which denotes the elements those sets have in
common. Picture such a diagram in which one circle represents infinite
power and the other infinite goodness:

Where these circles overlap, we find God.

Note that the second figure contains no representation of suffering. From a purely logical perspective, suffering seems to have no place in a universe governed by a God who is both infinitely powerful and infinitely virtuous. Put aside the question of what constitutes suffering, or say that suffering falls along a continuum that ranges from a shaving cut to death by torture. Put aside, as well, the question of whether any creature (saints, unborn babies, idiots, dumb animals) can be called innocent. As Nickles sings in Archibald Macleish's *J. B.*:

> If God is God He is not good,
> If God is good he is not God . . .
> I would have saved them if I could
> But for the little green leaves in the wood
> And the wind on the water.

One way around this problem is to posit that God is omnipotent but not entirely good. Say He's actively malign, as some of the Gnostics thought, or is so sporadically, is subject to mood swings, has His good days and His bad days. Some of which last for aeons.

Note how this hypothesis allows suffering back into the picture.

On the other hand, He may not be as powerful as we thought. In the Kabbalah, for example, we find the idea that in the act of creating the universe, God retreated or somehow contracted, like someone who sucks in his stomach while exhaling, creating a vacuum in which evil and suffering could come into being.

And then you have the Catholic notion that God made a special exception for free will, in the manner of those Turkish weavers who leave blank spaces in the pattern of their kilims. According to this proposition, the Lord orders everything in the universe except for our impulses and actions.

FREE WILL

Unfortunately, ever since the Fall, our actions are contaminated by sin—

—leading to the human proclivities for lying, fornication, self-abuse, murder, et cetera. Leading also to the inevitability of suffering.

Lest this proposition seem too depressing, the doctrine of Providence asserts that the Deity permits the existence of suffering but over the course of centuries and millennia turns it—subverts it—to His own ends. These are always good:

In other words, all suffering is an intermediary step in the progress toward a final redemption (a redemption made complete by the equally final damnation of the wicked), suffering is therapeutic, and the agony of past and present innocents is a mere technical difficulty, a speed bump. One imagines a procession of the murdered and tormented and enslaved, clad in emblematic garments—bloody pelts, togas, breechclouts, buskins, the swaddling clothes of infants, dhotis, the shabby suits of the passengers on the trains to Auschwitz,

Mao jackets and Vietnamese *ao dai*, the head kerchiefs of Bosnian women, the denim overalls of African American sharecroppers—all winding toward the vanishing point of Heaven, while alongside them a conga line of perpetrators—Roman centurions and black-clad SS men, knights in spiked breastplates, Spanish conquistadors and hooded Klansmen—moves in the opposite direction, into the maw of Hell. This cannot be represented by a Venn diagram.

There are other options. The clever Buddhists leave God out of the picture and envision a universe characterized by the unimpeded play of desire, governed only by karma, which is basically the Newtonian law of motion translated into moral terms.

And then you have systems in which the deity is supplanted by the laws of history or class struggle or psychological drives.

But by now the equation is getting to look a little cluttered. It lacks elegance. We might be better off factoring out some of its excess terms. Psychological drives can go.

And we can forget class struggle. That leaves us with only "history," otherwise known as Providence. Either way, it can be eighty-sixed.

We can eighty-six *God.*

But when everything else is factored out, there is still suffering.

It is what remains.

TWO

I know you've heard this one: "There was a man in the land of Uz, whose name was Job; and that man was perfect and upright, and one that feared God and eschewed evil." Note that verb *feared*. This is a story from the time before human beings learned to love God, before they came to think of God as their best friend. I believe that it is the most truthful story in the Bible. Most of those stories fall into the category of history or prophecy: They tell us what was or what shall be. But this story, Job, tells us about what *is*. Alone of the Bible's narratives, it is set in an unspecified time, after the Fall but before the Last Judgment. Its protagonist isn't even a Hebrew. He could be any of us, only better.

Along with being upright, Job is rich. The book inventories his blessings: seven sons and three daughters; seven thousand sheep and three thousand camels; one thousand oxen and five hundred she-asses. And because he is both virtuous and fortunate, he becomes the object of a wager. The wager takes place between God and Satan. Those of us who thought of Satan as God's implacable nemesis may be a little startled to find them getting along as famously as they do in Job. In this story Satan isn't the serpent in the garden or the commander of the rebel hosts. In the original Hebrew he's called *ha-Satan*, "the Satan," "the Adversary," a title that designates an angel who roams the earth, exposing human evil: a prosecutor. So he and God are colleagues of a sort, two guys chatting around the watercooler. God asks Satan where he's been, and Satan tells him: "Oh, you know, to and fro." Up and down. And then God asks Satan, "Hast thou considered my servant Job, that there is none like him in the earth, a perfect and an upright man, one that feareth God and escheweth evil?"

The Lord is boasting a little here. He's twitting Satan, that specialist in wickedness, with a perfect specimen of virtue. You can see how that might be irritating. Every boast is an implicit challenge, and Satan responds to God's with one of his own: "Doth Job fear God for naught?" That word again: *Fear*. "Hast not thou made a hedge about him, and about his house, and about all that he hath on every side? Thou hast blessed the work of his hands, and his substance is increased in the land. But put forth thine hand now, and touch all that he hath, and he will curse thee to thy face." Two thousand years of literature and folklore have taught us never to bet with the devil. But maybe that applies only to humans, whose souls are so small and vulnerable and so easily lost. God takes the bet. He's tempted. He says to Satan: "Behold all that he hath is in thy power." From that moment, Job is doomed.

At this juncture I'd like to tell you a joke. There's a Jew, a Cambodian, and a Bosnian. Or maybe it should be a Jew, a Kosovar, and a Tutsi. An Armenian, a Lakota Indian, and an African-American. It's hard choosing victims, there are so many of them. How do you decide who's suffered most? Say the Jews lost 6 million in the Holocaust, which puts them ahead numerically, but 800,000 Tutsi were slaughtered in a matter of months, with knives and machetes, mostly. Doesn't that sort of even things out? Is it more or less horrible that under the Khmer Rouge a million Cambodians were killed by other Cambodians? Does that count as genocide or fratricide? You see my difficulty.

Of all the calamities that follow, God is technically innocent. He never lifts a finger against Job. He just withdraws His—what did Satan call it?—his *hedge*. (An interesting word. A hedge often encloses a garden, like the Garden of Eden, the home we lost because we were foolish enough to let the devil trick us into breaking the lease: the home that is now hedged against us.) But with that hedge gone, Job is naked in the devil's wilderness. And Satan puts forth his hand and with staggering rapidity strips Job of everything—seven thousand sheep and three thousand camels, one thousand oxen and five hundred she-asses, seven sons and three daughters: all gone. Messenger after messenger comes to him with the bad news; it's like some gruesome version of the stateroom scene in A *Night at the Opera*. But Job holds fast to his integrity, a word that keeps recurring in this story with subtly different meanings. Even in the abyss of grief he blesses the name of the Lord—which confounds Satan, who predicted that he would curse God.

Which reminds me of another joke. An old Jew—let's call him Job—is stricken by a series of tragedies. Practically overnight his business goes bust, his house burns down, his children are killed in a bizarre accident. But when his friends come to mourn with him, they find him laughing. "Job, Job!" they cry. "What's the matter with you? You've lost everything, you ain't got a pot to piss in. What do you got to laugh about?"

And Job says, "I still got my health."

Maybe Satan knows this joke, because now he assaults Job's body. Once more God gives His permission—with the lukewarm caveat that the subject's life be spared. ("But spare his life." "Oh yeah." Wink, wink. "Sure! Don't worry. He'll be *fine!*") And the Adversary smites his victim with burning sores from the soles of his feet to the crown of his head. The noose of suffering has been drawn as tight as it can get. Destitute, childless, nerve ends shrieking, Job squats on an ash heap, scraping his chancres with a potsherd. His wife jeers at him: "Dost thou still retain thine integrity?"—and from her lips *integrity* becomes a term of derision, a synonym for moronic high-mindedness. "Curse God," she says, "and die."

So you have these three people, I don't know, a Cambodian, a Bosnian, and someone from Sierra Leone. The Cambodian's lost a leg to a land mine, the Bosnian was blinded by a Serbian paramilitary, and the guy from Sierra Leone had his hands chopped off. And the Cambodian says . . . the Cambodian says. What does he say? Help me out, somebody. I'm dying up here.

Now at this point something strange and radical happens. The *story* of Job comes to an abrupt stop, as though someone had hit the pause button, and gives way to a symposium—a wild, brilliant, bitter, oracular debate—on the riddle of divine justice. Why does God allow the righteous to suffer? On one side of the debate are Job's friends, Eliphaz, Bildad, and Zophar. They've come to comfort him. The way they do this is to tell Job more or less the same things that clergymen will be telling their congregants for the next few thousand years, whenever the lives of those congregants collapse or disintegrate for no apparent reason: to comfort them. They tell him that no evil can come from God; that God is always just, rewarding the righteous and punishing the wicked; that, given the inherent vileness of the human species ("What is man that he should be clean?"), it's likely that one falls into the latter category and has done *something* to deserve being worked over; that one should view one's misfortune as a divine reproof—as discipline—and accept it, be grateful for it, and repent the sin, whatever it was, for which the discipline was administered, so that God may restore one.

It's amazing. Here for the first time are all the gaseous platitudes that priests and rabbis and ministers have used ever since to anesthetize the grief-stricken—or shame them into silence. Here are the unctuousness and the sadism, the lubricant and the whip. What's even more astonishing is that the platitudes work: We suck them up, they make us feel better. Why should this be so? The only reason I can think of is that most people would rather feel guilty than feel helpless. Guilty for the baby dead in its cradle; guilty for drought, guilty for floods, guilty for plague. Guilty for earthquake, guilty for fire, guilty for Auschwitz and Treblinka; for the Middle Passage, guilty, for Wounded Knee, guilty; for Siem Reap and Sarajevo, guilty. Guilty for cancer, guilty for AIDS. Better to believe you brought this on yourself—*chose* it for yourself—than that it just happened to you. For no reason.

But this is exactly Job's understanding: that all that has happened to him has happened for no reason. "He breaketh me with a tempest and multiplieth my wounds without cause." In spite of everything those noxious comforters tell him, he insists he's blameless. Not just him but the countless others whom God humiliates and destroys. None of them deserves this. How can I convey the audacity of this position? Or its difficulty? When you come to understand that God permits evil to exist and even to triumph, there are two temptations: atheism or polytheism; to reject God or to fragment Him. (If you're an atheist, you believe that evil just exists by itself. And if you're a polytheist, you can blame all the horror and wretchedness of this world on an evil deity and attribute its sweetness and splendor to a good one. You can even claim that these deities are at war. You can, in other words, do exactly what Christians have been doing for two thousand years.) But Job stubbornly clings to one indivisible God, and stubbornly goes on arguing his case before Him. He's cranky, litigious, unappeasable—he's a pain in the ass, really. But this is the meaning of his integrity. The comforters try to shut him up and he shouts over them, up at the invisible figure on the bench, the judge he knows is dead set against him but from whom he still awaits justice: "Though he slay me yet will I trust in him."

"Though He Slay Me Yet Will I Trust in Him." Not a hymn but a torch song, addressed by a tormented lover to the faithless beloved, the beloved gone missing. A song of betrayal and absence. You picture her—because these songs are always sung by women—standing alone inside a cone of light, on display in her abjection. She's wearing a sleeveless dress of burgundy satin; her shoulders gleam like marble. In the dark beyond the stage men sit drinking at café tables, and her eyes seek them out one by one as she sings—Are you the one? Are you the one? Are you?—and then move on. "Oh that I knew where I might find him!" Her song is filled with accusation and entreaty, fury and despair, and finally with exultation, because if the beloved is gone, there's still this feeling he's left behind. Misery is his last gift to her, and she's drunk with it: He isn't any good, he isn't true, but I'll stick to him like glue. Can't go on, everything I had is gone. How could you leave me? How could you leave me? What can I do with this broken heart? You have no heart, Johnny. And I still love you so.

Job could also be a movie. It's a hard pitch, I know. The story's sort of a down, and there's no action in the second act. Here's my idea: Move the story from Uz—where the hell is *Uz?*—to Washington. Make Job a CIA agent, played by Sly Stallone; Sly could use a comeback role. He's a "black op" who goes behind the lines, in Central America, Afghanistan, Iraq, doing our country's dirty work. We need to establish from the get-go that this is a guy with balls, a man's man. But also vulnerable, sensitive: We should see him playing with his kids. His only connection to the Company is his Handler, the agent who briefs him for missions and covers his ass with the bureaucrats. Job is absolutely loyal to this guy, even though—here's the gimmick—he's never seen him. The audience doesn't see the handler, either. He's just a voice on the phone. I'm thinking Sir Tony Hopkins.

Anyway, one day Job comes home and walks right into an ambush. The house is crawling with terrorists. There's a huge gunfight, and at the end of it Sly's place is a smoking hole in the ground, his wife and kids are dead—make that one kid, we don't want people slashing their wrists. Sly tries to contact his Handler for help, but suddenly Sir Tony's not returning his calls. Maybe *They*'ve gotten him. Maybe he's *switched sides*. Job doesn't know. He's totally alone. Except maybe we give him these three sidekicks, like the Joe Pesci character in the *Lethal Weapon* series, who keep pestering him with lousy advice. A little comic relief. Okay, so Job tracks the Handler down to a secret headquarters, a stately old mansion in the Virginia countryside, heavily guarded. He makes it onto the grounds, but someone spots him. All hell breaks loose: alarms, guns, rottweilers. I'm seeing a helicopter chase. Finally he's outside the mansion, on the portico, exhausted, wounded, bloody, in tatters. He falls to his knees and hollers up at the balcony, begging the Handler to talk to him, give him some explanation. He's sobbing. "God!" he wants to yell. "God!" But all that comes out is "*Gaahhh!*"

There are still some third-act problems that need to be worked out.

●

Well, you can see how there would be. Not that Hollywood would find it all that hard to represent God; special effects have come a long way since *The Ten Commandments*. It's that there's no resolution, or rather, the resolution is so antithetical to Hollywood's cult of warmth. When God finally reveals Himself to Job, we want Him to *explain*: "That's for coveting your neighbor's wife." But the voice from the whirlwind explains nothing. It *asks*. "Where wast thou when I laid the foundations of the earth? Who laid the cornerstone thereof; When the morning stars sang together, and all the sons of God shouted for joy? Or who shut up the sea with doors, when it brake forth, as if it had issued out of the womb?"

There's no poetry that can compete with this. There's no argument that can refute it. Job asks, "How could you do this to me?" And God answers, "Because I can." Only not so matter-of-factly. This isn't an answer so much as it is a rebuke, thunderous, terrifying, sarcastic — sarcastic in a way that's recognizably Jewish. (I don't know if anyone remembers the old *Allen's Alley* radio program: "Vas *you* dere, Sharlie?") All poor Job can say in response is "Behold, I am vile. I will lay mine hand upon my mouth." This is where most glosses of Job end, with man's pathetic longing for justice coming up against the unfathomable power and mystery of the divine. Job wants to know why the world is unfair, and the Lord shows him the world — the entire world. The staggering vastness of earth and ocean, the secret dwelling places of light and darkness, the lion and the raven and the wild goat, the horse of the terrible nostrils, the monsters behemoth and leviathan. They're all here, not so much described as revealed. God slaps them down on the table, like poker chips of some impossibly large denomination. A bet you can't raise. What can Job do but fold?

I'd also like to mention some creatures that God leaves out of His peroration, though they're just as much His handiwork: the centipede with its poisonous fangs; the tarantula and the lung fluke; "tapeworms thirty feet long and roundworms so big and fat they block up your big intestine." This last is from John Updike's *Witches of Eastwick*. At the novel's climax, the devil — going by the rather obvious name Darryl Van Horne — delivers a sermon at a New England church. The title of the sermon is "This Is a Terrible Creation." He's right, of course; the devil is right. Creation *is* terrible, at least by human standards. But then, if you go back to the Creator's catalog of wonders, you'll notice that man is barely mentioned in it. He's a mote on the periphery, an afterthought. That's why Creation is so terrible. It wasn't designed for us — not for our comfort or even for our instruction. Not for our *wise use*. It is, in the deepest sense, inhuman.

Hey, what about Satan? Where the hell did he run off to? If Job were a conventional narrative, he'd come slinking back at this point, crestfallen, shamefaced: because he's lost the bet. Hasn't he? Job, of course, has passed the hideous stress test that was crafted for him; he's held on to his integrity. It's God who's been tempted, who's failed. We can't really say that He's failed Job. That would imply some preexisting obligation, and if this story makes anything clear it's that the Almighty owes no one. But no interpretation can disguise the fact that He's very nearly killed His servant, or allowed him to be nearly killed, out of, well, pride. The Lord Himself appears to realize this; He tells Satan: "And still he holdeth fast his integrity, although thou movest me against him, to destroy him without cause." For one moment He acknowledges the dreadful consequences of His whim. A moment later He disavows them: The devil made Him do it. Any literal reading of Job leaves us with the queasy intimation that God may be susceptible to demonic influence—that at any moment He may be conned into becoming our Adversary.

But the Lord deserves more credit, I think. Clement of Rome taught that He rules the world with a right hand and a left hand, the right being Christ, the left Satan. Father, Son, and Adversary: What if this is the true Trinity, a Trinity that both Jews and Christians once recognized but then discarded and ultimately repressed? Personally, I never got the bird. What if the wager between God and Satan is a contest between two aspects of a single Being? We might call them the Creator and the Destroyer, as Hindus call Brahma and Shiva. At the outset of the contest these alternate personalities are separate and opposed; by the contest's end they are one being. The Destroyer has been absorbed into the Creator. The Book of Job describes this wager from the point of view of its unhappy human marker—the die that is thrown, the coin that is flipped, the card that is turned over and over and over until its corners are torn off and its image worn almost beyond recognition. For Job the wager is a tragedy. For God, of course, it's a game.

Another way of putting it is that what to Job seems hideously unfair is, from God's perspective, just. Martin Buber says that human justice "intends to give everyone what is due to him," while divine justice "gives to everyone what he is." God gives each thing its nature, a gift even greater than existence. It is the nature of the world that creation coexist with destruction, that each mother forth the other. Magma boils up and cools to rock; plates of rock grind together like teeth, throw up mountains, collapse in trenches, are drawn down to the pit of the earth to become magma once more. Oceans drown whole continents. Everything splits and burns and rends. Lions with dusty golden skins eat defenseless grazing animals with liquid eyes. The raven feeds its young with rotten flesh. Somewhere in America religious psychopaths crash airplanes into skyscrapers and burn and crush three thousand strangers to death. And on the other side of the world American tanks roll through the streets of an ancient city and kill thousands of its inhabitants. It's all happening in a single instant, horrible and perfectly just. *And God saw that it was good.*

So say you've got a Jew, a Lakota, and a Tutsi. And they're hanging out comparing their tribulations. The Jew says, "I saw my whole family exterminated at Belsen. Mama, Papa, aunts, my sisters, two tiny girls. They were taken away to the gas chambers; they were burned in ovens, and their soot fell on me."

The Lakota says: "I saw many dead men, women, and children lying in the

ravine. When I went a little way up, I heard singing, and going a little way farther, I came upon my mother. She was moving slowly, and I could see that she
was very badly wounded. A strange thing: She had a soldier's revolver in her
hand, swinging it as she went. I do not know how she got it. When I caught up
to her, she said, 'My son, pass by me; I am going to fall down now.' As she went
up, the bluecoats shot at her and killed her."

The Tutsi says: "The militia had the people line up in the churchyard, in
rows. Then they would walk among the rows and cut us with their pangas,
swish, swish, swish, like they are chopping down maize. There is blood everywhere. At midday they get tired, they want to rest for a while. But they don't
want any of the people to get away. So they find the ones who are still alive and
sever the tendons behind their knees. This way they cannot run, and the militia can finish them later. Then they go off and eat lunch in the shade of the
rectory."

I know what you're going to say: *That's not funny!* But wait. It gets better, I
promise.

AN ORANGE GROVE, SOMEWHERE IN FLORIDA

I am weary of my crying: my throat is dried:
mine eyes fail while I wait for my God.

PSALM 69:3

WE were driving north, away from Miami, but not on the coastal highways. Instead we'd opted for the marrow of Florida, the flat, hot interior where oranges actually grow, on trees lined up like soldiers, in groves like regiments and divisions. Where the juice is actually made. Factories—Tropicana, Minute Maid, Sunny Delight—darken the road every few miles, and they stink worse than gas stations. Mashed pulp, tons of it, smells like anything else that has once been alive and isn't anymore. Rotten.

There wasn't much to look at besides the oranges. So when we spotted a school bus pulled over to the side, we watched it grow large in our windshield, transfixed. It was painted white with trim the color of a robin's egg, highlighted in rust. Across its backdoor someone had painted in a cursive hand, *"Get your praise on!"* But with its hood propped open like the beak of a hungry bird, the bus couldn't even get itself back on the road.

With visions of stranded gospel choirs shaking the trees with song just to pass the time, we pulled a U-turn and went back to give aid. But the bus seemed deserted. Maybe the choir had sought shade in the orange groves—

the sky was the flat gray of old bedsheets, but the sun's heat filtered through intensified. We walked closer, looking for clues, listening for hymns, but we heard nothing besides the *tick-tick-tick* of our car's engine cooling.

And then we saw the bus driver: a skeleton wearing skin like ratty leather, sitting at the wheel, staring through a bug-blurred windshield, watching us approach with what looked like lidless eyes. Then his bones rose as if pulled up by strings. He stood, crouched for the door, and emerged from the bus he apparently called home.

"James Simpson," he croaked. His tongue was too big for his mouth, and a white paste of dried sweat and salt ringed his lips. He wore high-top sneakers caked black with grease, oily blue jeans, and a dirty white T-shirt, out of which his bone-thin arms hung heavy as sash weights. His skin was sunned red and his tangle of hair was as orange as the fruit on the trees.

He looked like he needed more help than anyone could give. "Lord will provide," he said. He blinked, the pale, hot light of late afternoon proving too much for his cloudy blue eyes.

"Provide what?" we said.

"Gas," said James. "I ran out. I figured a police officer might come along, give me some." James looked over our shoulders, as if expecting to see a Florida state trooper glide to a stop in front of the bus, unfold himself out of his cruiser, and walk through the shimmering heat with his hands cupped full of gas. We couldn't help ourselves; we looked, too, even as James shuffled forward in his laceless sneakers, toward us or the angel in mirror shades only he could see. His eyes twitched back to us and our empty hands.

"That your church?" we asked, nodding to the inscription on the side of the bus. "Antioch Missionary Baptist Church, Opelika, Alabama, Jerry Dowdell, Pastor."

"I have come from Alabama," agreed James, "but I ain't from Antioch." He did not explain how he happened to be at Antioch's wheel. The Lord, he said, had taught him not to ask questions or particularly to answer them. He simply drove, waiting to be delivered to the church to which he said God had sworn his services. When he ran out of gas, he rolled to a stop and waited some more. Four days one time, he claimed, with neither food nor water. "Twenty-three hours behind a supermarket another time," he said. Sitting at that big, black wheel with its polish worn thin by his hands, waiting for God to refuel him through a sympathetic state trooper, or a grocery clerk with a heart for the Lord. Or us. Lord will provide.

"I aim to be a preacher," he said. "Soon. I'm studying. I ain't ready to start preachin' though. Word's still buildin'." One hand rose to his stomach. "In here," he said. He let his hand fall and stared at us, squinting in the sun. Something stirred the dust beneath the bus: a dehydrated white-and-brown pit bull. "Crybaby," said James. "That's his name." Crybaby lay spread-eagled, panting and struggling to keep his eyes from rolling to white.

"I'm hungry," said James.

The night before we'd stopped at a ramshackle Christian commune for junkies and winos, a compound of low, one-story buildings washed in gray paint known as the Circle of Love Ministries. Inside the circle—actually, a square of fencing topped with barbed wire—we had met a curly-haired drifter named Dennis, who'd plumped up on Jesus and government-issue cheese since he'd stopped "geeking"—smoking crack. He had strummed, with twisted hands, a few of his own songs for us on his guitar. Southern rock ballads, lyrics about a river that had lifted him off the streets of Jacksonville and carried him to this mosquito-infested dormitory-church just outside of Heaven. There were songs about loving the needle, and about being loved by Jesus, and about finally deciding he had to choose between them. "You can't just take," he'd said, eyeing the notebooks in which we'd scribbled his words. "You gotta give. Give something back to Jesus."

Easy for Dennis to say now that he lived in the Circle of Love, where giving and receiving was as simple as strumming a guitar. Beyond the Circle's borders, the transactions weren't so clear. It was hard to say what you should give and whether it would be received.

Not that James was proud. So hungry he said so, he looked ready to beg if only he could have found the words. But he couldn't. He was lost in a faith beyond asking, a black hole. He was inside it, in the dark, and he didn't even know that the air he breathed was suffering. What we call agony, he called God.

We put our notebooks away and gave James what we had, some twenty-five-cent packages of peanut butter crackers we found in our backseat and a bottle of water. He didn't want money, but when we offered to buy him some gas, he climbed into the bus and came out with a red plastic jug. As he handed it to us, we noticed the faded blue tattoo on his left hand. L-O-V-E, one letter per finger.

"How much do you need?" we asked.

"Whatever you can give," said James.

"No problem," we said, but it was. Neither of us had shaken his hand, and we were both afraid to ask him to drive along. Afraid of what? He was dizzy from the heat and his dog could barely stand. Together they might have weighed a hundred pounds. Maybe he had a knife, but not likely—it didn't look like he could've afforded one sharp enough to quarter an orange. Maybe he had a disease. Back at Circle of Love, Dennis had recited an alphabet of afflictions shared by him and his brothers, ticking them off on his fingers: "TB, hep C, HIV . . ." And yet we had been glad to take his hand and would've been honored to eat at his table if we hadn't arrived too late for dinner. James was different. Dennis's ministry may have been just a few cinder-block buildings, but at least it was real. James's church was running on fumes. His flesh had withered on his bones. His dog was too tired to protect him. The sun, hiding behind clouds, still managed to burn him. And he was sitting on the side of the road waiting for God in the form of a state trooper.

But the Lord didn't show. Just us, and we were scared of him, frightened of getting too close to his faith, of getting lost, of getting hurt like he had. He'd given his heart to God and God had spurned him; he was unlucky in love. He was an abandoned woman, a knocked-around wife, a child not so much forgotten as willfully ignored; he was a dog turned out on the road. Yet he trailed after his master: "I've been to churches," he told us. "But God ain't in those houses.

"Yesterday," he said, "I stopped at a Baptist church back there. You probably seen it. They gave me a sandwich and gas, too. They said they was a church. But there wasn't no God in their house. They just gave me the food and the gas so I'd go away. I didn't even ask them for it. I don't ask for nothing, I just take what God gives me. I told them I wouldn't ask for an invitation to come into their church and they didn't give it to me. They called law on me and preacher said, 'You got the wrong church, son.' "

Then there'd been the one in Tampa. The one he'd seen in a dream. He'd heard God's voice call him to this one. *Meet me there.* God's voice. It had been sweeter than cool water on a hot day, kinder than the girl who'd loved him when he was seventeen. It sounded, he said, like the sweet nothings God had whispered to him long ago through wind rushing over the purr of a 428 Cobra muscle car. James peered under the bus's hood, staring at its huge, cold engine. "I had a 'sixty-one T-Bird," he said, "that could outrun anything in Alabama, even the law."

But they don't just chase you, they sneak up on you. The sheriff had caught him unawares, thrown him in jail for Godspeed and reckless driving. James had sat in his cell, waiting for word from God. When it didn't come, he took a fork and some ink and into his own flesh carved the word of his own: L-O-V-E. "And I planned to do the other," he said, pointing to each of the blank fingers on his right hand and reading the letters that weren't there. "H-A-T-E."

"Like the movie?" we asked. James looked at us then his hand and frowned, as if we'd mentioned something long forgotten. "Maybe . . . ," he said.

Maybe like Robert Mitchum's murderous preacher in *The Night of the Hunter.* "Would you like me to tell you the little story of right hand, left hand?" he asks. He holds up his left hand to show off its inscription: "H-A-T-E. It was with this left hand that old brother Cain struck the blow that laid his brother low." Then he holds up his right: "L-O-V-E: You see these fingers, dear hearts? These fingers has veins that run right to the soul of man. The right hand, friends: the hand of love." His hands lock together, fingers intertwined into the shape of a temple. "These fingers, dear hearts, is always a-warring and a-tugging, one agint the other. Now watch 'em: Old brother left hand, left hand HATE's a-fighting, and looks like LOVE's a goner." Left hand wrestles right, the temple is tipping. "But wait a minute, wait a minute!" Right hand pushes, inches back to even ground. "Hot dog, LOVE's a-winning!" The hands struggle, left over right, right over left. "Yessirree. It's LOVE that won, and old left hand HATE is down for the count!"

"The fingers I wrote *love* on swoll up like sausages," James said. "And then they took my fork away." And then they took James away too. "A general called the jail, said I was AWOL. Said I was needed back in Vietnam."

When James had arrived in Tampa the week before we met him, the church God had promised him was no longer there. "They torn it down," said James. "I found my church and they torn it down." Since then he'd wandered. "There's a church waiting for me, gotta be," he said. Who hasn't felt the same? Who hasn't given up the looking?

We drove down to the gas station and filled up our tank, then the red jug for James. Inside we bought a gallon of water, a loaf of Wonder wheat, some jam, and a jar of Skippy. "Mm," said the woman behind the counter. "P B and J." It didn't seem worth mentioning that the food was for a man who was stranded on the side of the road and looked like he was dying of dehydration.

When we got back, James received the sandwich fixings and the gas with the same disregard with which he had endured the heat. So we said good-bye and started to leave. Then he stepped forward, and we moved back. He was close enough for us to see the sores along his hairline. "I wanna shake your hands," he said. Then he did. His grip was soft. If, when you were a child, you ever picked up a dead bird, a sparrow or a robin that you wanted to bury, then you've felt James's hand. Lifelessly heavy and lighter than it should be, and most of all *dry*.

He pressed his toothless gums together as he held on and nodded a little. Maybe he would be a preacher, maybe one day he'd hold someone still with the power of his cloudy blue eyes and the hollow bones of the hand that had escaped H-A-T-E, and whisper his secret into his victim's ear: the wisdom of Job running a finger over his own scars, the gospel of a sword-tongued street-corner ranter, shouting not salvation nor deliverance but disease: "You're just like me."

Then James let go, and his arms and ours fell slowly, and we stepped away from each other, all of us left with nothing to say. So we wished him luck—which he declined, explaining that he didn't need it—and got back on the highway. At the gas station, we stopped again to wash our hands.

SONG OF SONGS

BY DARCEY STEINKE

BOUGAINVILLEA petals blew around on the stone floor with a sound dry and melodic as you came into me. This was in that period of extreme weather. Heat waves followed by days of freezing rain. In that time of omens, large, medium, small, and extrasmall like the fact that your older sister adored cantaloupe while the younger one preferred sunflower seeds. And how in that small subterranean room with the twin beds and the walnut wardrobe, we were always cold. Staying under the comforter, both our bodies so thin that when we fucked our hipbones made a clicking sound a bit like a record skipping, and there was your pale skin, your heart beating in your chest with a wet sound like water swishing through a pipe. That sound along with the click of our hips illuminated everything, so I could see deep down into the hole, the fine blond hairs on my mother's cheek as well as bits of green glass in the dirt of Mrs. Johanson's garden. I saw everything all the way down into the night, drunk as I was on a thousand gin and tonics, because everybody wanted you, boys and girls. I desired not your body, which I already knew I could never make mine, but the you in the glittering asphalt, the you in the gas oven's blue flame, the you in the pattern of bubble in the glass of Coke. I had to convince you to come away from your computer and lay down with me on the futon because thinking has always been hard. I mean why make yourself into a clock when you can learn the names of the flowers. Once in the car, as we passed a bed of wildflowers, I exclaimed, forgetting your prohibition, *I love larkspur,* and you flew into a rage. You also claimed that sunsets, the raspberry sky over Brooklyn, didn't really affect you all that much. You loathed yourself more stylishly than I was accustomed to, and so at first when I loved you without knowing you it was like loving God.

Unable to sleep, you'd get up and stand by the fire. Nothing in the flame's light, not the mantel marble or the splintered mirror above it, suggested the modern world. You could have been a blacksmith in a La Tour painting, with your well-developed chest now gone soft in middle age. In the morning, we left the island and drove to a hotel in Norfolk, ate Chinese food, and watched *E.T.* at the theater. This was before pay-per-view, before even cable in that stone age when I ran around in my macramé bikini, my skin the color of milk chocolate. My white panties, your hard cock, our tan skin, we fucked every couple hours and got so high I put my hand through the headboard, through the wall, and into the chest of the man next door. His heart like a peony, and I knew he had found a little peace and so had I by loving your head of soft hair, your gray eyes, yours my first body and I was scared every time you took your shirt off, your narrow shoulders shocked me back into childhood and made me miss the subtle erotics of my family. My mother's cleavage. My little brother's belly button. My dad's fleshy upper arms. Light from the stereo illuminated the glass beads hanging over your doorway and sure it was sexy in there. All kinds of stuff happened. Later, after we both came two hundred times, you'd kneel next to the porcelain tub and read to me. Your body, pressed against mine, had the exact weight of a daydream as we lay down together on the flatbed boat, pontoons I think they call them, with a dozen red-and-white-striped seats. We lay together on the AstroTurf. Rock music from the other side of the lake, teenagers laughing, your body covered with freckles. Your pelvis like a bowl of clean water as you said the word *cacophony* and the radiators clanged and you tapped your empty cigarette box against my fingers which were clenched tight around a shot glass of bourbon, the liquid melting in several directions, and I knew we were over the guardrail parked in your orange Volkswagen looking out on the lights of the valley while terrible pop music played. We made out ferociously, the crotch of my jeans as wet as a washcloth. Oh, my love, my perfect one, my one of the seventies sideburns and redneck appeal.

Once kissing on a blanket spread out underneath a Sunday school bus you undid your pants and your cock slipped out. The prehistoric urgency of your hard-on and the sea-lamprey-like slit at the top haunted me so that later as I lay in my childhood bed I couldn't sleep, so I got up to watch television and there you'd be mending your fishing nets with a thick wooden needle. You'd tell by the movement of the cedar branch in your yard if that morning the fishing would be worthwhile. If not you'd load split logs into the woodstove and we'd sleep, your chest pressed against my back, your hand on my hip. This was around the time I locked myself into the ladies' room of the restaurant where I worked, sat down on the closed toilet seat, and said *I love you*, to no one in particular. Afterward I went into the walk-in with the bartender and we lay down on a flat of strawberries, and when I came out, the back of my white waitressing blouse looked like it was splattered with blood. But it was the milk in her breasts that haunted you, your wife standing drunk on the grass between your house and your neighbors', her panties stuffed into her back pocket, *milk*, as you said many times, *still in her tits*. You told this story in the holy space engendered after mutually fulfilling sex, as well as another incident. How you sat in a café across the street watching your father wait for you. After fifteen minutes he checked his watch, after forty he left. You looked like a paper doll cut out from the moon, and so during the blizzard I fled my parents' split-level and met you behind the Hardee's. You'd built a campfire. Brought a bottle of strawberry Boone's Farm wine. Ice crystallized on the rust stains of your beard. But you hated nature, and when forced to hike up Mount Lavernea with the German couple you kept stopping, hands spread wide, a cynical expression infusing your features.

These things stay with me, and so when I'm finally with you on the other side I'll remember how we went to the Log Cabin restaurant for breakfast but stayed all day drinking Bloody Marys. You were fascinated with locker-room slang. And you loved to sleep in your clothes, particularly your sweater vest and janitor pants. I remember as we sat in the red leather booth, bits of refracted disco ball light spinning, how I scanned your features—brown eyes with black lashes, thicket of silver hair, acne scars—for some clue as to why Paris is called the City of Light. When, up on all fours, your cock rooted inside me, I asked you if you felt *it*, you always said *yes*. After the second glass of wine, I noticed that your green eyes looked like tiny planet earths, and you told the waitress the soup was delicious, and me that my profile was killing you. Later you kneeled down to unbuckle my silver shoes, talking all the while about how if Eve hadn't eaten the apple there'd be no reason for language, that words were needed only to define our separateness from God. Later when I saw you pull the girl onto your lap, my heart broke and I threw my donut down and ran out of the loft, down the stairs onto the Chinatown street. I no longer had you to love so I decided to love the world. But that was hard, as the world, if you haven't noticed, is not that easy to love what with fast-food wrappers blowing around the subway tracks where I waited in my slip dress for the Q train. I rode that fucker all the way out to Brooklyn, where I ran past the picnic tables and the BBQ grills to the shore of the lake to see if the flowers were on the trees. Pitching squares of chocolate to the ducks, I said with each over-hand throw, My love, my own, I have looked for you everywhere, particularly in the pelvic region of the male species but also in red wine and hardcover books. Sometimes you make the back of my head tingle and subsequently I confuse being known with being obliterated. Why make me wait for union when I'm willing to crawl into the tree, grab hold of your blossoms, and fuck the dirt, my love, my beautiful one, quick before it's too late, grab my hand in the cab and kiss the nape of my neck and work that alchemy that changes everything into *you*. My beloved, my holy one, there is a melon in the fridge, split in half, covered in Saran Wrap. I got it from a gray-haired man who was anxious to get back to his book on genealogy. This melon is for you. I'm wait-ing to feed you this melon, chunk by chunk, right down to the rind.

NASHVILLE, TENNESSEE

Like clothing you will change them
and they will be changed.

PSALM 102:26

WE were eating ribs when we saw him, his hair long and brown, his beard thick and biblical like Christ's or Charlie Manson's. His eyes looked like eight balls with the numbers blacked out and his bony knees were white as skulls. But it was his ribs that drew our attention, pulling our gazes up from oversize plates to the half dozen televisions that hung suspended above the bar. The camera zoomed in on a photographic still of black-and-white bones pressed against skin, a rib cage like two skeletal hands just barely supporting what was left of John Walker Lindh.

The TVs were silent, but everyone knew who he was. The story of the California Catholic boy who had become the "American Taliban" had been in the news for weeks. Now came the report they were sending him home. Waylon Jennings's voice rumbled through the bar's sound system, a country twang standing in for CNN commentary: "Mamas, don't let your babies grow up to be cowboys."

Waylon had died just the day before, and now he was everywhere, on every TV and radio station in Nashville. So was John Walker. The "Ramblin' Man" and the kid who got lost in Afghanistan, joined for a moment by death, war, and the American belief that by changing your clothes—donning a black cowboy hat or a white Muslim kufi—you can become what you please.

"Don't let 'em pick guitars or drive them old trucks . . ." The picture on the TV changed: his thin, white body bound by black tape in what looked like a coffin, his gaunt face darkened by blood and dirt as if he'd been pulled out of a tomb instead of up from a basement flooded with water. A rag covered his eyes, a torn strip of cloth on which soldiers had scrawled curses. What did they write? The picture was grainy; we couldn't read the words. Mother-fucker? Cocksucker? That's what the men at the tables around us said as they glared at the screens. "Son-of-a-bitch," muttered one man. "Son-of-a-*whore*." Maybe there had been a wit among John Walker's captors, a joker, a sardonic ex–altar boy who had thought to inscribe "King of the Jihad" across his pris-oner's eyes.

We finished our ribs and headed out the door. We'd been making the rounds of both bars and churches in Nashville, watching for a story of overnight salvation, the kind country music is known for, the kind we'd just seen on TV. Somewhere in the city there was a man writing a song that would tell the story—

> I started lookin' around for a light out of the dim
> And the first thing I heard that made sense was the word
> Of Mohammed, peace be upon him
>
> STEVE EARLE, "JOHN WALKER'S BLUES"

—the pious light of Sunday mornings chasing dim and raucous Saturday nights; the constant cycle of putting on the fancy suit, then chafing and strip-ping and starting again. To John Walker his homeland had been as one per-manent Saturday night, too dark, too free, too naked. He must have wanted to start again.

It didn't seem an accident that there were as many bars as churches in Nashville, or that at least one was both: Greater St. John's Baptist Church, a white-brick box with two steeples like horns poking into the underbelly of an interstate overpass. A local porn king had bought Greater St. John's, rechris-tened it Confessions, and filled it with brass poles, pink neon, and naked women. Fifteen dollars got you a seat in the sanctuary, where the pews had been replaced by barstools, the baptismal made into private booths equipped with leather chairs, low to the ground and easy for a dancer to straddle.

We headed for the back of the building on a Saturday night. Down a short flight of stone stairs, through a locked glass door guarded by a buzzer and a closed-circuit surveillance system, in the same church basement that once held Baptist soup kitchens and Baptist potlucks, there was now a "bookstore," staffed by three women bound by too-tight black lingerie. When we arrived they shuffled into formation like they were line-dancing at a honky-tonk bar. One looked too young for this kind of work, her face pink and child-puffy, as if she'd just woken cranky from a nap. Another clearly couldn't give a damn or a fuck or even tell the difference; she was almost too drunk to stand. And then there was their captain, stocky from the hips to the knees, strong in the shoulders. She glared indifferently. Elastic garters sliced into her thighs, yellow bruises dotted her arms, a C-section scar ran up her belly.

"Twenty-five for every fifteen minutes," she said. "Plus tip."

"Out front? The stage dancers?" Too-Young cooed, "Those girls only tease." She took a step closer, leaning in. "We please.

"For three hundred," she added, "you get it all."

"But we only want an interview," we said. "We just want to know what it's like for you to do this kind of work in a church."

The drunk one laughed, snorting and stumbling. "Go talk to a nun," she said.

The captain shook her head. "Why don't you ask God?"

The next morning, on the suburban outskirts of town, we went to a mosque that had been bought and paid for with the help of a man named Yusuf Islam, also known as Cat Stevens. Inside, the mosque looked the same as any other middle-class American Islamic center: men and women lining their shoes up in the hallway and stepping sock-footed onto the carpets that covered the prayer hall, a big room cleared for devotion and adorned with the names of God in ornate Arabic calligraphy. The women prayed on one side, the men on the other, though they intermingled and whispered: Remember to pick up Pop-Tarts for the children! When is Mohammed's piano recital? Men dressed in robes over Dockers and women in modern, shoulder-length veils tried to help us as we fumbled through the routine, pointing us due east toward Mecca when we got down on our knees and tapped the floor with our foreheads, directing us with gestures like good-natured traffic cops to stand, to bow, to sit and listen.

"There is no difference," the imam said, "between the Christian God and the Muslim God. I am here today to tell you we love Jesus. We know he is a prophet."

The day we attended had been announced as one of "outreach" and "introducing ourselves," but it seemed as much a defensive strategy as an educational endeavor. Sharing wavelength with John Walker and Waylon Jennings, Muslims were on every TV and radio station in Nashville: Muslims harassed, Muslims arrested, Muslims assaulted, murdered, thrown from trains. "We love Jesus," the imam kept saying, because he had seen them on the news each night, he'd watched them as if he was a witness to the crimes: Three Muslim medical students are pulled off the highway in Florida, accused of "plotting an attack" at a Shoney's restaurant. In Houston, a Muslim-owned Goodyear store is set on fire. In Cleveland a man attacks an Islamic center by driving his car through its wall. There are shootings, there are shouts: Raghead. Towelhead. Sandnigger. "Arabs out" scrawled on Muslim houses. "Nuke them all" scratched on Muslim cars. There are hard drives confiscated; there are killers claiming "post-9/11 rage."

"We love Jesus," the imam said, because around the country there were so many racists threatening so many mosques you'd think that all the synagogues had already been graffitied, all the black churches already burned. "We love Jesus," because as close as LaVergne, Tennessee, managers at the Whirlpool plant were stalking the bathrooms, listening at the doors, preventing prayers to Allah from being said in the stalls.

"Jesus," the imam said emphatically. "Muslims love Jesus, okay?"

Half the people in the mosque were like us, lukewarm Christians or secular Jews or born-again Buddhists: "spiritual but not religious": infidels. Nobody said it, but it was true; not an accusation, a statement of fact. There were two kinds of people there: faithful, unfaithful; believers, unbelievers; insiders who lived Islam, and outsiders who'd come to learn. The imam moved his hands as he spoke, gesturing out with open palms, then drawing them toward his chest, not dividing the crowd but trying to blur lines he knew existed. Those outside of the faith fidgeted on the floor, trying to take pressure off pinched tailbones, raising hands occasionally to ask questions that would show them to be sensitive to the complexity of the situation. The other half watched the unfaithful watching, hoping none of the visitors were violent kooks in just-curious clothing. The imam droned on about American Islam, about how real Muslims were not like John Walker or the Taliban, repeating again and again that real Muslims did not respect Osama bin Laden. "No, no. Not at all. *Jesus*. We respect Jesus."

After the service, we got back in the car and turned on the radio. Waylon again, his slow voice still warning: "Mamas don't let your babies grow up to be cowboys . . ."

Back in the city, deep below it, we met two archivists from the Tennessee State Museum and followed them farther down winding metal stairs into the depths of the permanent collection, so vast it spread out from under the museum like catacombs. The archivists were the kinds of guys whose ages were hard to discern because their grins were so quick and expansive, changing their faces from old to new in the duration of a greeting. They were unshakably jolly despite the permanent dark of their basement bunker, in which the totems of the American South had been gathering for decades. We'd come to see depression-era pulpits carved from tree trunks, ivy-vine snake-handling baskets from high up in the Smokys, ritual objects of people too poor not to improvise.

In their spare time, the archivists told us, they were reenactors of the conflict they called, with a wink, the "War of Northern Aggression." "Used to be we had trouble finding enough guys to be the other side," the more burly and bearded of the two said. "Got so you had to bring a pair of uniforms with you if you wanted to participate: a gray and a blue. Last guys to show up had to be Yankees."

He smiled; he knew where we came from.

"Somebody had to do it, even if it wasn't as much fun. You mind dying less if you're Union, but then you're out of the action."

We walked by a grove of twenty-foot-tall concrete crosses, each designed to be dropped in the sea, hauled into the jungle, or shipped to the moon, to be seen a thousand years from now, reminders for the future of the faith of the past, just as the skyscraping Buddha statues of Afghanistan had been, before they joined the dust of the Bamiyan valley. Etched on the face of each was a warning: GET RIGHT WITH GOD. PREPARE TO MEET HIM.

"The battles are better lately, though," the second archivist said. "Lots of European reenactors are coming over these days. Irish. German. They don't care what side they're on."

"Just look at the Tenth Legion," the bigger one added. "All English. Back home a lot of them are Roman reenactors; they come and do the Civil War in the off-season. Gray, blue, whatever the heck centurions wear, it's all the same to them. Just another uniform."

We turned a corner and stopped in front of a mannequin dressed in an ancient-looking coarse-cloth robe with a veiled hood. It looked like it had once been scarlet and sturdy, but now it was closer to pink, its fabric linen-thin. On the face of the hood were painted crude features: a backward *L* for a nose, a mustacheless beard, and two comically arched brows smudged above two ragged eyeholes.

"That's something, ain't it?" the burly archivist said. "Oldest Ku Klux Klan robe in existence."

They couldn't be sure, but they thought it dated back to the days right after the war, the new fashion of the aftermath that never really ended. "Confederate veterans got home and couldn't wear the gray anymore, so some of them switched to red. Later they all changed to white, and those pointy hats, you know."

We stared at the robe like it glowed, trying to imagine the man who'd worn it. Small, by the measure of his shoulders, slight, maybe just a boy. With skirt and sleeves drooping toward the ground, it could have been a clown costume for a low-budget circus. Yet it hung on the mannequin like a tattered shroud, rags on the bones of a past not buried deep enough, naked in the archive's overhead light.

The archivists wanted to move on, to bring us deeper into the archive, farther below the churches and bars up on the surface. Spotting a bicycle that had once belonged to a great evangelist, they tried to coax us away from the robe. "But you all were looking for religious stuff, right?"

.Fallen, fallen is Babylon . . .

ISAIAH 21:9

ISAIAH

By Charles Bowden

WE'VE been dry too long and the thirst rasps our throats. The air here is wet, heavy with the taste of rain, and all the *avenidas* are lined with jacaranda trees lush with leaf. Our shirts hang limp off our backs and we suck down the air like nectar. We have come from the deserts to the land of milk and honey and endless spring.

The politician refuses to move fast as we cross the clogged street in front of the old cathedral in Guadalajara. We've got appointments with government officials, talking points to hone, clothes to press. But still there is no hurry in him. The traffic stalls in angry lines with the grilles like hungry mouths as he slowly moves, his eyes on the ancient temple. He is new here and this is his homecoming. The air is flowers and blue sky, the buildings ancient and stone.

The cathedral seems to be his target but my mind is elsewhere. I want to see the frescoes and paintings of José Clemente Orozco. I want the anger, the black fury, and especially the fire. When Orozco lived, nobody here could handle him and he had to leave and go to Babylon for eight years of brooding after his early ideas were denounced. He did not like it there and made a painting he called *The Dead*. He later wrote, "Something grave was happening in New York. People were rushing more than usual. . . . You could hear the sirens of the fireman and the Red Cross sounding furiously. . . . Wall Street and its surrounding area was an infernal sea. . . . The crash. . . . This was the crash, the disaster." He was seeing the economic collapse of 1929.

But I bow to the hunger of the politician as he ambles across the street. Exhaust fumes cotton on our tongues, and he looks here and there with deliberation. His skin glows a rich, dark brown, the hair a mat of black and the body solid and not to be hurried. Now he falls into one of those labyrinths of silence where he likes to wander. He'll be all words, a smile on the face, and then silence will descend like a curtain and he is gone, the pain is in his dark eyes and I wonder what hell he has suddenly discovered. He's around fifty, got some flesh on him, that gait of a solid citizen, the burgher safe in his city ways, but when this silence crosses his face and his eyes get narrow, well, then he is in another country and blazing with the kind of fire that blazes in the night thoughts of adolescents. He has always kept his wounds close at hand.

He suddenly asks, "Are you Catholic?"

"No."

"Well, I am deeply Catholic."

We've come from Babylon, but this name we never use.

Therefore my people are gone into captivity, because they have no knowledge: And their honourable men are famished, and their multitude dried up with thirst.

ISAIAH 5:13

I remember the first night our paths crossed. He'd just won the big election, the one he was not supposed to have a prayer of winning, the one where all the big money was aimed against him like artillery. He came from the wrong people on the wrong side of all the tracks. Yet, he won. I walked into the campaign headquarters with the money guy, the one who brings the envelopes election night so that they are not recorded before the vote. The money guy had explained to me that he gathered the fistful of checks with one simple argument: "If this asshole wins, do you want him not to know who you are?" And so, we walked in with all that money, all the checks written by the very rich boys who had tried to kill him in the campaign. He was sitting in this back room, a throng of brown people circulating around him. A mariachi band played, there were tacos and beer, and yet he did not smile. He seemed to glower, but when I looked closer, I realized that he was simply somewhere else, someplace beyond my geography.

Years before, I began a book with a Bible verse snatched from one of those bedside Gideons. I habitually prowl the Bible in lonely motel rooms as the wine bottle slowly flows down my gullet in the midnight hours. I'd cracked the book open to Isaiah 1:7, where he picked the scab of the loss of Jerusalem and the Temple, tasting the pain of the captivity in Babylon. And the voice said, "Your country is desolate, your cities are burned with fire; your land, strangers devour it in your presence, and it is desolate, as overthrown by strangers."

The book I was writing then was about speed and going over edges and living the fast life with no brakes, not a single thought of slowing down, and no purpose. I'd decided to capture the empty flesh pressing against me at all hours. But I could never put my real finger on my anger until half drunk I cracked Isaiah open and the wound drained right across my face. We have all lost our land to strangers and come to Babylon. We've grown fat here, but the pang of the loss remains. We are incomplete, especially around midnight. And we are angry, I know I am, because I'll be damned if I can understand why this has happened and what I ever did to deserve this fate. And though I want an answer, I do not pray for one. I never pray. I fucking refuse to pray.

In Isaiah, it's all pretty damn simple: The Jews go down, the Temple is torched, they're hauled off to bondage, they wail to God about the loss, and then the promise comes that they will be allowed, in the sweet by-and-by, to return home, that a stranger will come and bring them salvation, that God will square everything and create a new righteous kingdom. Done deal. Trust me. Made in the shade. Hot buttered soul.

I believe in the wound, the land taken, the temples burned, the bondage — that I believe with all my heart. But not the restoration, the righteous new kingdom. Not for the Jews, not for the gentiles.

The cathedral casts a cool shadow over vendors peddling rosaries, small pictures of saints, crosses, images of the Virgin. Indian women sit on their haunches on the steps, a child in one arm, the other hand out begging. The politician drops a coin in each and every hand. He knows the language. But he has never been this far before, never more than about 150 miles into the country. As a boy he would go to a provincial capital in the north and spend his summers there with relatives. The local kids would make fun of the way he talked, how he did not have the language down quite right. That is what he remembers. And that the north is dry, a place of sun and heat, and this place, this city with the cathedral, rests on a high bench a ways inland from the sea and is green, lush with green. He did not imagine home would be like this.

When he asked his father once why he came north, the old man said, "Toilet paper. They have better toilet paper over here."

Inside the cathedral is the usual high, vaulting ceiling, the naves like little caves off to each side, the various saints resting in glass cases, giant dolls with old robes and their faces always shiny from the paint dictated by custom. The faithful pray, leave offerings, sometimes light a candle, but mainly ask and ask and ask for that favor, for that caress of grace. The light is not bright, simply cool. Fifteen or twenty souls sit on the pews in silence. The scuffle of footsteps is the loudest sound. In back on a balcony, a huge pipe organ of rich woods and tarnished metal is still.

I wait in back for about twenty minutes as he wanders. Finally, he is done. As we come down the steps and back into the day, he says, "I've decided."

"Just now? In there?"

"Yes."

During the hard time of revolution, one in ten or one in eight died, probably at least a million. Then came the influenza, killing 300,000 more. Then came the revolt called Cristero, in which the righteous rose up and protected their faith and tens of thousands more died. And then came more hard times, and the pain kept increasing and so the people left, went north, and entered Babylon. And in Babylon they made the best of where they were. And yet, a part of them never forgot where they had come from, no one forgot, not those who had come, not those who had been born in Babylon. Especially those who had never been there. No one forgot right down to this present day. It is a wound, this leave-taking, one still fresh yet hardly mentioned. One always felt and yet never understood. Why were they forsaken, why did they have to leave? Where is the justice and mercy in this? And why did they have to come to a place where they were despised?

But it is promised in Isaiah that all of these lordly souls who despise others will suffer, all the empires will go to dust in the blazing light of the true faith. Comeuppance, that is the repeated message of Isaiah. As for Babylon, well, listen:

But wild beasts shall lie there; and their houses shall be full of doleful creatures; and owls shall dwell there, and satyrs shall dance there. And the wild beasts of the islands shall cry in their desolate houses, and dragons in their pleasant palaces: and her time is near to come, and her days shall not be prolonged.

ISAIAH 13:21, 22

Still, I reject the idea of special people with special truths. Babylon may be bad, but Jerusalem is fatal.

Over drinks, I say the Bible asks some good questions but I fall away when it gives answers. But this is a ruse. The Bible is embedded in my culture, the dreamsong of the zombies that we are, and so I know I must look at it if I am to understand the deeper rhythms of the talk in the churches and the back alleys. There is a single story: the faith, falling away from the faith, the punishment, the chance at redemption, and then someday the end time, when all is made right.

As a child I stopped believing this single story. Now, I fight it.

But this is the story I know in my bones from my life. The faith does not protect, the falling away is really the experience of being taken away, the punishment comes. And there is no redemption. And there will be no restoration.

Orozco once wrote that the revolutionary believes in "Justice whatever the cost." He made this statement to explain his painting of a revolutionary who stares out in defiance as a general stabs him in the back.

In Isaiah it is written, "For unto us a child is born, unto us a son is given: and the government shall be upon his shoulder; and his name shall be called Wonderful, Counsellor, the Mighty God, the everlasting Father, the Prince of Peace" (9:6).

That early whisper of the Messiah, the righter of wrongs. Orozco paints something he calls *American Civilization: Modern Migration of the Spirit*. The background is tanks, cannons, Greek columns pushed off pedestals and fallen to rubble, fires of war on the horizon, Buddha akimbo in the ruin, the headless statue of a woman with full breasts saying milk and succor, all this in the gray tones that grace the flesh of a corpse when we mourn our loss. In the foreground is a man in a loincloth. His flesh is yellow and orange and red, his cheeks dark blue, singing out about loss of blood. Huge holes are in his palms and feet. His eyes are somewhere between rage and catatonia, and these eyes say they have seen enough and will look no longer, so stop your praying. The man holds an ax, and behind him lies his cross, severed at the base by his hand.

Orozco, unlike Isaiah, never tells us what his work means. He sees, he paints, and then he leaves us to our fate. Much like the man in the painting who has returned in what looks to be a rage and cut down his own cross, announcing his renunciation of his suffering and of what has ensued from his message. The man has had enough of us and our ways and seems angry at what we have made of his life.

He does not bleed, but then corpses notoriously do not bleed.

Last night, the scheduled three-hour flight became twelve hours.

At the first stop in the north, we had hours between planes and so took a cab into the state capital. The restaurant was beer, food, and a mariachi band. The politician kept sending up requests for songs his father sang, and then he would sing along with them as we drank. After that, everything went strange. The next leg of the flight was late, and in some city farther south a woman got on and sat by me and told me as she drained double martinis that she was flying down to a coastal town, there was a deal in the offing that she might finance involving fish, special fish, and the special fish would be caught by brown guys in small boats and then air-freighted to Japan, where they'll pay a lot for this flesh. She wore a couple of rings on each finger and her thumbs also. Her boozed eyes peered from beneath a crown of blond hair and she explained how Buddhism had turned her around, as had this guy she'd met down here who'd steered her into this good fish deal. The plane broke down at the next stop, and after an hour or two, we were herded onto another aircraft, somehow she got lost in this shuffle, and we got to our destination about 2:00 A.M.

The politician disappeared into his seat during all this time. He'd never really traveled outside the country, had no passport, and carried a torn and brittle birth certificate. Every time he showed the ancient document for ID, another flake of paper fell off and drifted to the ground.

When we finally made it to the hotel, there was not a drink to be had. So we were left to the mercies of the in-room minibars.

> How is the faithful city become a harlot! It was full of judgment; righteousness lodged in it; but now murderers.
>
> ISAIAH 1:21

I can smell the rotten blood seeping out of the wet ground. It is everywhere because of all the conquests. And it is here, also. We live in a world where eventually all the temples go to the torch, all the people go to spend time in

Babylon, and the kingdom is never restored. This last is the rub. We keep licking this sore in our mouths and telling ourselves the kingdom will be restored. I part from Isaiah on this matter. I think we are already in the kingdom, ready or not.

In this place with the humid air and lovely jacaranda trees, the killing came early and so did the torch. The politician and I sit in a café, drink cold beers and eat *botanas*. Red tiles smile from the floor, and on the walls there are old photographs of dead revolutionaries from a dead revolution. But the real killing came five hundred years or so ago. Nuño Beltran de Guzmán rode into this green with five hundred Spaniards and ten thousand native allies. He found people who lived hither and yon, some in caves, people who had kept the central power at bay, failed to worship the pyramids with that blood running down the steps. Guzmán was a slaver, and many he simply killed, the others he put in chains. One local leader he dragged behind horses, then burned alive. By way of explanation, he said that the man had converted and then relapsed. Then there was the matter of disease, strange organisms brought by the strange men, and the diseases killed even more than the sword. The temple burns, the trip to yet another Babylon begins, the flesh and bone become ash and dust. Guzmán started a city, though the location shifted a bit in the early years. And then, he was hauled back to his homeland in shackles and vanished from notice. Close to five hundred years later, his hand is still on the land. The natives he found never recovered in number or in their souls. He was the first breath of the modern in this place.

Beads of moisture form on the cold bottles of beer. The big framed photographs on the wall hold a black-and-white revolution from almost a century ago. The blood brought no restoration, brought little beyond blood. Temples were burned and sacked at times in this revolution. There was a hatred of the faith among some who sought to fix this place.

The politician has fallen into one of his silences. He is home but he does not know his way around.

He rallies by remembering his childhood. His mother never learned the new language, his father used his back to earn a living. One day, the politician came home from school with a tattoo he'd inked on his hand. His mother put his hand on the kitchen counter, grabbed a Brillo pad, and rubbed and rubbed until all trace of his new marking was gone.

"My hand," he recalls with a smile, "was raw and open for days and days."

Thus saith the Lord the King of Israel, and his redeemer the Lord of hosts; I am the first, and I am the last; and beside me there is no God.

ISAIAH 44:6

The key thing is the anger over loss. Guzmán comes and destroys everything. The revolutions come and destroy everything. Hunger comes and it is north to Babylon and almost everything must be left behind and what little can be taken—language, custom, memory—these things are scorned, fall into disuse, and ebb away. New things take their place. Isaiah says the restoration will come, the world will be set aright once again. Babylon is a lesson, not a place.

But what if this thought is not simply the wrong thought or the old, used up thought? What if it is the fatal thought, the one not even to be dreamed, never to be desired? What if the destruction always comes, Babylon always comes, and this is always part of the birth?

You reach back, any of you, just reach back, all of us, and you stumble and we stumble into the tribe, and then the tribe starts talking and you learn of places now gone, of rites now dead, of powers now vanished, of young women with fresh scents now beyond your reach. You reach back and you start to believe in race, holy places, and if you linger, say you stay on the temple grounds or sit at midnight in the gardens with that demijohn of red wine, you swallow that magic word that floods your cells with ecstasy, the rave that hollows out nights for a thousand years or more, that syringe full of energy: destiny.

God has a purpose for me, this I know.

God exists.

God does not exist.

God exists but is unfit for worship because of the pain in my eyes.

God exists but does not require worship because he is my sister.

God is a word used by cowards, a babble of fear like that other word, *restoration*.

God does not exist, but if he did, Isaiah would not understand him.

God does not exist, but if he did, he would not talk to Isaiah.

God does not exist.

God has a purpose for me.

This I know.

Everything is crushed under the heels of the Guzmáns' belief in destiny. Every Guzmán, killing and raping and slaving, believed in destiny. World without end, amen, it is written.

> And they shall build the old wastes, they shall rise up the former desola-
> tions, and they shall repair the waste cities, the desolations of many gen-
> erations.
>
> ISAIAH 61:4

Her teeth gleam between her red lips, and her eyes flirt from face to face. She is our guide and takes us to the government palace. The building is new with old stone, a re-creation of the style of the conquest, when broad stairways and heavy courtyards stamped the new ground with the might of Madrid. Her skin is pale, and her body gyrates within the tight bindings of her clothing. The high heels click as we mount the steps.

In the conference room everyone wears suits and sits along the large wooden table, polished to an icy surface. The politician has been up pressing his pants, getting the wrinkles out of his shirt. He is nervous. He will be speaking the mother tongue, and he fears his barrio language will be found inadequate.

> And strangers shall stand and feed your flocks, and the sons of the alien
> shall be your plowmen and your vinedressers.
>
> ISAIAH 61:5

What I remember of the meeting is not really the woman's glowing skin or scent, or all those suits lining the table with notepads at the ready before them, or even the presidente reeking of power. What I remember is that the politician was the only man of color at the table and how his brown skin melded into the varnished surface of the wood. The business at hand hardly mattered. The skin color mattered. Outside on the sidewalk, beggars leaned against the government palace, women with dirty, long skirts, the hands out begging. And every beggar looked like the politician, that same rich brown, and everyone at the table of power looked like snow.

After the meeting and the exchange of gifts, the obligatory photographs, the good cheer, the pats on the back, we went out into the streets again where all the brown people strolled, and then off for drinks. We never mentioned this matter of color.

He asked me, "Was my Spanish good enough? What do you think?"

I think Guzmán still runs this place, that the killing has never ended and the wounds still bleed.

The presidente had given us each a plaque, silver plates with Mayan figures. Mine means grace and power. I know this because the politician can read the ancient figure language, a symbol-talk as dead as the temples themselves.

Isaiah is useless to me at these moments. He is about punishment, suffering, and then restoration through God's mercy. I am standing in the real restoration, the mixing of blood, the beggars and rulers, the flow of time down hard, stony paths. There is no going back for anyone. Isaiah's prophecies are so much trash. But that is not the issue. It is about now and the day after now. Or it is about ruin forever.

But ye shall be named the Priests of the Lord: men shall call you the Ministers of God: Ye shall eat the riches of the Gentiles, and in their glory shall ye boast yourselves.

ISAIAH 61:6

Isaiah says the lion will eat straw like the ox. No, he won't. The lion will eat the ox so long as a tooth remains in his mouth. Just as the ox will murder grass all the days of his life. And the men will want the women and the softness of their forms. I know this absolutely as I hear the woman's high heels click away on the stone. The leather red, like her lips.

Going through the walls of Salvation and entering the gates of Paradise has led us to Hell. The prophets have done us no good. And it is dishonest to say the prophecies are simply metaphor since we know that these metaphors have been iron and blood and ruin.

We want meat and so we go to a grill featuring the food of Argentina, and that food is large slabs of beef. We drink, God, do we drink. The days have taken their toll what with the procession of offices, functionaries, and that caste system based on color, the man with the broom always dark, the man with the suit always light, that race judgment that we constantly notice but never mention to each other. We dine like wolves and drink like men from the desert.

The meal is all bloody chunks of steak and ribs, condiments of the pampas. There is much gnashing of teeth, the fine sheen of juices coats our faces.

The politician relaxes after a fashion, and he tells a story about the time his grandmother died.

When she died, the politician's father went south, crossed the border, and attended to the burying. He finally found a priest who would speak over his mother's corpse. Some had been reluctant because of her marrying three times without the sacraments of the faith. But even this priest still spoke of her life as a series of moral lapses.

Afterward, he and his brother drove the priest back to town, the politician's father sitting silently by the window as the priest rattled on. When they got to the town, the father took a wad of money, the promised payment for the funeral, and he stuffed it into the priest's mouth and then cast him from the pickup like a plague.

His son tells me this. He also notes his father went to mass each morning.

I say nothing. I am the unbeliever.

I did not lose it at the movies, it was in a green field on a spring day with my mother's dress clinging to her body as she hung clothes on the line. A snake slithered through the grass, I stumbled after it with my two-year-old legs. My mother screamed, grabbed me up, and I have never caught up with that snake disappearing into the green under a spring sky.

So do not talk to me about the restoration. We are restored, the slime of the sea courses in my cells, my eyes stare out from under dinosaur lids, and the lion will not eat straw like the ox, but the lion may eat me. And I may eat the lion. We may have sinned, that is true, but we will not be redeemed. We are the redemption.

All the people who want to go back, to achieve the restoration, they are fighting life and they bring death. We are going forward, and we are following a snake into the tall green grass.

Now, finally, it is written.

Or this way. I have to get to this unease within me, I have to take a knife and stab myself and rip out my entrails and bring this unease out, lay it on cold marble, the flesh still quivering, that sticky, warm feel of flesh as the heat finally begins to leave it. There is a backbeat to all this, and this backbeat is in the stones of the field, the weeds nibbling at the edges of our vineyards, in the fossils being retrieved from their long-lost graves, the backbeat is in everything that ever was and will be. Isaiah sits down at the snares, picks up the sticks, but he cannot play this backbeat. Ever.

The Indians die, the culture goes to dust. The peyote brings dreams but nothing comes back. There is no restoration, it is not part of the arrangement. Inside my body, there, those organs I've ripped out of my guts and plopped on that cool marble, yes, those, now reach out and touch them, don't be afraid, touch them and feel all the lost ones, the tiny creations swirling in the first days of the primordial soup, the smoke coming off the pyramid as the incense burned and the still beating heart in the priest's hand made the sun return and life continue, Orozco looking dour as his brush moves across our minds, the lonely species of pine clinging to a lost stronghold on some crag, the whale sounding in the deep blue sea with all the Jonahs tumbling like dice in his belly, my dead father, the mega fauna gone from land, everything, there on the marble, touch it, there.

So don't talk to me of restoration. You are going to get us all killed. I'm meeting her for drinks, and we are going to do the backbeat until we die.

> For, behold, the Lord will come with fire, and his chariots like a whirl-wind, to render his anger with fury, and his rebuke with flames of fire. For by fire and by his sword will the Lord plead with all flesh: And the slain of the Lord shall be many.
>
> ISAIAH 66:15, 16

Orozco came back to Mexico in the thirties, and the government in Guadalajara gave him the commission to paint a fresco in the government palace. I drag the politician to it, practically propel him across the empty Plaza de Armas, lazy in the midday sun. I want to dispel the pall that has settled over me from our time in the cathedral. The church was too smug for me, all the answers on the lips of the dead saints far too pat. I am not good at certainty and I have no stomach for the promises of all the Isaiahs. I am not a heretic, that would make me of the tribe. I am a different species, deaf to the enchantments of the fall, the punishment, and then, of course, the worst for last, that damnable restoration.

Decades have passed since I last went up this stairwell. The steps are polished stone, the entire building states the new order brought so long ago by Guzmán and his sword and slaving. The palace is the boot heel of the new order smashed into the faces of the natives. The politician has been trained up on the conquest, the rape of the nation, and then the long struggle, all those revolutions, for justice. And of course, the restoration of the original world, the one fabled and kept in a drawer in velvet cloth, the heavenly realm where all was in balance and love hung from the trees like ripe fruit. The politician feels Isaiah in every cell of his body.

Orozco does not.

So we enter the building, turn the corner, and he starts up that stairwell, and after two steps, maybe three or four, stops dead in his tracks. The huge head of Father Hidalgo, the spark that started the revolution before the next revolution, stares down with a face of wrath, his hand on that brand crackling with flames, bodies crumpled at his feet, the bodies gray, lifeless, and rich with rot. And off to Hidalgo's right are the bishops and generals, all gray, and they have created death and ruin, a landscape forsaken by God and littered with carcasses. To his left is a landscape of Nazism, capitalism, and communism, and it also is a landscape where corpses scream, and the ruin of all hopes. The huge fresco says: Everything we have tried has failed, all our ideologies have proven lethal. And the huge fresco says: We must try again and again and again, try forever, not until we get it right, we cannot get it right, we are incapable of getting it right, we are animals, but we are animals with dreams and perfume and fine teeth to tear asunder choice meats, we will never eat straw like the ox, we will never enter the walls of Salvation and wander the city of Paradise. But we will go toward it and we will fail and we will love and we will kill and we will take the color from the sky, the kiss from her dead lips, the breast from the cold mouth of the dead baby, we will. That is it: We will. And whosoever promises us Paradise, that is the traitor. Whosoever offers us Salvation, that is the killer in our midst.

Because in the middle is the man of fire, old Hidalgo, who in 1810 came out of his godforsaken village with thousands of Indians at his back and walked the land with murder, killed the invaders, cast out the evildoers in his lust to restore the kingdom, brought justice to the enemies. And wound up with his head in a cage suspended from the city walls and in his wake a vast death. He is the primordial hero of the nation, and each year on the sixteenth day of September the presidente of the nation gives out Hildalgo's cry, the fabled El Grito, the presidente spits in the face of all the infidels, screams at each and every one of the Babylons, and invokes the cause of freedom. Then the presidente retreats inside his palace and wallows in the rot and corruption of his life and our lives. Such is the custom of the nation.

The fresco offers no answers, paints all the false paths, and yet the walls insist on the man of fire, the burning brand in his hand, the necessity of the quest and damn all the ruin it has so far brought.

The politician falls into one of those pools of silence he so loves, wanders there and leaves me behind, and for twenty minutes he seems to eat the fresco enveloping the stairwell. And then, after that, we never speak of it, because there are things beyond the words. If you go to the words in these matters, you wind up with Isaiah and that list of enemies who must die to pave the way for the restoration.

We go to the ancient market town where the crafts of the Indians are still preserved like holy relics. The politician eagerly haunts these streets. He buys special keys with his initials carved into them, a tablecloth with the symbol of the nation, that eagle devouring a snake; he buys dolls for nieces, little statues for others. His bag sags with small treasures.

We pause now and then and sit in the cantinas and drink. The air is hot, and the trees are so very green. Music fills the air. We are far from Babylon here, the maps insist on this fact, we are in the very loins of the mother, of the perfect homeland that once was and, of course, once must be again.

He has reached that decision, the one he made in the cathedral when he sank into prayer while I watched various communicants struggle toward God in the sterile air that priests always seem to leave in their wakes, that astringent air that denies the aromas coming off all the kitchens, the perfume wafting up from between her legs, banishes all these fine things, and insists on a scrubbed world and a virgin, always that virgin, insists on a place before and after experience, a place where nothing happens and there is simply duration. And this damnable sterile air. I have never been in a sanctuary where I did not want to bust up the pews and light a cook fire, fill the air with smoke and savoring stench of burning grease.

The politician has decided to run for congress back in Babylon. He says simply that it is time. I do not ask questions. I tell him I will help. I know why he will run. Because he feels his people have been slighted, because he feels things have been taken away and he has been made a captive in Babylon. But I also know he is a man of Babylon, not of the villages down here, across the border, in the other country. Nothing will be restored, but maybe some things can be made better. No regrets, no resentments, but the hungers are forever, or as long as it takes us to end it. I fight, that is true, but I also accept. And I have never wondered for a single instant why my ears keen to the click of her high heels on the cool stones.

He savors his tequila.

We do not talk of the man of fire. He is not written, he left no prophecies, he offers no restoration. But the eyes will not release anyone who looks upon them. The temple must burn. Once, twice, yet more times. Burn to the ground, burn forever. We will rebuild, that is true. But then we will simply burn it down again.

It is the only way we can go on.

It is a true matter of faith.

Hey, buddy, they're rebuilding the temple. Got a light?

We've been dry too long and the thirst rasps our throats.

MOUNT VERNON, TEXAS

A horse is a false hope for victory.

PSALM 33:17

SOME called him "Two Foot" George, to others he was "Hawkeye" McVay. He was a geologist by degree and a onetime rodeo champion, a preacher by birthright—"my dad was a Methodist minister, my granddad was a Nazarene"—and by virtue of the call that had brought him from Louisiana to look for a ranch. He bought 450 acres, leased 300 more, but what God really wanted him to find, he came to believe, was a temple: an abandoned livestock auction house on the south side of the interstate, a drafty box with long barns extending from both sides like wings.

"Something intrigued me to it," George recalled. He put down what was left of his life savings, cleared out the bats and the skunks and the possums that had moved in when the cows had moved out, and put a new coat of paint over the wind-worn boards of the exterior. Inside he set up tables and covered them with red-checkered tablecloths, and with his wife, Stacy, he opened a country diner. He invited fiddlers to play and led his customers on trail rides, and soon enough he had himself a regular congregation. So he began bringing in preachers; and on days they didn't show he began preaching. The crowd dwindled, people wanted to eat in peace, folks asked him if between the Baptist and Holiness churches in town he couldn't find a church that suited him.

"Long story short," George told us, "I went out of business. But it was a blessing-in-disguise kinda deal." He put the chairs up on the tables, pushed them into the corner, and retreated to the big room at the center of building, the one with the windows looking out into the livestock stalls. He tore out the metal gate through which cattle once bustled and declared the wooden benches rising to the rafters to be pews. Threw down a plywood platform over the dirt floor and built up a pulpit where the auctioneer had once called. The smell of beasts remained, so he hung rotating fans from the ceiling. Strung up two bare lightbulbs above them. Where you might find a picture of Jesus in another church he put a painting of a caramel-colored Texas longhorn, standing strangely serene against a pale yellow sky, tall grass slanting past its knees. Out front he planted a cross made of whitewashed horseshoes.

"My God," George told us one afternoon as we sat in his parlor. "He's a God in the business of restoring things."

George did with his church just what he'd done with his diner, started bringing in fiddlers and guitar players and honky-tonk holy rollers. Turned Prairie Station Cowboy Church, as he called it, into a stop on the Saturday night–Sunday morning circuit traveled by musicians hoping to make it big in country or Christian recording.

"Cowboy Church" as de facto denomination began in the open air of rodeo arenas, but as a faith with actual foundations it has grown strong in Texas. There's Crooked Pine Cowboy Church in the town of Humble, Cowboy Church on the Move in Abilene, churches all over rural Texas with names like Rugged Cross and County Line and Silverado. There's Living for the Brand in Athens, the All Around Cowboy Church of Sealy, the Cowboy Church of the American West in Midland, the Cowboy Church on Fire in the town of Iraan.

The Cowboy Bible, a folksy translation of the New Testament with western scenes on the front and back covers, opens with a set of ten directives for a cowboy and his horse. Number 10 reads: "Horse—accepts all! . . . Rope, bridle, blanket, saddle, rider." The lesson being that the whole truth of Christianity is that a person must be as obedient to his God as a horse is to its cowboy.

"It's in the heart, see," George said. "Anyone can follow the creed of the cowboy."

But not just anyone could claim the name. George led his congregation of thirty booted-up mailmen and physician's aides on account of the fact that he was the real article. People called him Hawkeye because he was a fine judge of horseflesh and seemed to have a second sight for where an animal wanted to move. Old rodeo riders remembered him as Two Foot for his skill with the bulls. Soon as the chute gate swung open, he'd throw both feet out wide as a split and yank them back to jack his spurs into the bull's shoulders. This earned him extra points from the rodeo judges but made him no friends in the bull world. Once a brennel bull named Number 99 threw George into the dirt and dropped his hoof on him like a one-ton hammer. Nearly split George's liver in two. Another bull hooked his lip and sliced it in half, leaving a scar that gave George a kind of friendly sneer. Then there was One Jump George, so called because no rider ever held on longer than a single buck of his hind hooves.

George versus George: One Jump bucks free from the chute and throws his rump into the air. Two Foot makes good on his name, kicking so that his heels would click if not for a thousand pounds of muscle between. Three seconds into the ride—a rodeo aeon—and the two Georges are still together. Four seconds: George the bull spins and jumps. George the man hangs on with his right hand, his left in the air like he's blowing a kiss. Five seconds: One Jump looks back, surprised to see a cowboy still holding on. He swings his head over his left shoulder, down then up, and catches Two Foot's face with the point of a horn. Bare cow bone drives into George's left eye and back out like a spoon scraping a bowl. Six seconds: George McVay is on the ground.

"If God didn't want me to have that eye," George told us, "I don't want it neither." He petted an orange tabby in his lap and squinted at us from behind gold-rimmed spectacles through his right eye alone; the other was glass and didn't move. His voice was deep and twangy. He wore a black down vest over a salmon-colored western-wear shirt, lean jeans, and cowboy boots caked with mud. He believed you could tell a lot about a man from his hat: His was black and dusty with a red-and-green cord tied around a crown rounding out to shapeless. He took it off whenever he sat down, but he was most comfortable with his hat on.

He wore it when he preached at the church, and it must have helped, because despite his lack of ease in front of a crowd he managed to give a good sermon. "Growing in faith," he preached when we sat with his congregation, huddling in down jackets because the heat wasn't working, "it's like being Michelangelo, carving *David*. You do it by not by accumulating doctrine, but by shearing it away. It's hard work, cuttin' marble. You don't get it done fast."

George had cut most of the frills out of his service—he'd sent the fiddlers packing, he no longer bothered with Nashville-bound gospel singers. Instead he relied, week after week, on a single sobered-up cowboy named Ron, a onetime one-hit wonder of mainstream country with a handsome but thin voice that didn't quite fill the barn when he sang one of his own compositions, "Praise You with a Twang."

"Growin' in the Lord, it's like cuttin' a cow out of a herd," George preached, shifting his weight back and forth up on the stage. "Which is why you need a cowboy to do it. Tough. Patient."

Back at the ranch, though, George was feeling anxious. Six foot four and broad in the shoulders, bearded, handy with any tool you could name, George did not seem like a nervous man. But he admitted that calving season kept him up at night. "Just thinking about those mamas out in the cold." So we climbed into one of his trucks, a white Ford Lariat XL loaded with stiff, heavy chaps, a braided bullwhip, a blanket, and a lasso, and went looking for calves.

"Most beef cattle aren't really built for birthing," he said as he drove. "Take your typical cow and mate her with a fifteen-hundred-pound bull and like as not you'll end up with a calf you'll need to cut up inside of her if you're going to get it out and not kill the mama. But the Texas longhorn is one of the few that has a pelvis that's made for birthing a baby steer. She'll drop her calf in fifteen, twenty minutes, while she's standing in hard rain if she has to, and if it's healthy that baby'll be bounding about in half an hour."

George turned left off the packed dirt of the ranch road, and we rolled through an opening in the post-and-plank fence that kept the herd from wandering toward the interstate. The prairie spread out before us. The windshield filled with dark gray sky.

"There's some question among Christians whether cows go to Heaven," he said. "To me it ain't much of a question. Think about it: What's creation all about? What's a mama got for her baby? Compassion. That's all it is. Say we see a baby with extreme deformities. We gonna have compassion up on that baby, 'cause it's one of our own. Well, this here? What I call my ranch? These cattle? It's all His own, the whole outdoors."

George drove in silence for a few minutes before he continued speaking. "Tell you something. A secret. I'm thinking of giving up my ranch. More church I do, less comfortable it sits with me. Way I look at it, it's animals suffering for man's sin."

Which was why evolution sat no more comfortably with him, despite his training as a scientist. "I don't see what a monkey's ever done wrong to end up a sinful man."

He had another theory. "So we know the Lord created Adam and Eve and all that," he said, "all them plants and animals we have around now. But there's no real way of knowing which *cycle* of creation Adam and Eve were." George glanced over with his good eye, the brow above it arched with something close to scientific curiosity.

"Shoot," he said. "A thousand civilizations coulda come and gone before then and for some reason the Bible just don't mention it. But that don't mean what it does say can't be true."

It was a strangely Hindu approach to Christian fundamentalism; maybe he learned it from the cows. What are they but four-legged samsara machines, walking wheels of life and death, grinding grass into meat generation after generation just as we kill and eat them to do what we do, driving pickup trucks, building churches, reading books? When did it all start, why should it stop? Call it Christianity if you have to, but the faith of the prairie is one of unnumbered beginnings and endings, alphas and omegas coming and going like flash floods and drought, surprising you even when all the signs are there.

"Well, there they are," George said. The pickup slowed at the edge of a moving acre of hide: brown, black, and white, in a dozen mottled combinations; one hundred head of longhorn cattle, huddled together shoulder to shoulder, snout to flank, like steaks packed tight in a walk-in freezer.

Outside the pickup it was bitter cold, no protection in sight from the wind that scrubbed the plains. We cracked the window anyway, and the cab filled with pungent air. There they were, and there *it* was: a whiff of the insides of the animals we eat, so sour it clogged our noses, made us close our eyes and say, Whew! But then we breathed it in deep as we could. Ah, let there be manure. Let there be cows. Let there be the reek of waste and growth and possibility. The prairie drops hints that maybe Eden wasn't a garden at all but a thick-mudded shit field, dark earth softened to a mortar so thick even God must've had four-wheel-drive.

George stopped the truck but kept it running as he leaned over the wheel, squinting at the milky gray sky. High above the herd, black dots circled in clumsy figure eights, spiraling down one and two at a time, growing larger and faster as they neared the ground.

"Buzzards," George said. "They come around calving season, try to kill both mama and calf when they're vulnerable. Try to eatem while the calf is still hanging out its mama's behind."

Not twenty feet away, a stand of cattle parted to reveal what it was that had the birds so excited: a newborn calf, white and pink-nosed, slouched in a puddle of rainwater and blood, black buzzards tearing at his legs, pecking dots of red into his snowy hair. The calf's mama, a brown-and-white-speckled beast, her hair matted and her ribs heaving from the effort of birthing, roared and stabbed at the birds with her horns, but her baby just lay there and took it. What else should he do? Ten minutes old and no reason to believe life was otherwise.

Every minute was learning. The lessons were the cold of wind, the wet of mud, the pinch and snipe of bird beaks. A buzzard dug into him behind the joint of his knee and flew off with a few ounces of hair and blood he'd never have a chance to use. A tongue more blue than pink slipped out of his mouth, and his eyes rolled toward the sky, watching as bits of him were carried away on the wind. *So that's what my legs are for.*

Two Foot George thought something different. The pickup's door swung open and startled the birds, scaring them high into the air. The door slammed shut, and George was out in the mud in his boots. We followed him out of the truck but hung back as he waded into the sea of longhorns. Each one had a span of tusks that could spear and lift him from the sternum like a bale of hay, but George slid through undaunted and untouched, crouching low, talking quietly all the while, feinting toward the calf but keeping his eye locked on its mother's. She didn't so much moo as growl. George backed away, his eye still on hers, and pulled his whip out of the truck. Her eyes darted from her baby to his hand to his eyes, one squinty, one wide and blank, then back to the whip in his hand. He held it coiled, more a symbol than a threat, and approached the calf again, whispering to the mama sweetly even as the other cows surrounded him, until he was gone from our sight but for the black hat bobbing amongst the horns, his words blending with the grunts and bellows of the cold, angry cows, the squawks and cries of the vultures, the whistle of a cold, sharp wind, and the tapping of rain turning to hail: a high plains polyphony. "You know I'm a-gonna help now, mama," George whispered. "We gonna save this baby together now, mama, I gotta get in close now, mama . . ."

George's arm shot out beneath the mama's horns and snatched the hind legs of the calf. The mama wheezed; in her four stomachs, the sound's pitch rose as its last strains squeezed past her teeth. She scraped her hooves in the mud and switched her tail. A few strands of hay clung to the horn she dipped low and up, low and up, testing the motion. George stood his ground, out of courage or resignation—*so that's what my eye is for*—we couldn't say. But the mama backed off. George hoisted the calf onto its front legs, trying to plant the rear ones in the mud as if he was building a house of cards. If the calf couldn't stand, it couldn't nurse; without milk, soon, it would die. But all the calf could manage was to buckle and fall with a splash back into its puddle. Every minute was learning.

The cows crowded around went back to chewing grass with bovine indifference, forgetting in an instant what they had been so excited about. Even the mama looked away. She wandered off to pass the afterbirth, walking slowly with a sack of pale red fluid drooping behind her. "She'll spit that out in just a minute," George said. Soon as it dropped, she turned around to eat it. That's what they do.

George looked on the scene with his one good eye, tugged down the brim of his hat, and deadpanned the shortest sermon ever spoken in the mud of the East Texas prairie. He trusted Scripture as far as it went, but today his text was all around him, the story of a heifer devouring her placenta as buzzards swarmed to do the same to the calf she had nourished for nine months.

"Well," he said. "There's creation for you."

George bundled up the calf in straw and a horse blanket, hoisted him in the air, and carried him back to the pickup. Placing the calf inside, he turned up the heat, directing the vents so they'd blow directly on the calf's shaking limbs. Then he circled around to the driver's side, planning to bring the calf home, where he'd wrap him in a quilt and feed him by hand. Only then did he remember that today he was not alone with the creatures in his care.

Two Foot George looked at us from behind his glasses. One eye dead and gone, the other still looking for life, he kicked the mud from his boots as he asked us, "Y'all mind riding in the back?"

As I looked, a great stormy wind came out of the north;
a great cloud with brightness around it and fire flashing
forth continually, and in the middle of the fire, something
like gleaming amber. In the middle of it was something
like four living creatures . . . and they sparkled like
burnished bronze.

EZEKIEL 1:4–7

Mortal, eat this scroll.

EZEKIEL 3:3

EZEKIEL

BY MELVIN JULES BUKIET

THERE is no God and the Jews are his chosen people. What a great word that is: *chosen*. As in choice, prime, grade A meat electro-prodded into marching up a slanted ramp to a mechanical hammer which hums and burps before slamming down onto the ridge atop bovine eyes, which flutter and close as the creature slumps among splinters of bone and brain fluid, after which the floor's hinged support beam tilts and drops the carcass into the processing room, where steel band saws whine and slice off part after section after part, conveyor belts sending them hither and yon to the fertilizer and dog food divisions and, most profitably, wrapped, packed, and prepriced, $8.99 a pound, bound for the tables of the nation—as a new victim shambles into place.

I'm no vegetarian, mind you. I run a carousel, not exactly a job I expected, but the one delivered to me.

"Hot dog," I shout to the vendor who passes by every day at exactly 4:15.

He knows his regulars and has already whipped his long fork out of the tin cube of briny fluid in which the sausages steep to spear me one and set it to rest in the center of a soggy, scroll-shaped bun preslathered with mustard and a dab of minced red onion, just the way I like it.

On the next revolution, I grab the bun and slip the vendor a twenty for the next month. I'm the only person on Manhattan Island who keeps a hot dog salesman on retainer.

"Mommy!" a kid atop a galloping white stallion calls to a woman in a gray suit by the perimeter, worried that the operator has left the controls. A minute ago, the kid was delirious with glee, hands thrown courageously outward from the reins, but the second I abandoned the cockpit in the island in the center of the carousel, he clutched his steed's leather straps and started to fret. I could see it as I reached for my lunch. His eyes grew serious and he stopped screaming, his silence more troublesome than his noisy ecstasy. Kid's a faker. Worse, he's a young lawyer, already thinking about a possible tort, a claim, a class action suit by the children of America. The hell with him.

The hell with all of them, the howlers, the whiners, in long pants or knickers, public school kids in torn jeans or private school brats in navy blue blazers, boys or girls in belly-revealing T-shirts or plaid skirts and lace collars. I'm fed up and hungry.

I slip back between Winky, one of whose marbled eyes is missing, and Silver. They have dumb names, but what can you expect? This thing is designed for five-year-olds circling round and round as they slide up and down bronze poles that give the illusion of flight as the rest of, or at least my little portion of, God's great universe spins past.

There's the quaintly cobbled plaza in front of the carousel, where lines build up on weekends and a wedge of Central Park greenery may be glimpsed as we turn, clockwise, ever clockwise, for a moment eastward, toward Jerusalem, to give out over the roadway that bisects the park at 65th Street onto the macadam path that leads to the zoo.

At least they call it a zoo. All it consists of is two red-tailed foxes that hide in the underbrush, a slothful polar bear who rolls over and yawns once a season, a family of monkeys who live on an archipelago of rocks in the center of a pond, jerking themselves and each other off to the shock of the tourists, and the insanely popular seals. Pardon me, sea lions, because they have ears, which really are noticeable because they're the only protuberances from their bodies, which resemble nothing so much as vast, nippleless black breasts. Boring.

"Don't worry, kid, I'll get you in for a safe landing." I push the shift that starts the carousel to slowing.

But now he's louder than ever. "We're stopping!" He cries out the obvious as the blur of trees gradually resolves itself into individual trunks, limbs, and branches. He feels gypped because the ride has been shortened due to his own obnoxious behavior. His mother is walking clockwise, keeping pace with one of my favorites, Sigmund, a black pony with a playful pince-nez atop his snout. "If you think we are ever coming back here . . ."

I can't tell whether she's threatening me or her son, who lingers as if he's expecting a rebate, but I answer anyway. "Only game in town, folks. You don't like it, go to the zoo."

"Hmph." The mother sweeps the boy under her arm like a shopping bag and whisks him away.

"No!" he screams plaintively.

What does he have to complain about? What other kids can pay a buck seventy-five for a two-and-a-half-minute ride? Do the math. That adds up to lawyer's wages. Now multiply the hourly fee by the forty creatures of my domain and it's a veritable firm.

A fairly odd firm, mind you. Of course, most of my partners are horses; that's traditional, but at some moment the original Coney Island carousel maker—all of the finest carousels were built in Coney Island at the turn of the century—must have felt bored with the equine form and started to experiment with different animals. I've heard that he made one carousel that consists entirely of birds, and one of bears for an amusement park in California, but mine is the biblical carousel.

All the creatures on it are mentioned somewhere in the Five Books of Moses and attendant lore. Besides a dozen horses, one pair of which is attached to a pharaonic chariot, I have Duke the donkey, Robbie the ram, Charlie the camel, and one stationary cow for the tots too young to bob up and down as they turn round and round. Still, the service animal motif was clearly too dull for the creator. Thus he produced Lenny the lion out of Daniel's den, with his glorious mane, and Sammy the three-seater snake, and Wally from Jonah, the weirdly slim whale—one does need to straddle these beasts.

Yet unsatisfied, the creator then leapt out of the realm of zoology and began to explore the bizarre world of biblical mythology. He made the ziz, a rooster-like bird with red crop and real feathers that have to be replaced every two years; the behemoth, more or less a supersteroided bull; and the shamir. According to legend, this last creature could gnaw through anything. He was used to cut stone blocks for the Holy Temple because war-adaptable metal tools were enjoined. All we otherwise know about the shamir is that it was as small as a grain of barley, so the carousel maker produced a horse-size grain of barley with google eyes and scary, sharp teeth; it's the least popular of my attractions.

Still, moving or still, as fabulous as they are, at heart they're dry wood. Drill a hole from collar to core and all you'll find is sawdust to sawdust, ashes to ashes when it's burnt.

Can these bones live?

Never mind. Carved and sanded out of oak and ash, their haunches and chests, wings and scales, press against the wind. Eyes are rounded, nostrils flared, ears glued on, tails of genuine horsehair stapled. Usually testicles are kept off the creatures, but certain kinky manufacturers appended realistic organs—unlike the entirely fake organ on the carousel. My jolly calliope is actually a false front, beautifully ornamental and utterly functionless. The music emerges from hidden speakers attached to a tape recorder behind the pipes.

These people, they have no shame. I take a chisel to the testes, place it tenderly at the base, where human males are most sensitive, aim my hammer carefully, and lop them off in one swift blow.

Then I tend the wound, touching up—it sounds pornographic—the bare spot, dabbing on paint to match the streaks and shadows of the first artist before the hydraulic lift starts pumping the brass pole up and down and the revolving platform picks up speed.

The kid I kicked off the carousel is still on my mind, and his last howling "No!" seems to echo, but I pay it no heed. There's always a new crop. They're hovering about by the shingled ticket kiosk that's designed to look like a miniature cabin. Some have mommies, some nannies, and some are all by their lonesome, just waiting to fork over seven shiny quarters in return for the strange thrill that I alone offer. Where do they think they're going on their

equine or feline or mythological steeds? And are they disappointed when it
turns out that their ride has taken them nowhere?

A shy little girl in a navy blue jumper cut just above her dimpled knees is
first in line. She comes once a week on Wednesday afternoons and always
chooses the speckled roan in the middle row. She rubs a hand over its neck,
pretending she's calming the creature before jabbing her saddle shoes into its
sides and whispering, "Giddyap."

Others scurry for the best mounts, preferably in the outermost of three con-
centric circles, because only there can they hope to grab the brass ring—good
for a free ride—that dangles tantalizing inches out of reach. A tough-looking
kid with a cowlick leaps atop the lion, and a pair of identical twins help each
other onto Sigmund while the slow kids are paralyzed, at first by choice and
then by its lack, as horse after camel after ziz is claimed. A tall boy whose
stature alone ought to give him an advantage shuffles worriedly left, right, left
again, a pathetic dance step.

"Room for all," I say, because the kiosk will sell only as many tickets as there
are seats, but that's no comfort. These kids don't know that the best tactic is to
head immediately for the far side of the carousel, where there will be a moment to make a decision. All they know is that the laggards get the stationary
horses, whose hooves never leave the floor and who do not have poles that
pierce their bellies to reach the gilded ceiling, or the whale or the snake or,
most humiliating of all, the cow. Look at it, waiting for the slaughter.

"Take your seats."

Sadly, the tall boy slumps onto the cow, his knees practically grazing the
floorboards.

Sometimes parents stand beside their children, pretending that they are
only there to reassure the young ones but actually cadging a free ride for themselves. I know their games, their tricks. I've seen it all before. Kicks are where
you find them.

I've seen two giggly teenagers on a mount (both paid in full), the boy invariably behind the girl, rubbing up against each other as if accidentally, and
once a couple gave me two hundred dollars to open the carousel for a private
ride at midnight. She sat with her back to the horse's head, he leaned forward,
inside her, and her hair splayed out, mixing with the mane. Giddyap.

I've seen a lot, not only cheap sex and cheaper sentiment, but greed and
gluttony and sloth and wrath, every one of the seven deadly sins and several
more. Worst of all, I've seen an utter lack of faith. These people have sated

their stomachs and their groins at the expense of their spirits and their souls. They engage in idol worship that is more despicable than that of the ancient world because their idols are sports heroes and movie stars who have taken the place of priests in a corrupt society, and instead of prayer they waste their precious allotment of days in frivolous search of free time, which they call leisure, some of which is used to ride the merry-go-round.

As for me, I have higher things to think about in my home in the control room behind the calliope facade. It is full of gears and levers, cranks and cams and the tools necessary to repair them when they break. The space is cramped in the summer and freezing in the winter, but I don't care. I sneak off to relieve myself in the woods when necessary and live off the leavings of my patrons: half-eaten chocolate bars and bags of popcorn and sandwiches brought for alfresco summer lunches and, of course, hot dogs. Physical deprivation doesn't bother me. What matters to me more than anything, the reason I stay here, is The Voice.

What voice? Well, I've never heard it, but I know that it's there, somewhere beyond the whistling of the pipes. When my wife died and I abandoned our apartment, I wandered into the wilderness. Month after month, I walked the streets and avenues until one day, standing at the corner of Fifth and 63rd, I detected faint music coming from somewhere inside the park. Obscurely compelled, I followed the music's trail until it led me here, where I found my destiny. The operator at the time was drunk and slovenly, and the concessionaire was berating him for some prior irresponsibility. "This is the last straw!" he screamed over the music. I inched closer, fascinated by the calliope. Keys and pedals moved up and down as if played by an invisible organist, and cabinet doors flapped open and closed, and every once in a while a dramatic gust of steam jetted out of a hidden aperture atop an array of different-size pipes, but for all the moving parts it was obvious that the contraption had nothing whatsoever to do with music. It was the perfect counterpart to the horses and other beasts that pretended to independent motion, simultaneously ludicrous and delightful. It was the most beautiful thing I'd ever seen or heard in my life. I strode straight past the kiosk and mounted the merry-go-round, mesmerized and ticketless.

"Hey, you!" the angry boss shouted.

I put a forefinger to my chest.

"What do you want?" he raged.

I don't know what I was about to say: Music? My wife? The Voice? Instead I said, "A job."

He paused for a moment, looked me over, and said, "You're hired." And that's the way it's been for years now. I strain my ears, but all I hear is whistling.

Can this God speak?

For as long as I've been listening and waiting, I've never heard anything more than the rinky-dink melody of the tape recorder as the horses and other creatures ride and ride and never get anywhere. Surely there is more. I know that it must be there. Yet revelation comes at odd moments. That's its nature.

And then I take a bite of the hot dog just as I'm distracted by a pigtailed little girl in a pink frock riding sidesaddle. That's been a big no-no since five years ago—or was it seven, who knows? time flies like horses—when a kid fell and broke his spine and the insurance settlement nearly put me and the herd out to pasture. I start to shout at the girl, and a chunk of frankfurter wedges in my throat. I gag and wheeze like a teakettle through the reduced valve. Instinctively, I squeeze my fists as hard as I can, and the rest of the offending sausage squirts from between the halves of the bun. And the bun itself opens, unrolls, unfurls like parchment, and mustard lettering appears in the blurry stain of red onions. A message.

I am choking, perhaps fatally. My face is probably red and my eyes abulge, yet they remain focused on the writing on the yeasty scroll as I stagger into the pole next to a child in a maroon vest. The writing on the bun reads, "Eat me."

A command.

At the risk of further clogging my throat, I obey the divine mandate and stuff the bun into my mouth, and a miracle occurs. Instead of killing me, the soft bread pushes the hot dog down and I breathe free.

And The Voice of the pipes finally speaks.

Son of Man, tell them what you know.

How do I know what I know?

You know because I tell you.

So I tell them. I tell them what had been on my mind since I first landed here. All of my complaints burst forth in a torrent of language that I didn't know I had in me.

"Harlotry, usury, venery," I declare. "The Lord gave Himself unto you and you gave yourself unto others. He gave you children and you made them wicked. He gave you a Temple, and you defiled it. He entered into a covenant, and you broke it."

The pigtailed girl stares at me.

I continue. "You pray to false idols and never acknowledge the true God of the carousel that has made you and the eternal go-round. All you need do is open your eyes, but instead you close them and give unto others what is due to your Maker, and you must be punished."

Where is this coming from? And to whom am I addressing my screed? To children. The boy in the maroon vest angles away from me, and the twins twist around from their single seat like a double helix unwinding. Still I speak. I am a fountain.

Thus sayeth the Lord: *I will be a scourge. Your skin will blister, your hair fall out, pustules will form and spread. I will whip you and hound you and drive you forth from the Temple you do not deserve, and you will die in exile, and the sun will bleach your bones.*

Can these bones live?

Sayeth the Lord: *You will suffer. Your children will be torn from you and thrown over precipices. Your old people will be set adrift. Your spouses will be presented unto your enemies for their pleasure. You will be pierced, jabbed, and needled. Your skin will be flayed and displayed in the homes of your enemies. Your stomachs will churn, your intestines unwind, your breasts shall be burned and your penises chopped off with chisels.*

Wait, where does that come from?

Sayeth the Lord: *Your homes will be sacked, your bedsheets torn, knotted, tied around your necks, and you will be hung, wrung out to dry.*

Holy cow!

Sayeth the Lord: *You have made your choices, and they will have their consequences. As you sow, so shall you reap. As you write, so shall you read. As you think, so shall you dream. As you are, so shall you be.*

And the visions, they keep on coming. I foresee ruin on a grand scale—individual, social, national, civilizational, universal. I see death and exile.

But wait again, I want to reply to myself, what does this mean? If exile isn't home, what is?

"Jews!" I scream, which is ridiculous because most of the riders aren't Jewish, though one small boy in a yarmulke winces. Never mind. In a larger sense they are all Jews, because they are all in exile from their personal notions of Zion. Whether that notion is attached to the miserable sliver of land between the Jordan and the Sea makes no difference because every one of us is, whether we know it or not, merely biding time until local weaponry advances from stones to knives to guns to dynamite to the inevitable. The land—Jerusalem or the Upper East Side—is never ours. Nor should it be. Exile is freedom.

And that's when I realize that I'm not voicing a warning, or rather it's not the warning I thought. I'm not warning them for God; I'm warning them of God. Why? Because we haven't violated the covenant; God has, unilaterally. Because mortality is the first sin against creation. Because all sacrifice is human sacrifice. Because He loves cataclysm, calamity, and catastrophe, performed to the ecstatic tune of the calliope.

A little death here, a little death there, we can take, make our peace with, but He went too far. And the stronger, more fervent our faith, the worse our loss. The mistake we've made for as long as He's killed us is that belief does not entail the necessary corollary of worship. If I wander into Fifth Avenue traffic and get run over by a bus, that does not mean that I should hobble to my knees and pray to the bus.

Forget the land of milk and honey, you kikes, or the old sod, you micks, or *La vida splendida*, you spics. You're all doomed because He loves blood. It's His idea of ink. And Jews have always provided the best plots. That's why He chose us to be protagonists of the tale that moves from the Destruction of the First Temple to the Destruction of the Second Temple to the Crusades to the Inquisition through expulsions and pogroms and on and on and on to the twentieth century, and glimpsing beyond today on to the glorious future that will culminate in one gigantically big bang, so that a radioactive Tel Aviv will look the way it did when my forebears looked on the wilderness, so that another race can rise from the cosmic stew to birth again and die again, to go round and round like the horses on a carousel. No wonder we're driven crazy.

Son of Man, The Voice says privately. *Stop thinking and speak.*

But I can't. It's unspeakable. Can these bones live?

That depends on your definition of life. If the deity is the prime mover, then the creations on my carousel must qualify as lesser movers. And if you ask for something more than mere existence, say the two greatest possible attributes—beauty and morality—well, these creatures are beautiful, more so than the immortal, intolerable deity who informs them. And as for morality; well, they do no harm, so they're ahead of the game in their endless circle, striving, striving, and never advancing an inch, just like people.

Giddyap!

The horses' painted wooden coats begin to take on an odd texture that could make me swear individual hairs were growing out of their wooden cores, rippling in the wind. Their curved wooden muscles are gaining depth and nuance. Above the calliope, I hear a neigh.

The Wednesday girl looks scared, the twins are screaming, and the tall boy on the cow is suddenly much taller, his knees leaving the ground, the cow lowing and, unencumbered by a brass pole, lumbering to its feet.

Jesus!

Lenny the lion is snarling, and children are desperately unwrapping themselves from their thin leather belts, installed as protection. Sigmund snaps his head up, and his glasses fly from his nose. The faces of the parents and caregivers are changing, too, as they realize that what they thought were bizarre daydreams arising out of the mesmeric whirl of horses and other beasts and waving hands and smiling faces are quite real. Duke the donkey, otherwise known as Alan the ass, brays and bucks, and knocks his brass pole into another, which topples into another like a bowling pin, and the carousel is spinning faster.

The girl in the Wednesday dress, first onto the carousel, is first off her mount, running for the edge, but a brown mare jostles her toward Wally the whale, gulping air in search of water and plankton, commencing to flop over onto his side.

One horse, rearing, smacks its foot against the calliope and opens a gash, from which blood as red as onion paste spills, and an ivory white shaft gleams through.

Can these bones live?

No, no they can't. I've had enough. My ministry is over. I hit the stop lever, but it snaps in my fingers, and the merry-go-round goes round more wildly.

I dash out of my enclosure onto the spinning platform. I'm like a speck of dust on an old record turntable, kept in place by the gravitational field, trying to release the screaming children, too late to save them, too late. God is here and there is no escape. As they throw themselves off the edge, the centripetal force hurls them out of their intended path, to the paving stones. The tall boy flies headfirst into the ticket kiosk and lies silent.

Can this God be?

The dizzy lion leaps off the platform and stands on an outcropping of rock, roaring, while the runaway chariot clatters over a curb, dragged into the path of a hansom cab filled with tourists, who also start to scream. The air is filled with noise and the snake slithers into the underbrush and the barley-shaped shamir buzzes through the base of the fake pipe organ, and the pipes crash and bang against each other, the first sound they've ever made.

And I can make a sound, too, a single syllable, a word, and the word is the same word spoken earlier by the vulgar, spoiled, stupid child who worried because there wasn't anyone in control of this ride. It's No. No, I've waited forever to receive The Voice that I can finally deny. No to torture. No to death. No to any form of control.

Look at the manes of the horses, fine as spun silk, look at the carved nostrils, flaring so widely you can practically hear the intake of breath. Look at their finely marbled eyes, glittering in the last rays of the sun, taking the light of creation and spitting it back. There's something worth worship, because it was made by a person.

So the people sculpt and prostrate themselves before idols. Fine. So they fornicate. Great. Greed is only another word for desire, which implies hope; wrath is righteous anger. Slander is the same thing as fiction, which I love. Every sin is a virtue, because it is human, and every virtue a sin because it belongs exclusively to the deity who does not exist and has countenanced every evil since Eden.

Listen to me.

No.

Listen and obey!

No! Take your voice back to the mountains. You had your chance and it got us nothing. God of chance, we are Chosen indeed—by ourselves.

At last, the carousel grinds to a halt. The children are gone, the animals gone. I stand alone among the ruins of my very own Temple. I grab the brass ring.

CRESTONE, COLORADO

But you laugh at them, O Lord . . .

PSALM 59:8

BEFORE we left Texas, an older friend gave us some advice for writing about God, which is to say, for telling stories about what people want and fear and what they think will happen when they die. Our friend knew something about it; he'd written books about those kinds of things. "People are gonna want to hear wacky stories," our friend said. "The folks back home are gonna ask you to tell them about the crazy things people out in the provinces believe.

"Here's what you do," he said. "Tell them a story. Any story." We'd already told him a few, and he rattled them back at us. "Tell them about the strippers in the church in Nashville, or about the Buddhists dropping food on each other. Tell them about the Dickheads and the waitress who wants more. Get them waiting for a punch line." We nodded. "Then tell a few more stories. Tell them about the serial killer in Florida. About the girl's mother and the preacher and the choir singing for the electric chair. Then tell them about the calf in the mud with the birds picking it to pieces. And then here's what you say. You say: 'Getta laugh outta that one, asshole.' "

So there was this witch, and three times a week she drove fifty miles and back to play rehearsal in Salida, Colorado. She looked just the way you'd want her to look: She was forty-two with hair as black as a bat, her eyes big and spooky-beautiful and surrounded by makeup like it had been applied with a Sharpie. The show was *Damn Yankees,* and she had the female lead: the devil's handmaiden. Seriously. This witch, Debra Floyd, was starring in a musical about Satan put on by a town so Christian people wrote letters to the local paper demanding the theater change the first word of the title to *Darn.*

And get this: the town Debra lived in? Not Salida, where the play was, but where she actually lived? Crestone, Colorado. This place was a zoo, an interreligious petting zoo. A three-ring multifaith circus. Catholic monks and nuns shacking up together, three kinds of Buddhists on one long dirt road, an ashram tucked away on a dead-end street, and this Japanese art cult sitting at the top of it all, polished rocks and fake streams everywhere, like some kind of Frank Lloyd Wright Shinto ski chalet.

The woman who runs all this—no, not the witch—the rich Danish lady who hold the keys to this menagerie is an oilman's wife who discovered Native American spirituality by reading *The Last of the Mohicans.* Now she gives her land away to seekers. All kinds, she says, she doesn't care what they call themselves, though she hasn't found any Jews that fit in yet. People say her husband, Maurice Strong, has got a bunker under the valley, where he and Henry Kissinger will run the world after global warming melts the ice caps.

Assuming, of course, the aliens don't come first. There's this group called the Arcturians who wanted to build a pyramid in the desert outside town, so the mothership would know where to land. Forty stories high. Hot pink. The zoning board said no. They didn't like the color.

But you'd have to ask the local alien expert about that. He wrote a book on Crestone and its surroundings, *The Mysterious Valley,* about UFOs and cattle mutilations—you know, livestock found in the desert with weird patterns carved in their haunches, poor cows sucked dry by Martians in search of bovine blood. That's what he writes about. Did we mention he used to date Debra? The devil's handmaiden. For a while, they were like the prom king and homecoming queen of Crestone, but they couldn't make it work. Nothing mysterious about it—they couldn't stop fighting.

When we met Debra we'd been trapped in a car together for four months, and had been getting along about as well as you'd expect. Every day a new reason to hate each other. One of us shouted; one of us grumbled and stewed; both of us were tired and wanted to stay put for more than a day or two. In Crestone, we met a nice young couple who ran the local video store and were building a house made of straw outside of town; they gave us a place to stay and probably saved our lives by keeping us from killing each other. Debra lived up the road, in a black-roofed A-frame with a shingle hung out front that declared VILLAGE WITCH. Inside was cluttered with a piano, drums, a guitar, a dog, two cats, two mice, a pink python, a rat with an earring, and a scimitar Debra used in her belly-dancing routine, all of it covered with the pale red dust the wind worked in through the cracks of every house in town.

Back in Somerville, Massachusetts, where she came from, Debra used to manage an occult store called Arsenic & Old Lace. Read every book in it. Took a course in witchcraft at community college. The instructor brought her out to his coven in the country. Back then, Somerville was still a tough working-class town, run by a thug named Whitey Bulger and his Winter Hill Gang. Debra was like a Fresh Air Kid, walking among wildflowers for the first time. Soon the witches had her in a garden, planting herbs, and in a big roomy kitchen, baking bread, and sitting under the trees in the evenings with guitars and banjos and tambourines like it was a special camp for heathen. They taught Debra how to channel her natural power, taught her magic was no different than the prayers she'd said at Catholic mass. They stripped her naked, bathed her, blindfolded her, bound her hands, dipped a magic knife in a magic cup ("Yes," Debra said, "it's *that* Freudian"), and consecrated her to the "dread Lord of Shadows," the "God of Death and Rebirth," the "Bringer of Fear who maketh men flee," the "Giver of wine and vine and ecstasy." Debra worshiped He or She of many names: Pan, Venus, Odin, Isis, Mars, Mary, Lucifer—the devil, right? Not really, said Debra. "I mean, what's in a name? We put gods in costumes because we can't understand."

The day we met her she was wearing patchwork jeans and a purple velvet top of her own creation, covered in roses, scooped low to reveal toned muscles and smooth skin. She sat out in the sun with us, offered us cigarettes. Took her about two minutes to size us up and figure out we'd been fighting. So she read our fortunes, palms and tarot cards, told us everything would be fine, and even gave us a love potion in a little turquoise pouch, told us to hang it from our rearview mirror. She noticed our eyebrows raise as she put the pouch and a small vial of magic oils in our hands. "Oh, it's not just for romance, it's for harmony. Trust me, it will make things better."

She said she had proof of her powers. Once, back when she was still new in town, she went hiking up in the mountains. Nobody told her about spring storms, so she was going along in shorts and a halter top when out of nowhere comes snow. It's May or June, she can't remember. Anyway, she wants to keep going, so she thinks, If only I had a hat. And what do you know? Up ahead, she spots a little blanket snagged on the branch of a tree. She takes it, wraps it around her head, and keeps going. And the snow keeps coming. She reaches the lake, but when she turns around to go down, the trail is gone. The snow is coming hard. Snow *and* lightning, zapping rocks and bushes, and Debra's the tallest thing standing. So she fixes her big black eyes on the cloud, her head wrapped in the blanket, her bare arms and legs shaking, and says the magic word: *"Please can you just go over there for a minute? Please?"* And—according to Debra—presto, the cloud jumped away from the mountain like it was playing hopscotch. Debra was amazed. "These things don't always happen when you try," she said, "but when you're in desperate need sometimes they will." Then she laughed, a cute, benevolent cackle, all witch plus a dollop of teenybopper.

Then there was another time, back when Debra really was a teenager, still kind of Catholic, only a little bit magic. Her father had been a drunken bum, and he'd left her. Her stepfather was a loan shark, and a drunken bum; he beat her. So one night, while the family was out on a miserable vacation on Cape Cod, Debra's mother wakes her up in the dark. They're leaving. They race back to Somerville, pack up their things. As soon as morning rolls around, her mom heads to the bank. While she's gone, Wicked Stepdad shows up. "Our dog had just had puppies," Debra remembered, "and my stepfather came in, really drunk, really enraged, and he tried to come in my room, where the puppies were, I was protecting them, and I screamed at him not to, and there was a pair of scissors, and he laughed at me"—Debra did that cackle again—"and said, 'Well, I have a gun.' "

Then? We don't know. After a while, he left. Debra wouldn't explain. All she'd say was that the puppies survived.

A couple weeks later, he showed up at their new house and stole the whole litter.

Debra had this problem you see sometimes in people who've been abused. It's sort of like stage fright, but it happens all the time. Debra said it made her fall down. "Like, kerplop." It was worst, of course, when she was actually onstage. So she had this trick to help her stay on her feet. She made her own costumes. She threaded her own belly-dancing bells and made a dog suit once to play the lead in *Sylvia,* and when she auditioned in Denver for a reality show, she brought along her five-foot-long pink python, Sheesha. For *Damn Yankees,* she made herself sparkly shoes. Spent hours gluing sequins on a pair of heels, just so.

We caught the show three days into its sold-out run at the Salida High

School auditorium. Debra was a hit, all Fosse flips and belly-dancer hips, eyelashes so long and thick you could see them flutter from the back rows. She played a sexy demon, Lola, summoned by the devil to seduce a mark, a man about to sell his soul for a song. "Straight seduction job," the devil tells Lola. No problem, she says, before launching into her big number: "Whatever Lola wants, Lola *gets*."

Afterward, we were relaxing at the devil's apartment, which was over a flower shop on the quiet main street of town. The devil's name was Greg West, and he was the only pro in the company, a costume designer who'd grown up in Salida, fled, and returned twenty years later for reasons he couldn't himself explain: "I guess at heart I'm just a small-town queen," he said. Greg was a big man, neither fat nor muscular so much as simply of very large proportions. His hair was a bowl of carrots upside down, and he spoke in a rolling baritone rich with the accents of every city he'd ever lived in. He sat in the corner and lit a small blue pipe while the rest of us shared a jug of tequila. We praised the show and laughed over the bloopers and apologized to Debra for failing to make the previous night's performance, for which she'd reserved our tickets. "Couldn't be helped," we said. "We flew off the road."

Debra's eyes, drooping a bit, went wide.

"Yeah," we said. "On the road to Salida." It was a straight shot of blacktop lifted off the desert floor by a low berm, no shoulder, no rail, nothing to get in the way of ninety miles per hour. We hadn't been going that fast; we'd slowed down so we could read the map while we drove, to figure out how far we had left to travel. Then we'd looked up and there it was: not a UFO, not an apparition, just a jackrabbit in the road. We swerved hard, but there was no room for mercy, and before we knew it we were airborne, the hum of the tires weirdly gone. We thought, calm as could be, Well, that's it.

Neither of us could remember the landing, just the cloud of red desert dust that surrounded us for the ten minutes we sat there, wondering if we were dead or alive, Debra's turquoise pouch of twigs and leaves dangling from the mirror. Blessed be: The car was still running. We turned on the radio—thin but perceptible, a pop song we couldn't name. Well, shit. Guess we'll just drive out of this one. We hit the gas and got ready to go, but nothing happened. Spinning in the sand, maybe; a little digging and a shove and we'd be off to the show. So we got out to inspect, and we'd about guessed it right, the car looked fine. Only there were no tires. We'd knocked off three out of four.

Debra was staring at us while we told her all this, so we tried to reassure her that it was no big deal, nobody hurt, kind of funny. She shook her head slowly but didn't say a word, so we kept going. We told her about how we stood out on the side of the road for half an hour, waiting for someone who could go for help. A small fire truck came out of the dark, two volunteers in the cab, completely soused. They put in a call on their walkie-talkies or their CBs or whatever, and then set off in a hurry, weaving away before the cop got there. "Real sonofabitch," they warned us.

An understatement. He was the local state trooper, all crisp creases and barrel chest. First thing he did when he saw the wreck was put his hand on his gun and order us up against the car to be frisked. No small talk for this guy— it was just us and him and wind. "No explanations now, gentlemen, I'll determine what happened here."

"Lucky thing," we told Debra. "He wants to know what we're all about, so we tell him, writers. Wants to know what we write, so we tell him that too— and it's like we've said the magic words. 'Writing a book about religion.' He invites us to hang out with him in his cruiser while we wait for the tow truck and he just starts telling us stories. Says go south, down to Chimayo, and there's people who eat dirt because God blesses it, and he says, truth be told, he's one of them. Go north, he says, Crestone, they have Buddhas in a monastery there. That's what he says. 'Big, fat Chinese Buddhas.' Then he says, 'I'll tell you something strange. Really strange. I was out here other night, right here, for another accident, just about this spot.' "

If we'd been paying attention, we probably would have noticed that Debra had gone pale and that Greg the devil was sort of chortling. But instead we just kept talking.

"He says *right* where we were, car did the same thing. But a total wreck— a grandmother and her granddaughter. Grandmother's dead on one side of the road, and apparently the kid was sitting there by herself on the other before the cop got there. Right where we were."

Finally Debra spoke. "She wasn't alone," she said. "I was there." We both kind of half-smiled, not sure how to take this claim of magical omnipresence. Debra shook her head, a quick little dismissal this time, and then she told us a story.

It was opening night of the show, 1:30 in the morning, Debra's cruising home in her beat-up Toyota, replaying in her head the applause of earlier in the evening, when something interrupts. "I saw it before I knew what it was," she said. "It was a half-moon, bright, and I saw a dark mass. I was almost past when I thought, That's a car wreck. There were people there. There weren't any ambulances." She screeches to a stop and throws the car in reverse and goes back to see if her eyes had been deceiving her. No. A car, upside down, some kind of big American monstrosity. A body beside it. And a little girl, squatting by the wreck, holding herself and rocking. Debra gets out. The body—it's a woman.

"Oh my god," says Debra.

"Nan went through the windshield," says the little girl, her voice so cool and unemotional Debra knows she's in shock.

Nan's head looks, simply, broken. In place of her stomach there's a basin of blood. And yet she's alive, trying to move her head, trying to speak.

"What did you say?" we asked, waiting for the witch's wisdom.

"What did I say?" Debra's eyes went wide again, not with magical wonder but with the amazement one reserves for talking to fools. "I said the stupid things you say when you don't know what else to do."

She strokes Nan's cheek and tells her it'll be okay, and in her heart gives up on her, and goes to the child, rocking, and asks her what has happened. The girl says she has a classmate who was in an accident, but all that happened was that she broke her leg. That's the interesting thing about accidents, says the girl. *Sometimes,* people die; *sometimes,* they do not. You could see it right there. *Nan* had died. *She* had not.

Debra sits down in the sand, gathers the little girl to her, and waits on the side of the road.

"Did you try to use magic?" we asked.

"What? What? Hop on my broom?" She laughed—a harsh, embarrassed sound. "There just wasn't anything I could do. I didn't even have a cell phone."

"Kind of weird," we said, "how we crashed in the same spot the next night and survived."

"You're right. Interesting . . ."

"Total coincidence," we said.

"I don't think so."

Greg the devil flicked his lighter, held the flame by his face, and in his most demonic baritone, said, "Spo-o-o-ky!"

It was pretty funny.

I will read the writing for the king, and tell him what it means . . . MENE: God has numbered the days of your reign and brought it to an end. TEKEL: You have been weighed in the scales and found wanting. PERES: Your kingdom is divided . . .

DANIEL 5:26-28

Then the king gave the order, and they threw Daniel into the lions' den.

DANIEL 6:16

DANIEL

By EILEEN MYLES

IN the second year of the good girlfriend we spent Xmas with her family. It was a horrible Xmas; her stepfather, the doctor, had many children and many grandchildren and they all hated him because his mother had died when he was young so he had the bitterness of a man who grew up without sweetness—so in the face of adversity in the lives of his children he would judge them harshly and cast them out. He was a rich man who kept assembling a family again and again, and the next family would fail him and he would judge them, and so on.

The girlfriend I had at that time was good, very good, and so was her sister.

So these women had never been cast out by the doctor, and their own mother, who had died a long time ago, had been a peacemaker among the wives and the children and the grandchildren, and she had helped the doctor with his heart toward all of them but now this mother was dead.

Still all the children and the grandchildren would return to the old doctor's house for Xmas because this was the house they had known, and now the old doctor had a new wife. And she would probably get all the money when the old doctor died but the habit had been established in the time of the loving wife, the good girlfriend's mother, that everyone would come on the holidays to the home of the old doctor, but now it was not a loving home and the holiday was really not such a great one. The doctor's house was large and outside were many trees, but the house was not cared for. There were small animals dying in the walls, and you could smell their death and the trees crashing around the house and the heart of the old doctor was very bad and everyone watched and waited for his house to crumble and his heart to stop and his things to be distributed among the children and the children's children though each in their heart suspected the new wife would get everything and so everyone sat around the holiday table that groaned with turkey and cranberry sauce and beans and they would think, Those candlesticks are mine and This is my chair and That painting on the wall is mine, but everyone thought these things in silence and the tone of the room was sad. The good girlfriend's mother was buried outside.

My own name is Daniel, I am a poet, I came to the house of the old doctor that Xmas because I was then part of the heart of the good girlfriend so it was important I take this journey with her. She wanted to see the old doctor, and her sister would also come and their mother's mother would journey there and at the house all these women would go to the mother's grave and we did. The mother was buried behind a bush under a tree.

It was illegal of course in Long Island to put human remains in the ground of your own land, but the old doctor had a lot of land and had lived there for a very long time and no one would question anything he would do.

So it was sad, the spot where the good wife was buried, the weirdness and the wrongness of burying a woman's remains on private property, like a dog's. But the doctor's power was very great, and everyone drank deeply of red wine at dinner that Xmas Day, and I, Daniel, do not drink wine or any other spirits. Nor did the good girlfriend drink. But her mother's mother was herself a good woman and yet she did drink a lot of the wine and her son was a man named Nick. He also drank a lot.

And this Nick, who was the good girlfriend's uncle, was strange and had lived in the house since the dead woman had married the doctor many years ago, in the childhoods of the girls, during the reign of Jimmy Carter.

Nick had done something bad in the land that President Carter had come from—the South. As a young man Nick had committed a crime in his land and he came north and joined his sister and the two good daughters and their stepfather. Nick was a chef. So he cooked for them all in the house and he took care of all the animals. There were horses and dogs and hens.

No one knew what his crime had been but he lived in this way, a man in hiding; the legend was that when Nick was young, even before his crime, he had loved a woman but his mother and his sister got in the way of the love, they stopped him from becoming full and complete, this was the story.

So perhaps he was a man who had never grown up, was partial, was spoiled even before he committed the crime which he did in the South, and now he lived in the doctor's house and would sometimes speak for the doctor on the phone when the good girlfriend would call.

Think of how anger spreads in a man when he is not grown whole and he leaves his home and is in exile, it makes of him a thief. Now because Nick spoke for the doctor when the good girlfriend called the house—to the point where she sometimes would not recognize his voice—she would go: Is that you, Nick? You-Nick, that became his name and he was the prince of the servants of the house.

You-Nick was the good girlfriend's friend when she was quite young because she lived in the children's side of the house which was separated by a great door from the loving mother who sadly lived on the other side of the house with the doctor once she became married to him.

You-Nick lived on the girls' side, the children as well as the food and the animals of the house all being in his charge and he would ask the girls about their feelings and act in loving ways toward them, particularly toward the good girlfriend who was the older of the two. And You-Nick began to go into her room in the night. Once he had become drunken he would go to her room on the dark side of the house and many many ticklish things would be done.

This being of course the same house we now spent the holidays in, the tone of the house was bad and I did not drink of their wine. And my girlfriend's family did not accept me as a man. Daniel is not wealthy, they think, and yet he is content to write his poems and travel with the women on holidays. For these reasons the old doctor's family cannot accept Daniel. And yet I could not be cast out because still I was the girlfriend's guest. And I did not drink of the wine.

But the mother's mother drank it and You-Nick always drank of the wine and the doctor drank like a man of wealth and power and so did his new wife. Like people who perhaps do not know each other in their hearts, not minding it, they talked mostly about the things they owned and were making larger and also of what they were reading in the paper.

This new wife had already made one change in the house. She had men come and make a pink bathroom for herself in the doctor's house which was similar to the bathroom in her own house she had lived in before she married the doctor. For this reason she became known as the pink wife.

All this was in the second year of the good girlfriend. The great tree shook outside the window, it would fall on the house, the doctor's heart was bad, and these people that year were reading in the paper about Woody Allen. He had gone to high school with the pink wife. And so she intermingled her own greatness with his. And when Woody Allen took his lover's daughter to lay with him, the doctor and his wife laughed and drank the wine and everyone seemed to think it was okay ("Good for him!"), and they displayed a clipping of Woody Allen and the girl on the refrigerator and the good girlfriend felt deeply sick since the same story had occurred here—I, Daniel, am speaking of the many many ticklish things in the dark of the house—and so I tried to comfort her yet I also sat in the bathroom and trembled and prayed to the God I knew and the great tree was dying outside.

Accordingly all the presents that were exchanged that first Xmas felt like the great many things slipped in with the coffins of the dead. The doctor himself was soon covered in scarves and gloves, and a very fine blue sweater was given him by the good girlfriend and her sister.

I did not see these events truly, for still I sat in the bathroom shaking. Daniel, Daniel, my girlfriend called so that I would come and join them.

I asked the God I knew for the courage to be there and a great peace suffused my insides and I was emboldened to leave the bathroom and go sit down and watch the living corpse of the old doctor smile and laugh and open gifts and I saw the many leaves of secret feeling of the family covering him: the books and the scarves and flattery and tickets to recitals of great music in New York. This last one was given to him by the pink wife, who would just go and hear the cymbals and horns with someone else if the old doctor suddenly keeled over and died. All the gifts were intended to come back to the giver when the old doctor died so I felt fortified in my conviction not to give gifts in this house.

And I sat there on the old dark hairy rugs with the good girlfriend, who did now have a present for me, which she had some men deliver to the house.

I opened the long and enormous box which turned out to hold a telescope. Which was good because a poet does like to look at the stars.

Isn't *that* nice, drawled You-Nick, then walked outside to have a smoke, and the new wife whispered something to the old doctor.

Sam, the doctor called to one of his many grandchildren. Help Daniel get his wonderful telescope up. Sam was one of those geeky guys—he had the telescope up in about a minute. The great telescope now pointed outside. So tell us what you see, Daniel, demanded the new wife. I asked God for some courage and I stepped up to the eyepiece.

I see a great tree, I said, and everyone laughed. It's not doing so well, I said, wiping my lips, for my mouth was dry.

Tell us something we don't already know, pushed the pink wife. Sam, will you take a look? And he leapt to the charge, shoving me aside. The geeky Sam made a great production of focusing and adjusting the metal beast. He turned to the family and shrugged. I see birdshit all over your cars.

The Canadian geese have had their say, pronounced the doctor. Thank you, my dears, that was lovely. Now how about some more wine, and some pie, he called into the kitchen, to anyone. And the house was filled with servants, and everyone was his.

Incredibly, in the third year of the good girlfriend, she wanted to return to Long Island. She wanted to go to Long Island because certainly the old doctor would die this year—she knew it, and her sister knew it, and the wives and the many grandchildren all knew and saw the same thing: The great tree might fall. And her sister had moved to California since the last year and she also wanted to go to the doctor's house. It might be the last year my sister and I can spend Xmas together in the house of the old doctor, my girlfriend said, and if you are truly in my heart you must also come to Long Island with us.

I watched TV the night before Xmas. There was a nature show on the glowing tube. I watched a lion devouring its prey. A beautiful golden lion with reddish hair. In its jaws was some little brown bear, later a screaming hyena. I, Daniel, was sprawled on my red couch transfixed by this spectacle of something living—a breathing, pulsing creature—being devoured. What is it to be in the jaws of a lion, how must it feel to be eaten!

In some ways I knew. All day I had been buying gifts. Though I had insisted for weeks and months I would not go to Long Island again—because last Xmas had made the good girlfriend so miserable—the doctor and the new pink wife were crazy, they ignored the good girlfriend, and You-Nick was creepy and covetous toward her. The good girlfriend understood all this, she agreed. But still she had to go, and her sister was going, and because this was "a relationship," I had to go too.

I got in my car and I drove to the east, slowly crawling among a great many cars on the L.I.E., still thinking about that lion, and I got there on Xmas Eve.

The doctor's oldest and first daughter lived in the North and she had three sons. All of these were men grown and this daughter herself shared her bed now with some alcoholic wretch named Frank, who'd had an affair this year and the oldest daughter left him. And then her mother, the old doctor's first wife, a great ancient woman with wild hair who herself had wealth (and owned a great many dogs which she trained), this woman sent her first and oldest daughter on a boat trip so that the daughter would forget her pain. That daughter was now looking at distant water and warm sun and meanwhile this woman owned a dog. A big blond golden named Lundy. An old dog of about twelve years who was spending that Xmas at the doctor's house since its owner was away.

My girlfriend had arrived at the doctor's house with our own dogs the night before. The three dogs met and intermingled. Yet something was amiss.

On Xmas Eve the youngest pup couldn't sleep. He kept looking out the window at the moonlit night, pacing the room, jumping on the bed, jumping off. He was driving the older one crazy. And Lundy, the oldest and largest animal of the three, the one owned by the doctor's first daughter, was roaming freely around the house. Sometimes sleeping outside our door. I could hear his mammoth breath. We took the dogs on a walk the next morning, which was Xmas Day. All three had blazing red velvet bows around their necks. You-Nick, the animal keeper, had done this. Rosie was pissed. And this was my dog and Rosie was of nine years then. And yet she had seemed at least two score and ten the day she was born. Rosie's eyes were not the same as God's, yet they were always so sad and forlorn because Rosie knew we were all compelled to do the completely wrong thing and she had to watch. So she accordingly scowled around the perimeter of the field in a red velvet bow, and Hoover the puppy then began doing something interesting, which was warning I, Daniel, something bad was about to happen. Hoover was part shepherd part chow and in keeping with this nature he began herding me away from the dog Lundy.

Hoover! laughed the good girlfriend, for as many times as I would try to chat Lundy up, this orange puppy Hoover would cut me off at the pass. I think he's jealous, the good girlfriend teased. Hoover thinks you're *his*, she said, squeezing my arm.

Then the girlfriend and I went for a run. On that same Xmas morning. The paved hills gleamed black in the daylight of the neighborhood in which she grew up. There's where I went with Mariah Carey, sang my girlfriend, and we ran past an old red high school. The warm black hills challenged us, were hard on our legs, and we began to fight:

Daniel why don't you control Rosie more?—because the dog kept running into the yards of the neighbors—and Why are you so unhappy about spending time with my family? and Daniel you think so much about yourself— And I, Daniel, turned to her with my swirling gray poet eyes, and she said: See, you are not even listening to me now—

I said nothing, seeing the white columns of the doctor's house peeking from the bottom of the hill. And in my heart I began to feel dread, about all of it, and I felt I should not have come.

After our run on Xmas Day, I went downstairs to get some clothes out of the car. My girlfriend was upstairs lowering her strong, white body into the tub, a nice steaming bath. I held some shiny pants on hangers, a suit jacket, a soft, expensive shirt, and a small wool hat from Agnès B. with a pom-pom. It was a gift from my girlfriend. And I had given her a CD player to listen to while she ran.

Lundy was strolling around the circular driveway surrounding the house. Trees were dying in every direction. You-Nick stood with his schoolteacher girlfriend tugging shopping bags full of brightly wrapped gifts out of the car. Lundy was decorated in a red velvet bow. I, Daniel, closed the car door with clothes hanging off me. *Click.*

Lundy shouldn't be in the driveway, complained the new wife. She was in a pink quilted coat, policing the grounds as I turned toward the house, one foot already on the concrete front stairs. Lundy doesn't *know* the neighborhood, the pink wife continued.

This crazy big dumb dog from Maine, so casually strolling out into the road across from the high school—Mariah Carey's high school. In front of the whole world, this famous *place*, Lundy, poor Lundy, will get killed. You-Nick was being summoned into action. He would help. You-Nick of the animals. You-Nick of the House.

What *would* You-Nick get when the doctor died? He would absolutely get *some*.

Lundy, I called. For they did not think I was a man. I was certainly *more* of a man than You-Nick. And I could do his job. Lundy, hey Lundy. I grabbed the dog's worn leather collar. In a moment I was on all fours in the snow. I kneeled helplessly, and dark red blood gushed from my wrist as Lundy's huge fangs plunged deeper and deeper into me.

The trees crowded in. Green, green, smothering.

I slurred, "Oh baby," words slurped out of my mouth: nonsense words, *Mene, Mene, Tekel, Upharsin.* My wrist was a foghorn. I radiated: numb, numb, pulsating waves, waves of something tiny riding far from some time-less spot in the distance on the other side of pain. Over it and past. Like all of time was a recording of this pain, a wavy bacon of me. Give me drugs. Oh, wine.

It was fine and reedy, a radiating feeling. *Oh baby.*

Lundy struck again, teeth sunk into the fat underside of my left forearm. I collapsed, threw my whole body on the dog's body, and the new wife did this too. Whip, whip, whip. The trees began springing back. The pink wife saved me. Strangely, she did it, she totally saved me. I got up and staggered away from the animal. My blood in the snow. I was sobbing.

The good girlfriend was upstairs puking in the toilet. Because of her mother's death, she could not tolerate physical distress. Meanwhile my girl-friend's younger sister wiped my face and held my hands and found my gloves and held on to them. The old doctor half blind came stumbling out. The trees crowded in. It's not so bad, my dear, just clean it up.

He looked into my eyes, gleaming.

Oh yeah I know your stepdad, the emergency room doctor told my girlfriend as he was sewing me up on Xmas Day.

The woman in triage had followed me with her eyes as the two good daugh-ters led me into the lobby and up to her window. I held my arms out before me with huge bloody bandages taped to my wrists.

So what's up, Daniel, she said. She was talking really tough. She slid me a chart. I can't write, I told her. I had gauze piled three inches high on each of my wrists. I'm a holiday suicide. I'm a gift, right?

My wrists hurt today. As I write. Each word pulls these veins and ligaments, a caravan of pulsing thought—these words appear before you, like my heart.

Under the white lights of the operating room the doctor explained, We don't want to stitch this too tight because dogs' teeth are very dirty—it's almost impossible to avoid an infection with this deep a bite.

A few hours later I was back at the house. In my running clothes, my arm in a dark blue sling, and the dumb pom-pom sitting on my head. Later we washed it and it shrunk and my girlfriend's sister had a baby and we gave it to him. Maybe it's quietly sitting in his drawer. In California.

The pink wife continued to show concern. Before dinner she invited me to join her in the den. The chairs were thick leather and dark. I loved the chairs and so did my girlfriend. It was a pediatrician's office. He had a good practice. A way with kids. That's how he got the good wife.

The walls of his office were dark and old.

So what do you do? she asked. I told her I write and her eyes looked deeper, waiting for the truth. She was looking all around the room. The pink wife was kind. Do you work? she asked. I teach workshops, sometimes. Oh, she said, seeing me now. You teach. And she breathed again. *I teach.* We just want to know that you're going to be okay, and she patted me on the shoulder and walked out. I liked her. And I think she liked me.

I was sitting on the bed with the good girls after everyone had gone to bed. We were having some tea.

Do you think she was wondering if you were going to sue? my girlfriend's sister asked.

God, do you think that's why she was talking to me?

She looked at me, and she looked at her sister. Yeah, I do.

EAST L.A., CALIFORNIA

My tongue is the pen of a ready writer.

PSALM 45:1

I N the barrio people like to say buildings painted with murals of the Virgin don't get fucked with, and it's not just a play on words. Marked with Our Lady of Guadalupe, brown-skinned and emanating a thousand beams of light from her blue and gold robes, at once an Azteca maiden and the mother of the Christian savior, they're as safe from graffiti and break-ins as the homeboys who etch her on their arms hope to be from gunshot wounds.

We'd heard the section of East L.A. we fell into could be as lethal as a lions' den if you were so bold or so foolish as to go there at night without a god or a gang getting your back. It wasn't long before we made a friend, though, a guy named Pablo, who giggled when we met him for no other reason than that he found it funny to shake hands. He shook ours with a smile that suggested it was a real novelty to him, and took genuine pleasure in the act, moving his arm in the herky-jerky way of a puppet, like he was being tugged by a string.

Pablo had landed in East L.A. when he arrived in California a few years before, an Argentinean immigrant thrown by circumstance into a neighborhood with roots in the less prosperous, more dangerous corners of Latin America: Mexico, El Salvador, Guatemala, Honduras. Light-skinned and soft-spoken, with hair just long enough to tuck behind his ears, he stood out despite all efforts to blend into a landscape illuminated by murals of ghostly Mexican revolutionaries, Aztec warriors plumed like peacocks, dead Latin Kings haloed in gold. Colors were important here: His bandanna was neither red nor blue but turquoise, bold both in its effeminacy and in the question mark it became in the grammar of the gangs. It was the kind of thing that could get a guy into trouble. But Pablo understood colors, he knew what he was doing. He wanted to study art; he'd spent his whole life with a ballpoint or a pencil close at hand. "I draw always," he told us. "I draw in Argentina. I draw here." Drawing held the two places together, connecting different languages, different lives. It made him feel powerful. But it couldn't keep him safe: Since he wasn't in a gang, he'd found he needed another form of protection.

He had it now. Pablo's right arm was covered with open-jawed skulls, their eye sockets glowing like embers. A red-and-black dragon wrapped his left arm, climbing from his elbow toward his shoulder, sliding up under his sleeve like a lover's hand. Pablo smiled at the monsters he had inscribed on his skin, and spoke of them in hesitant English. He didn't want us to get the wrong idea.

"I am no Antichrist," he said. The word tripped over his lips and his cheeks flushed, as if the sound of it made him uncertain it was the one he wanted. "No," he said, then scratched his ear, closed his eyes, and tried again. "I like skulls," he explained, "but I believe in God, too."

He offered his heart as evidence, stretching his T-shirt down with his left hand, rubbing his right over smooth skin a few inches below his collarbone.

"Here I will put Jesus," he said, then shaped his thumbs and index fingers into an oval the size of a pack of cigarettes. "Just a small Jesus though. I need some others and there is not much room."

Other tattoos, other gods, crowded onto an altar of flesh. We'd met Pablo in their temple: a storefront tattoo shop tucked in among the mercados and botanicas of East L.A. White cinder-block walls, harsh fluorescent light, blue neon OPEN in the window, the shop was covered floor to ceiling with samples of various body art styles: thick-lined birds and stars and lightning bolts; daggers and roses delicate as spider silk; big-breasted devil women with doe eyes and pointed tails. Cartoons as illustrations of the strangeness of our inner lives, and black inked words to mark our bodies as parts of a larger whole. "Mafia Mexicana," "Longbeach," "Mi vida está en tus manos," *My life is in your hands.* Most of the artists in this shop seemed to specialize in a gothic script favored by the local gangs, but at least one had a knack for cursive as well. His talent was displayed in a Polaroid close-up of a fat girl's ass. Left cheek: *try,* right cheek: *me,* divided by a satiny green line of thong. An exclamation point rounded out the phrase; whether plea or challenge, it was forceful in its symmetry.

We leaned in close to read the writing on the wall, wondering if somewhere in the middle of all this we might see God: on the waiting canvas of Pablo's chest, in the pen-drawn patterns that decorated the shop, in piles of snapshots stacked like decks of cards by the cash register. Pablo turned them over for us, dealt them out: Praying hands grip teardrops strung like rosary beads. Jesus wears a bloody crown of thorns. Our Lady of Guadalupe holds a flower. She holds an infant. She holds a body pocked with bullet holes.

Pablo flipped through the photographs like he was reading scripture, handling each by its edges. Body after body, tattoo after tattoo, he glanced and moved on, skimming for something new. Then he stopped and stared at one. He lifted it toward the light for a better look: a close-up of a bare and muscular back, flexing like that of a carnival strong man, arms up at right angles, bent at the elbows. Across this canvas was painted a full-color crucifixion scene, Christ's skin a shade darker than that of the man who wore him, his muscles more pumped, his blood leaking from wounds so finely drawn even the picture looked like it needed a Band-Aid.

Pablo studied the photograph for a long minute, bringing it closer to his face to examine the tattoo's details: Jesus' hands impaled on the strong man's shoulders; Jesus' feet tucked at the ankles under the strong man's belt. Pablo smiled and shook his head, not jealous of the artwork, or of the physique, but bemused by the excess displayed in each.

"Belief is good," he said. "But maybe some believe too much."

Behind him the door clanged open and two glowering homeboys walked into the shop. The older of the two wore his loyalty inscribed on his forearm: three gothic letters telling the world to watch itself. The two men looked Pablo over and sneered at his lack of affiliation.

Not far from the tattoo shop there was another temple, the Dolores Mission Catholic Church. At the rear of its sanctuary, the church featured a mural that looked like *Scarface* meets *Animal Farm* in stained glass. In the lower left corner of the scene, two blue, pig-nosed gangsters enter a crowded church. One, wearing a suit, is pointing with a hooflike hand; the other holds a red and yellow tommy gun and shoots a bullet past worshipers painted in dark pastels. The bullet screams across the altar and into the priest with a burst of blood like a flame. His arms flap out sideways as if he's trying to fly. Another man unprotected by faith; another whose prayers only saved the lions the trouble of saying grace before their meal: Archbishop Romero of El Salvador, gunned down by government men in 1980, in a world the mission's parishioners left but could not leave behind.

On its shoulder, in the corner to the right of the altar, the church wore another martyr: a girl named Stephanie Raygoza, killed in front of her house a block or so away. Her neighbor had tagged some buildings in a rival neighborhood, Cuatro Flats, branding their barrio with the mark of his gang, The Mob Crew. He'd walked in and out of enemy lands without notice or a scratch, painting out the locals' graffiti and then tattooing everything with three bold letters—*TMC*—not just the initials of his gang or a talisman of protection but barrio shorthand for "I got balls this big." Try me, cabrón.

They did. Stephanie Raygoza was out riding her scooter when a van pulled up and five Cuatro Flats homeys piled out at the end of her street to do some tagging of their own. Glocks instead of spray cans, bullets instead of ink. One ricocheted and put Stephanie Raygoza's image permanently on the church wall. Now she stands there forever, older and taller than her ten years, staring out with eyes aged by the wisdom only martyrdom and a mural painter can give.

The sermon at Dolores Mission the day we attended was on Thomas, the Doubter, the disciple who in the Gospel of John insists on putting his finger into Christ's bloody wound. "Thomas is also called the Twin," the priest said, "because he is always of two minds. He'd like to believe, but, God, would it hurt to give us a reason now and then?"

A woman in the front row nodded. She was dressed head to toe in deep Lakers purple. Her jogging pants made crunching noises when she shifted on the pew's hard bench. On her back her shirt was marked in gold, BRYANT, 8. Even her hair was purple; chicana black hennaed red with surprising results. She closed her eyes and shook her head at "give us a reason." Later, we would find out why: Her brother was in prison for a gang-related murder, one of her sons was dead.

"Jesus is an immensely physical person," the priest offered. "All through the Gospels we see him touching, feeling, reaching toward people. He spits in his hands and holds you to restore your sight. He caresses the sores of the leprous. By touching he makes us whole. So when Thomas wants to touch his wounds to be sure he is who he claims, Jesus just opens up and says, Touch me, enter me. Know me."

Stephanie looked down; Romero looked down; the Laker woman looked down at her purple shoes. Those who know.

The priest continued, "Better you should believe without evidence, Jesus tells Thomas, but if you need this, go ahead."

Try me.

It was time for communion. The purple woman crunched into the aisle in her nylon pants, bowed to the cross, and joined the priest at the altar. Together they turned to face the congregation, he with a gold bowl filled with wafers, she with the chalice of wine. Instead of the usual words of presentation, "The blood of Christ," when she offered the cup she whispered simply "His blood" to every communicant, and every communicant answered, "Amen." His blood. Amen. His blood. Amen. "His blood," two dozen times, but each time she said it emphatically, each time a little different, as if it was not just a ritual phrase but an entire vocabulary of grief.

His blood.

Amen.

Whose?

Amen.

Why?

Amen.

Would it hurt to give us a reason?

Pablo rolled up the right leg of his jeans to the knee, then reached out and grabbed our arms to keep his balance. On his chest he had made a space for Jesus, but he would leave the shop today with the Virgin on his calf. He had already made a rough start of it: the face of a woman like a candle flame, her body below in robes that dripped like wax; thin black lines waiting to be filled with color. "After she is colored I will put roses, something good all around." He smiled at the thought, tracing a finger over the flowers and vines he seemed already to see.

"I can only afford a little at a time," Pablo said to explain the partial tattoo. He looked again at the two gangbangers, then added softly, "But still she is protection."

After their entrance, the gangsters had presented the tattoo artist with a drawing of the artwork the younger one wanted, black shapes on blue-lined paper. We'd seen the artist shake his head.

"I don't do gang tats, man. They get me in trouble."

"It's just letters, bro."

With a shrug the artist had shown the gangster to his bench. Sometimes acting like you believe but knowing better is the best protection around.

We watched then as the artist's needle buzzed to life, and the gang kid's eyes narrowed at the sting of it. He bit his lip and tilted his head back, looking down over smooth cheeks and a wisp-covered chin to see trenches of color dug into his forearm. Cutting a pattern of holes opened with metal, filled with ink, the needle's hot finger shot in and out of walnut brown skin. Three dark letters, outlined then thickened, a single dot at a time; a thousand tiny entrance wounds that made him wince and scowl and put his free fist to his eyes. Maybe the pain was the point of it: Each black dot was a spell, a prayer, the controlled suffering of the temple, given by the artist, his priest, meant to protect him from the uncontrollable kind, waiting always outside.

Pablo stood there watching, anxious for his turn at the needle. He motioned again to the tattoo patterns on the wall, the snapshots by the cash register. "I would like to learn this kind of art too," Pablo told us. "I like to work with other . . ." He stopped and asked in Spanish to anyone who might help, *"Cómo se dice 'material'?"* And someone answered "Material." He looked embarrassed that it was the same word but carried on. "I like to work with other material. I come here not just for my tattoos but to see how the pictures are done. To learn the machines. How to draw on skin."

The tattoo artist grabbed his customer by the wrist and dabbed his latest artwork with a pad of gauze. "Stay still," he commanded and the kid obeyed. Pablo seemed pleased by the artist's power: his needle, his lines. Whether it was a crown of thorns or three gothic letters, what mattered was the fact that flesh could be remade in the image of anything at all.

We once knew a guy who had a crush on a girl so bad he had her face tattooed on his arm. He was a nice guy, he rode a motorcycle, he liked to bake, but the girl wasn't interested. She moved away and the guy took a job at a Dunkin' Donuts. He got so fat, you couldn't recognize the girl's face on his arm. A few years later he shot himself.

Expressions of immutability, so many instants sustained, and yet if you look at tattoos closely all you can see is how they age: how they fade, how they widen as arms swell, how they crack with scabs and battle scars. The guy we knew tattooed a girl on his arm in the hope his devotion could keep her from leaving or not loving him, keep him from getting fat and killing himself. A tattoo on the surface seems so devil-may-care, but underneath, under the skin, it's the striving for permanence of someone who knows it's impossible. So the gangsters say, Fuck it, I'll be dead by the time it starts to sag.

Pablo turned again to watch the art of it, the writer rather than the written-on. They controlled the streets, but he would control the ink.

"They tell me first practice on pigskin, or an orange, with letters and numbers," Pablo said. "Then I will be ready."

Still wiping away beads of blood and color from the gangster's arm, the artist looked at Pablo, then at us. "Who's next?"

Pick me up and throw me into the sea.

JONAH 1:12

JONAH

By Rick Moody

NOW *the word of the Lord came* unto Jonah Feldman, of the Feldman family of Maspeth, Queens, which regional name in the language of the native population connotes *place of bad waters*, his father being Hyman Feldman, Orthopedist, whose business was at the clinic near the Mount Zion Cemetery. Hyman's father was also Jonah, whose father was Abraham, and so on, Jonahs and Hymans and Abrahams and Zechariahs helixing into the past. Anyway, the word of the Lord came to this Jonah Feldman, but why this guy, what qualities proved him deserving of such a visitation? What made this young adult, Jonah Feldman, different from, say, Stanley Rabinowitz, just up the block, much smarter, made his parents happier, went to a fancy Ivy League school? Almost caused his mother to have an aneurysm she was so happy. Why Jonah? *If you pursue honor it will elude you:* The word of the Lord had not come unto Stanley, bypassed him entirely; nor had the word of the Lord come to Louise Luchese, three blocks down, who wanted to take the vows of a nun in spite of her enthusiastic wantonness; nor to anyone else in Maspeth, nor to anyone else in the entire borough of Queens. No, the word of the Lord came unto Jonah Feldman, only young man in his neighborhood to have printed business cards for himself on his twenty-fourth birthday that said *Kosher Fag* on the back, by which he intended to disseminate through an elegant but unprepossessing font the fact that he both kept kosher and liked boys.

Though lately he seemed like he was less often Kosher and more often liking boys. He ate the occasional cheeseburger, which would have infuriated his grandmother, and he felt in these dining experiences a fine disgust and admiration for himself. And he went to the Hispanic butchers in the neighborhood, and he drove on the Sabbath, et cetera. He was putting more energy into the Fag part of his plan. For example, the delirious and profound word *cock* was his companion, his spur and staff, the word rather than the thing, its Middle English origins, *to mete with Cocke they asked how to do*, its blunt Anglo-Saxon simplicity, *what man are thou, when thy cock is up*, its endurance as slang, its flourishing as an image in his image repertoire, *Ere his small Cock were yet a fortnight old, how with majestick Vigour it should rise.* In boys he saw it, the word, and its syllable rang in his ear, a transgression in want and a transgression in name; it was the name that gave him to wanting, he had come to wanting now, could put it off no longer, and the wanting made the name ring in his ears like the church bells of Maspeth. Jonah Feldman was a Kosher Fag, for his fealty to cock was perfect, his love for cock, his nurturance for cock. A *hot cock has no conscience,* it is said, yet still he worshiped it, though most of the clubs that he frequented with their thundering breakbeats and handsome but narcissistic regulars did not take kindly to a Kosher Fag from Maspeth, Queens, more Maspeth than queen, alas, with his kinky dark hair already receding, his soft middle, his proofreading job at Price Waterhouse. His eyebrows met in the middle, despite nervous and painful tweezing. He would buy any reasonable clothes at Century 21. He knew nothing about style, he liked sports, even baseball, he couldn't stand Liza Minnelli. He would have been happy in sackcloth or polyester, eating locusts and cheeseburgers, as long as he could wear his yarmulke. The boys in the clubs did not get the yarmulke, they did not know that in his neighborhood it was a dignified thing to affix this symbol upon the male pattern baldness of his genetic tribe. The yarmulke was strong and noble, and it could make courageous such a one as Jonah Feldman, to whom the word of the Lord came now. And why not, because he loved by the word, the word was with him and in him.

The particular messenger of the Lord, that night, it should be admitted, was a young blond fellow by the name of Carolina, or this was the name he gave, though it was clearly an assumed name, for the very air of these nightclubs circulated with assumed identities, with calculated anonymities, with the sorrow of cast-off selves, with the shadows of things glimpsed only between songs in the clamp light of the deejay's booth: the bartender in the black light by the cash register, couples appearing and then vanishing into the men's room, faces pressed together in the cadences of a strobe. All assumed identities, all assumed masculinities, in leather pants and mesh T-shirts, while afflicted selves like Jonah hovered just out of range. The particular heartache of Jonah Feldman was to come to this place and to see love whirling about him and to know that he would not likely participate in full, as with the gelding who stands off from the herd.

Nevertheless, one night among the breakbeats at a certain club, West-World, very far west in the city of New York, Jonah Feldman of Maspeth, Queens, managed to find himself dancing with a blond boy from the Bible Belt. It could not be, this cavorting, as many months had transpired since last he had known love. And yet it was. Carolina smoked unfiltered cigarettes, was too thin, was possessed of a large, severe nose and a cruel laugh. Yet behold that one incisor that jutted out in the front part of his lowers, behold that cowlick. Carolina said, *Here, take some of this*, proffered a certain controlled substance. *Frolic with me, Queens boy.* It was all too good to be true, dancing to the hurtling of the music, dancing to the cascading of machines, all too good to be true, because it *was* untrue, in a way, for now no other man was in the room, they had all vanished, there was just the music and the boy called Carolina. When the word of the Lord comes to a room, it is as if none other inhabits it.

The somewhat soft and somewhat slovenly Jonah Feldman pressed his lips against those of the pseudonymous Carolina. Carolina's tongue was now in his mouth. It should have been impossible for the blond to talk. The controlled substance was beginning its navigations in Jonah's bloodstream, the controlled substance whose name started with the letter k, or which had a k in it, though maybe it seemed so just because of Jonah's preoccupation with the word *cock*, which also had a k, as did *kaon*, an unstable meson particle, *kaph*, the eleventh letter of the Hebrew alphabet, *katzenjammer*, *kestrel*, *kiddush*, *kaddish*, *Kislev*, *kitsch*, *klutz*. They were kissing, and at some point the controlled substance was collapsing them, and that's when the room began to seem kaleidoscopic. For if you have wondered at the circumstances which are congenial to the word of the Lord, trust that an unearthly light always comes from within, and trust that a voice calls out where none should be. The voice of God should not have come from Carolina, as it should not come from a West Indian woman who cleans people's apartments in wealthy neighborhoods, as it should not come from a tottering disabled man lurching from an ambulette to the front doors of his special education school, nor from famine victims of pagan countries, nor from the twittering birds.

Carolina, in this epiphany, was saying something to Jonah Feldman, the words were becoming clear now, they were becoming audible, they were in the process of revealing themselves in the field of music playing in the room. Here they come now. Empiricists and doubters, take note, the actual word of the Lord, as spoken in a certain nightclub in New York City, in a year of done darkness,

Arise, arise! Neglected servant, arise!
Jonah Feldman, of Maspeth, Queens, arise!
For I have a favor to ask of you, young Jonah, forsaken Jonah,
I have a favor!
Lend to me your ears! For I am not in the habit of talking to you
in this way!
I'm asking for you to lay aside your cares, neglected servant,
I'm asking for you to draw near to my request..
I'm asking if you might consider performing the following task
as my representative.
I'm asking if you would prepare for a long journey, to a certain village,
A village by the name of Lynchburg,
Where you should search out those with poor reading skills,
those who cannot read.
And there you should instruct them in the matter of reading,
young Jonah.
Because in Lynchburg the standardized test scores are
astonishingly low.
They are not hearing the different ways I spill my name on the page,
They are not hearing the many poems in which I conceal myself,
They are not hearing the many soaring melodies in which
I am so various,
My melodies of ecstasy and profligacy and enthusiasm and woe,
They are not hearing that I am in all words,
That I alike fill the household measuring cup and the mighty ocean,
That I adorn all empty places, and that I dwarf all mountains
and all skyscrapers.
They do not know the many pronunciations of my unspeakable name,
Jonah,

So I ask if you will go to Lynchburg, when you are finished with the
oblivion of this
Particular kiss, there to deal with the splendid wickedness
that I have described.
I pick you for this task for no reason but that I love you!
So remember while you are in Lynchburg, in a whole lot of trouble,
as it is already written,
That I love you. Travel safe!

His hangover the next morning, for it was now the next morning, was an af-
fliction such as Jonah had rarely suffered in his short life. It was as if he were
molting his very skull, his jellied eyes were shish'd on flaming skewers, and he
was sorely afraid. He was in Maspeth, Queens, trying to reconstruct the night
prior, and his mother was banging on the door, wanting to know if he was
going to take the morning repast, his favorite, which she had made especially
for him. It wasn't safe that he shouldn't eat, et cetera. With the scrofulous but
pragmatic logic of the hungover, Jonah realized, for he was indeed sorely
afraid, that he needed not to be living at this address any longer, he needed not
to wake with bite marks on his nipples, pained in certain nether regions the
pleasures of which his mother knew nothing about, as she pounded on the
door, he needed not to have his favorite breakfast prepared for him each and
every morning by a mother who no longer knew him in his entirety. The plan
in which he saved for a down payment on a condominium through the
largesse of Price Waterhouse was no longer a valid plan. He could not talk
about the half of his life of which his parents did not approve, a portion of his
life now growing to be more like two-thirds. Indeed when he got up and put on
his terry-cloth robe and slippers and went into the kitchen to face his parents—his father with newspaper and bagel, his mother with spatula and coffee—they were looking at him with a noxious disappointment. His mother
was going to cry. Why were they looking as if they might cry, when all that he
had done was kiss a beautiful, elegant boy called Carolina and take a drug
with *k* somewhere in its name, after which he'd had a tongue in his mouth, followed by some events he could not remember, including bite marks on his
nipples—wait!—there was also the strange monologue that Carolina had
whispered into his ear.

The words were unforgettable, notwithstanding the fact that Jonah had forgotten much else of the evening. They came back to him now, and the heart of
Jonah Feldman was heavy with dread at this fresh remembrance. These

words, perhaps, were the thing that had made him sorely afraid, that made his somewhat occluded arteries skitter as with an SOS. He tried to eat breakfast as usual, but there was a weakness in him whenever the words returned to his ailing consciousness. Of course, this was evident to his beloved mother, who kept intruding. Are you feeling well? Honey, will you examine him? There's something wrong with him, I can see it. However, his father, the excellent orthopedist, who erred on the side of medical disbelief where his children were concerned, would not examine his son, as even Abraham himself would not give his son a reflex test, nor perform a throat culture, unto the moment when the Lord said that the sacrifice should now be performed. On weak legs, Jonah Feldman, in slippers and robe, walked out of his house in search of the copy of Newsday on the front step, but transmogrified now, pressed into the service of the Lord.

It would be best if it could be reported that Jonah Feldman of Maspeth, Queens, was such a faithful servant of his recent apparition of the divine that he immediately, in his bathrobe, embarked on the purchase of plane tickets from the airport called LaGuardia, from which a commercial airliner would then take him to our nation's capital, where he would board a commuter flight to Lynchburg. There, he would descend into the pit of wickedness called Lynchburg, so as to prophesy variously as to the thousands of words hidden in each and every word, the secret languages of the Lord hidden in plain sight, et cetera. Unfortunately, it must be admitted that Jonah Feldman instead walked up the block, halted before Kaplan's delicatessen, tried to dial Carolina from a scribbled phone number in the pocket of his robe. Number out of service. His intention was to ask Carolina, if indeed this was the name of that blond, to repeat those numinous things Jonah believed he had heard the night before. For if he had not heard them, was it not the case that Jonah had been selected for a great and terrifying burden, namely the burden of hallucination?

Jonah Feldman, in the convexity of worry, made as to flee from Maspeth, Queens. The fleeing came as naturally as breathing or eating, for he was scarcely observant these days, nor was he old enough to bear the word of the Lord, and he was not a professional success, nor did he have the fire in him which might make him a logical spokesman for the poor or spiritually challenged. So he fled. His destination, on this particular morning, was the township of Port Washington, of the island which stretches easterly into the sea, where a certain high-speed boat, the Ledyard, owned and operated by the natives of this land, served as a ferry service purposed upon their sovereign tribal nation, which in turn featured an emporium of games of chance. Good business for all involved, boat, casino, taxes, jobs. Since it was yet early, and likewise the Sabbath, the *Ledyard* would be sparsely occupied, except by the most grizzled of habitual gamblers. They'd be making their way to the casino in an attempt to win back large parcels of gold and real estate they'd lost the week before betting on sports events. Yes, this would perhaps be a place that the Lord would not chance to look for Jonah Feldman, formerly of Maspeth, Queens, now a slightly disheveled man wearing terry-cloth bathrobe and slippers, clutching a hundred dollars currency that he had not used the night before to secure the services of a male harlot. So he paid the fare and went down into the boat, in order that he might journey to southeastern Connecticut, far from the presence of the Lord.

Amazing how quickly that tempest was upon them. The high-speed boat, the *Ledyard*, designed to be faster than the clotted federal highway grid in transit to the heavily taxed casino, was equipped with all useful conjuring devices, with a global positioning system, with loran, with radar, with depth finders, forward thrusters, et cetera. It even featured the Weather Channel, on a monitor in the cabin. Yet the spokesmodels broadcasting from the Weather Channel could not explain how this new weather event, soon to collide with a northeasterly storm streaking down the eastern seaboard from Newfoundland, had so quickly cohered into an unpredictable category-four hurricane, name of Katherine, just as the mariners of the craft were steering off of Port Jefferson. The tempest, when it neared the coast, unleashed waves so high that they disappeared into clouds, gales that betimes lifted the boat from the very sea, rain and hail, all manner of precipitation. The tempest was ancient, timeless, and the mariners despaired, for their high-speed boat was disabled and adrift and they no longer could divine their position. They each shouted to individual gods, which gods had as many names are there are words to describe them, they shouted to their money managers and insurers, their polarity therapists, their yoga instructors, their talk radio hosts, their acupuncturists, their chiropractors, their psychopharmacologists.

And then they began throwing things over the side. They threw overboard the magazine rack from the cabin of the ship, they threw out all the sweetmeats and foodstuffs from the snack bar, they tossed out television monitors, they threw out their expensive overnight bags, they threw out the benches, they threw overboard at least one small dog. For the ship was going down and, if so, would go in a denuded state, that even one life might be thus saved till the last. The dread of the Lord was heavy upon the mariners of the *Ledyard*, likewise the passengers.

Jonah Feldman, who knew finally that there was no locale to which he might flee, nonetheless attempted to secret himself in the *Ledyard*'s men's room, the comfort station, even if doing so were unlikely to impede the all-seeing omnipotence of the Lord. He drank flat Cherry Coke and muttered that his parents would never forgive him, his neighborhood would never forgive him, his employers would never forgive him, never mind he had done nothing, had never asked, by way of supplication or through any other means, to become a servant of the Lord. In consideration of these requests, he fell fast asleep, because he'd kept late hours the night prior. It was here, asleep on a commode, that he was discovered by the captain of the aforementioned craft. Wake up, buster! One of those taciturn mariners with hands like catchers' mitts, with a ruddy, striated face, with a knitted cap, with a scar running perpendicular to his jawline and down to his breast. Might as well have had a wooden leg. The captain wore a complete uniform of foul weather gear. Wake up! And get your ass above! We're going to draw lots to see who gets the life jackets! The ship again listed violently to one side. In a timid voice, Jonah inquired if there were not lifeboats enough for those onboard. But the captain chastised him with popular and offensive terms of derision for the unmanly, and then he additionally remarked, *Just get your fat ass up top, if you want to live.*

Above, in the cabin, where the windows had all been shattered, where passengers bled and moaned and gnashed their teeth and huddled in a small maintenance closet, the captain laid out his vision for orderly abandonment of the craft: *I have a number of these matchsticks that I use for toothpicks, and I have busted one of these very matchsticks down to a nub, and we are going to draw lots from these—one person, one matchstick. I propose that we outfit with these remaining orange life jackets all those who manage to avoid the accursed nub.* Of the twelve miserable gamblers in the maintenance closet, all agreed to the plan, naturally, as it had a betting aspect. They cast lots, and the nub, as if the captain had fixed the game, fell to Jonah Feldman. Gamblers are readers first and foremost, they are readers of the skies, readers of the faces of dealers, readers of auguries, of birds, of dates, of numbers, of names; gamblers are diviners, no flock passes overhead that is not portentous to them. These gamblers had their schemes, therefore, they had their racing forms, they had their ideas about the order of things, they knew prophets and prophecy, and when Jonah Feldman was revealed, through instantaneous possession of the nub, as a man of particularly dark luck, the gamblers fell upon him in a fierce inquiry into his significance. An older man with cracked spectacles and excessive amounts of cologne offered a brief kind word before demanding, *Just clue us in here, what's with the instantaneous hurricane, and what's your job, and where do you come from, and where are you going, and what is your ethnic and racial self-description and why have you brought us to this dark place?*

Jonah Feldman cried out to them all, *I'm a Jew and I'm a homosexual person, I am both, and I won't dissemble here, even if you should throw me over the side. And I fear the Lord, I mean the actual God in actual Heaven, author of both sea and the dry land, also author of the results of all games of chance and presidential elections, likewise author of the stars and equations of physics, including Planck's constant.* The gamblers saw immediately, at least according to their Manichaean philosophies, that having a Kosher Fag onboard their boat was a very bad omen, even if in public settings they professed a certain acceptance of both categories attested to by Feldman's ethnic, political, and religious self-designation. They didn't want to throw Jonah to his doom, because they figured it too would be impossibly bad luck, and because it seemed morally dubious, but neither did they want him on the boat. So Jonah said to them, *Take me up and throw me into the sea, since it's for my sake that this tempest is upon you.* By which he meant that there's always a tempest, and always a culpable party, and he was willing to be done with the brief interval of his promising life and proofreading job at Price Waterhouse, he was willing now to be courageous and dead, for tempests are full of revelation. He had done what he ought not, he had avoided his duty, and so he must perish. Just then there was a violent rolling of the craft and a wave of such magnitude that it was as if a sheet were drawn over them, and gamblers and crew and captain alike knew that their destruction was imminent. They picked up Jonah Feldman, humbled and resigned, and they shoved him through a shattered portal, into the fathomless deep, into the dark draperies of the underworld, and he was gone.

Whereupon the sea ceased from raging.

Immediately, the high-speed ferry, the *Ledyard*, in its grim, senseless course, came to a halt, too. Ahead were the splendid cliffs of Block Island. Gulls fluttered above the breakers, sentries at the entrance to this more pacific kingdom. Twenty miles or more the mariners must have come by chance, buffeted by the tempest, soon to wash up on the rocks here had not the storm vanished. The sun peeked from behind a riot of clouds. The gamblers were prepared to cash out. There would be no five-card stud today. No blackjack. No craps.

In the meantime, the Lord had prepared a great fish to swallow up Jonah. It is possible, of course, that the Lord might have beached him on Plum Island, nearby, where the federal government was torturing monkeys and baboons with *Bacillus anthracis*, where they refined and aerosolized dengue fever and hantavirus and Ebola and plague. This would have been appropriate recompense, but it did not come to pass. The Lord did not beach him there, did not let him wonder about grace and mercy while scraping off ulcerated nodules in the twilight of some hemorrhagic swoon. Likewise, the Lord might have imprisoned him in a nearby East Hampton restaurant, working without benefits alongside a number of foreign nationals, washing dishes and bunking with these foreign nationals in a trailer park. There he would have had time to rethink his resistance to the Lord, his disinclination to undertake the work that had been given to him to perform. Or the Lord might have allowed him to be gored by a deer buck, or set upon by the ticks feasting themselves on this deer buck, or the Lord might have condemned him to live in Bridgeport or New London for many seasons. Instead, the Lord prepared a great fish.

Into the water Jonah Feldman tumbled, into that tempestuous water according to which there was no up and down, nor east and west, just expanses of darkness, which compassed about him even to his soul, and he felt the last bit of air in him bubbling forth, he saw the jumble of images from his life, his *tuckus* smacked in the Long Island Jewish hospital; his bar mitzvah, and the speech he gave there on the subject of the New York Yankees and their relation to certain passages from the Talmud (such as: *It is forbidden to live in a town that does not have a green garden*); the first older man who, behind a druggist's in Maspeth, Queens, begged to be allowed to part the mysterious folds of Jonah's trousers; likewise the girl his parents nervously found to be his associate, perhaps one day to be his bride; then her contemptuous whispers to him at a temple dance; an incredibly good jar of spicy pickles opened like it was a prize on a summer night in the mountains; weeping one night after taunts from school yard friends; awake later, wandering the second floor of his house in Maspeth, Queens, encountering his grandmother, her hair uncoiled about her shoulders, whispering of the war; male prostitutes solicited on the avenue down by the subway, some of them gentle and loving; a hundred dates refused; remonstrances from his bosses at Price Waterhouse; and then, again, dancing with Carolina, until the voice came to him, the recollection of it, *Arise! Arise!*

The fish was leviathan; in particular, it was the blessed blue whale, hunted to the edge of its elimination from this world, and it bore down upon him. Preliminarily, the Lord had actually contacted the blue whale, asking for indulgence in this matter, *Friend Whale, can I bother you to swallow this particular human being for a brief interval? I know you are an eater of plants and a peaceful being, and I know you fear for your life, as there are anglers in pursuit of you, but this human being needs some three days to reflect and atone, and I would prefer him to spend time where the surroundings provide for both revelation and the great delicacy known as fish cheese, which in the northern countries is considered a delicacy.*

The whale replied, *Happy to serve, as I must,* its melancholy eyes downcast. Taking a mighty breath into its awesome lungs, the fish dove deep toward the arc of Jonah's fall and swallowed him up, sweeping in alongside Jonah a healthy portion of plankton and some automobile tires. Its teeth were not so much knives as brushes, Jonah recognized, or so he felt coming out of the reverie of his afterlife, that purple corridor populated by dead acquaintances described on television programs. The throat of the fish was not so much gullet as waterfall, in which whole swamps of vegetal life swirled and mixed in a stew of nutrition. Before he even had a chance, he was swept over these falls and pummeled by the squeezing and dousing of fish peristalsis. It was an hour or so in that esophageal coil, and it reminded him of the time he had the MRI, though without sedative. But the entertainment had not even begun, for after the hour of acid-drenched peristaltic massage, he fell end over end into an unlit room about the size of a domestic recreational vehicle, spongy floors, about one-third full of liquid as well as marine life and plants and man-made plastics. Among the finds: a shortwave radio, still functioning; a cardboard box, containing red rubber gymnasium balls; a beach cooler, housing a six-pack of a bland domestic beer; and one human skeleton. Before long, he resigned himself to the temperature of the mixture, to yet another shower of surprises that would rain down upon his head from above, including the occasional muffler, or other injurious missile, as well as live eel or skate or harvest of seaweed.

And there was the smell! The rankness of the fish cheese, of death, of eternal decay, where every fishy thing began its decomposition, where living things were scorched and liquidated into a sequence of vitamins and protein chains. It was an awful smell. Jonah Feldman had been in a nightclub in the West Village only the night before, where every man looked like an angel, where the lighting was low and the promises perfect, and now he was in the belly of a whale that ate auto parts and shat them into the North Atlantic when the spirit moved. It would be only so long before he was himself excretory. A miracle that he lived thus far, to be sure, that he lived inside the stomach of the whale, but what good is a story of prophecy if it doesn't have a miracle in it? Prophecy is a kind of language, and language is a kind of imagination, and imagination is a kind of desire, and desire knows no containment, wants what it cannot have, and in wanting it sees. So Jonah Feldman, having three days in the belly of a fish in which to think, reflected.

On the first day, after being bitten by something, some predator that he had to squeeze to death with his bare hands, Jonah reflected, and in the night he likewise reflected, though strictly speaking there were no days or nights there. At first, these reflections had the cast of his own life, and he saw the silhouettes of the Catskills, he saw his parents playing cards, he recalled the night on which he was assaulted on 21st Street, he saw various academic contests, from elementary school, from Hebrew school. Then the cast of these reflections took on, instead, the rosy tones of desire, the physiques of certain boys and then certain men, the curve just above the hip of a man when he is no longer wearing any clothes, likewise the lips of men, and the tendons in the necks of men busy about their exertion, calves of men, abdominal musculature, and these particular reflections were good and many hours passed according to them. But then, without companion with whom to commiserate, he thought of the Lord, conceived of that thing inconceivable; he worked around the edges of the Lord, felt the impossible heft, or at least pointed in the direction of the Lord, by enumerating such things as the no-hitter, the paintings of Mark Rothko, the film performances of Judy Davis, all of which seemed to suggest the Lord, and amid his reflections he composed a prayer for the forsaken, memorizing it until he could call out the words in his foul-smelling imprisonment:

Thou celestial agency,
Who smiles on boys beaten senseless in the gymnasiums of America,
Cleave near;
Cleave near to the contused, both those who in their disgrace
tell tell tell

And those who mutter nothing and enfold memories deep
in the filing cabinets
Of dark juvenilia, thou celestial agency,
Perform not thy vanishing act again;
Shower infinite compassion on those who know polysyllabs
But rarely utter them;
Love all lovers in exile;
Love the impossibly obese, love the leprous, love the homely, love the
Embittered, love transsexuals, love eunuchs and pedophiles,
Love all abdicators and deniers;
Love all those with unusual gaits and bad speech defects,
Love Jews and Armenians,
Palestinians and Tibetans, love Chechens and Albanians;
Let the names of hatred be made into names of
Delight,
Thou celestial agency,
Until all degradation is past;
Bear up accretions of words and names of disgust,
And build a new ocean to contain them;
Thou celestial agency;
Thy ideas are sometimes bunk,
But thou hast bisected day and night and thus fabricated the dusk and
the dawn, the perfect
Poise between things;
Love thou the disenfranchised who crowd around thy absent shadow,
unable to
Finish their business;
For thou hast made masculine power and made
the football coaches and
Posturing, steroid-addicted simians who are drunk with it,
Bear up those who lie awake at night, pacing the floor in convulsions of
Exile, who weep such torrents that dry fields everywhere are
irrigated with the
Floods of their misery—which tears are more numerous?
Give the batterers a stern talking-to, thou celestial agency,
For they have bilked every shareholder;
For they have staffed and directed every army,
For they have directed every dictatorship,

For they have purged every dissenter,
For they have applied the electrodes to every political prisoner,
For they have committed every genocide.
How the hour grows short, celestial agency, there will soon be
only the batterers
And their veiled wives,
Show us thy justice and we will lay down our vanities.

When Jonah had finished his prayer, there was a sigh in the world, and the Lord caucused with the blue whale and gave him instructions, and the fish then vomited up Jonah Feldman on the coast of Virginia, next to an expensive and ill-decorated hotel. The whale, now beached, was immediately photographed for the nightly news. However, the man at the site in the fouled terry-cloth robe went unseen into the bush, with no camera nor reporter to demand of him that he tell the story of the miracle of three days in the entrails of a North Atlantic whale.

What is the greatness of a great person? That person is not ashamed to say, *I don't know.* This was the predicament of Jonah Feldman, of Maspeth, Queens, who now smelled like the secret life of a bulimic! Whose slippers were torn! Whose beard was three days grown out! Whose thinning hair was matted against his scalp! Jonah Feldman, prophet of the Lord, now resembled most a deinstitutionalized schizophrenic, and the citizens of the commonwealth where he had washed up knew not what to think of this, a St. Jerome in the wilderness, a holy man whose martyrdom is to make known the word of the Lord. And they therefore feared this new ghostly presence in the countryside. Nevertheless, the fashion stylings of the itinerant psychotic were favored by the Lord, and if man were indeed made in the image of the Lord, might one not conjecture that the raver in the countryside was most what the Lord Himself looked like, or else why such a prevalence among men?

In the course of his march, Jonah meanwhile chanced upon the most beautiful place he had ever seen, for there were not many beautiful places in the borough of Queens, not like this wilderness at the seaside, with its wild horses. It seemed scarcely possible that he could have come from the belly of a fish, only to walk but two or three miles away from an ill-decorated hotel to find himself in pristine wilderness, where horses gamboled and galloped and did not take the bit. He saw the pack of them, their manes stirred in the breezes, their haunches as sleek and perfect as anything made by the Lord, rearing up onto their hind legs, so that the adolescent stallions could engage in tests of skill and disport with the females. They trampled an open meadow, and then the males and their mares disappeared into a coniferous wood, thundering across accumulations of soft pine needles. What better emblem of the imperial reign of the Lord, the movement of noble beasts upon their free ramble? Jonah Feldman was sure he was dreaming by reason of his ordeal. For in a moment, Jonah again heard the word of the Lord, almost as if the voice came from a talking horse, although he was pretty sure that talking horses were confined to television situation comedies: *Arise! And go to Lynchburg, Jonah Feldman, for I believe that we had an agreement that you did not honor. Go and preach to the failed readers and interpreters. Do as I have bid thee.*

Jonah, the prophet of the Lord, had not had a decent meal in days, excepting sea scallops that he had eaten in the Japanese style while inside the fish, and he was hoping to have some Chinese takeout, or perhaps a curry, anything but seafood. Yet now he understood that ignoring the voice in the wilderness was no longer an option, that is, unless he wished to see earthquake, flood, volcanic eruption, bioterror incident, et cetera. Through a variety of means of transport, including rowboat, freight train, eighteen-wheel truck, and of course the lowly pedestrian means, Jonah, in three days' time, traveled directly from the islands of the mighty ocean, across the bay, past crabbing operations, shrimp boats, deep-sea rigs, past the naval mariners in their crafts, inland, across the James River, past hunters and moonshiners, farmers of tobacco, farmers of dairy, truck farmers, agriculturalists of all varieties, through counties with names like Dinwiddie and Amelia and Appomattox, until he was in the interior of the state, in the shadow of the Blue Ridge peaks. Then along a county road strewn with franchises, he came to the city of Lynchburg. Here he recognized a fiendish cloudbank above him. He felt rain begin to fall. Around Jonah Feldman there were the portents of the imminent destruction of Lynchburg. He could see. For he was a prophet. He made his way directly to a certain chain store that specialized in office supplies, and there he begged for a felt-tip marker and such items as might be fashioned into signage, and then he walked into the town. He commandeered a milk crate at the rear entrance to a supermarket. Farther he walked.

At length, he came to the television broadcasting facility of a televangelist. When he reached this place, he knew that his life's journey had culminated according to the will of the Lord. There was a great evil there, and much neglect of the millennia of prophecy that had been organized into the books of the Lord, for example the words of lovers, *Come, my beloved, let us go forth into the field; let us lodge in the villages. Let us get up early to the vineyards; let us see if the vine flourish, whether the tender grape appear and the pomegranates bud forth: there I will give thee my loves.* These words had been forgotten, in this spot and many others besides. And Jonah Feldman took up his signage, and he affixed language to it with the felt-tip marker known in these lands as a Sharpie, as follows:

Free remedial reading lessons! Apply herewith!
(In forty days, Lynchburg will be consumed by fire.)

Then, in a tattered robe, through which his capacious belly was sometimes protuberant, and wearing slippers fashioned from cast-off newspapers, smelling like vomit and human soil, unshaven and raving, Jonah Feldman, of Maspeth, Queens, preached the glory of reading in front of the security gate of the television station. This went on for many days. At times, the workers of the television station fed Jonah Feldman with fast-food snacks that they purchased on their lunch breaks. He thanked them effusively. He said, *I know I look pretty bad, and I'm sorry to be a pest, but I am doing the work of the Lord. I will try not to frighten your children.*

Perhaps the arrangement would have persisted, were it not for the sudden arrival of the overlord of this empire, the king of blinders, autocrat of poor reading skills and antievolutionist, scheduled to perform that day on his television station for cameras national and global. He was due in makeup, to have his comb-over combed over, to have his Pan-Cake applied, to have lipstick faintly smudged across his lips, though he had decried all harlotry and excesses in the matter of appearance. Jonah wondered as follows: What did it mean to this man to be a lover? Did it mean to care for the indigent with the love that the Lord cared for them? Did it mean to awake with worry? Did it mean to attempt perfect compassion? And could this guy read at all?

In his cavalcade of limousines, the king of blinders paused for a moment in front of the security gate of the television station, and in that moment, he glimpsed the repulsive freeloader in front of his place of business, who no doubt, according to this king of blinders, was a product of miscegenation or bastardy. The king indicated, then, with the faintest of gestures, that an aide in the limousine was to incline an ear to him, and thus the king spake: *Have that guy removed.*

The beating, when administered to Jonah Feldman, was prolonged and merciless. A soft answer turns away anger, it is said. Not in this story. He was carried away by men who set records in their high school football leagues for sacked quarterbacks. They took him to an alley behind a dry cleaner's, long past nightfall, and they knew no sympathy. First these men impugned Jonah's dignity, telling him that he no longer smelled like a man but now instead smelled like an animal, and then they told him that he was no man, since he would not fight like a man, and many bruises were administered, and there was cracking and crunching report that issued from Jonah in the region of his nose, and then perhaps also from his jaw, and the men said he was lucky that they didn't fuck him, just to show who was boss, but they preferred to fuck things that smelled a lot better. Lids of trash cans in the alley were used as righteous instruments by these men, until Jonah's head was abundantly swollen and his eyes shuttered. He had much internal bleeding, and now he was naked and alone. It occurred to Jonah, in his suffering, that it was all madness, that he was a mad person, that the drug that had a k in its name had kicked his ass, he had been beset by Klansmen, or their confederates, and that, though he was a keepsake, the Lord had been replaced, in this instance, by the knavery of this world, where all was knock-down and drag-out, where all was knuckle sandwiches, where all was kidney punches. All his imprecations, his requests for mercy came to naught. His madness was clear, it was in the obsession with words to the exclusion of things, his obsession was with sounds that rang in his head, as though the sounds themselves were the Lord. This was not enough. He was bereft. Without the Lord to intervene, without a compassionate soul to tend to his wounds. He was abject in the sight of the world.

And by what reason? For what cause? Might have been the pain; might have been the ordeal; might have been three days in a fish's belly; might have been the drugs; might have been the loneliness of many years; might have been the abuse of older men who loved him and abandoned him; might have been the vilification of generations, the vilification that was like a second heartbeat in his breast; might have been the night; might have been the South; might have been an illness of the soul that had taken root in his father and forefathers, the illness of insight, might have been dumb luck or chance, or operations of the universe that were no more than mathematics, might have been the quotidian happenstance of the world. How else to explain why for some prophets it just got worse? How else to explain the decline and fall of Jonah Feldman, Kosher Fag? His days had all been trials. He had inexplicable vexations. Why did the Lord one day ameliorate his sufferings and then, on the next day, visit sufferings anew, as junior high school was followed by the even more fiendish tortures of high school.

Was it simply that a lover of nightclub habitués might fall, in torment, into the testamentary language so beloved of the Lord? Was it so that, as a prophet from the outlands, he might expatiate upon the paradoxes of the Lord for all future generations?

If so, then we are in luck. For in this abjection—days before Jonah's father and mother came to the city of Lynchburg to bear away their firstborn to the hospital in Queens known as L.I.J., days before he was given drugs so that he might forget—Jonah Feldman composed a second prayer, mumbling it so that it was like an imperceptible breeze in the city of Lynchburg:

> Thou art a gracious celestial agency,
> Merciful and slow to anger, and of great kindness,
> But why spare
> A town full of bigots? Why spare those who
> Hate their wives and belittle them?
> Why spare callousness and violence?
> Why spare agents of oppression,
> Especially such agents of oppression as specifically invoke thy language
> And thy tradition as
> A bulwark for the meting out of unjust punishment?
> Why lobby for enlightenment one day
> And tolerate ignorance the next,
> As though thy attentions were enfeebled?
> As though thy methods were imprecise?
> The fuel of all murders and wars, ignorance, is seemingly
> blessed in thy sight,
> For it exists in abundance.
> What ever happened to nonviolence, celestial agency?
> Was that just a political formulation?
> Where I should have served to enlarge the notion of compassion,
> I have instead been broken upon it,
> I have seen things driven apart;
> My bones are shattered,
> I am all disfigurement, all suffering, all chastisement, all neglect,
> all exile,

I am the end of a simple faith, therefore,
Take, I beseech thee,
My life from me,
For it is better to die than to live.

Now *the voice of the Lord came* one last time to the delirious prophet Jonah Feldman. The voice of the Lord, voice of compassion, voice of tenderness, voice of infinite care and nurturance, whose capacity it is always to have the last word, and thereby to insist on the perfect repetition of all His narratives, saying, *Why shouldn't I spare Lynchburg, which city houses more than sixscore thousand persons and many more presently being born? And if not for them, for the wild horses on the beach? And if not for the wild horses, for the swaying reeds they trample down? And if not for the reeds, for the crickets which linger there, and if not for the crickets, for the aphids which they disturb?*

UNINCORPORATED TERRITORY, OKLAHOMA

Lift up a song to him who rides upon the clouds . . .

PSALM 68:4

WE left California and returned to the interior, not so much going anywhere in particular as roaming around the American underbelly, the flat, hot, still spaces south of the wheat-filled plains. In the town of Wichita Falls in West Texas, we drifted to a stop at a hotel called the Tradewinds, once prosperous, now located beneath an interstate overpass. Its guests were mostly families who'd temporarily moved out of their cars and into neatly kept rooms surrounding a pool that hadn't held water in a decade. They paid their bills in spurts of five and ten dollars and occasional chores, and the Tradewinds seemed content to have them. We stayed there for a week, splurging on separate rooms, dozing in the courtyard of busted-up blacktop and cottonwood trees, at night walking over to the deserted main street of town for barbecue and beer at a joint that advertised itself with a neon nuclear bomb; West Texas is where they make such things.

One night we walked out of the bar and found the street strangely aglow, a pale orange light coming from around the corner to the west. We followed the light until we came upon its source, a brick building a block long and a block wide, bright yellow flickering in its windows, a black plume curling up from its roof like the whole thing was a chimney. We were the only witnesses, and we saw the building like that, a container made to fit perfectly its contents; then it blossomed, the walls nearly disappearing in flames that ballooned, cinched to a tight belt, and exploded into a mushroom twice the height of anything in the city. Heat tumbled toward us, so hot and sudden we could see it coming, watch the air ripple and distort with temperature and then feel ourselves become flotsam and jetsam in its ocean. People speak of the roar of a fire, but this one didn't sound like much of anything. We could see it, smell it, even almost taste it, but we heard nothing. It was like watching a silent movie. Then sirens broke the calm and firemen pushed us back and hoses burst into stream. They had no effect at all. A fireman told us the building had been under construction, an old warehouse in conversion, it was filled with buckets of paint and varnish and other oily substances that burn slick and hot and quickly; it wasn't long before first one then another wall of bricks seemed to lose its courage and crumble into flaming rubble. We watched for half an hour, then returned to the Tradewinds while the fire was still burning.

Later that night a West Texas thunderstorm rolled in over Wichita Falls, and rain beat down the flames, turned the smoldering bricks into crumbs and red mud, and washed the spent chemicals intended for rebuilding into the gutter. Opinion in town was divided over the timing of the storm. One school of thought held that it was fortunate, the saving grace of fate and perhaps the touch of God; another noted that it had, in fact, compounded the damage, made what was merely ruined entirely unrecoverable; and a third point of view, popular with the guests of the Tradewinds, believed that it didn't matter, since after all, the course of the weather can be accounted for, but its *meaning,* that's inscrutable.

As to the building, we couldn't say; that was a question for insurance investigators. The storm, though—impersonal, arbitrary, and unconnected to the flames—that made us wonder. We packed up our bags the next day and left Wichita Falls with a new mission: to find someone who could read the subtext of the sky.

Dr. Jason Persoff leaned over the steering wheel toward the windshield of his rented minivan, looking for directions in the dirty white clouds. "The weather is a lot like language," he said. "We think and we talk in words. But we don't see those words. We don't see the letters." He spotted a slightly darker patch on the horizon, faint as a fingerprint on glass. "Yet we're able to process language. We talk about things that are completely abstract, and we recognize them instantly."

Jason belonged to a tiny sect the doctrine of which revolved, literally, around tornadoes. There are thousands who share their passion, high holiday weather watchers, but true storm chasers are a rolling denomination only about three hundred strong, the high priests of nature worship. Of the two dozen whom we contacted via their Internet chat rooms, Jason alone agreed to share his secrets.

A video camera and a case of Diet Pepsi rode shotgun in Jason's minivan, so we were crowded into the back as we cruised down the spine of Tornado Alley, the north-to-south corridor known for the most destructive weather in the country. Every year around the same time, late spring, the plains stretching from central Texas to Nebraska and Iowa become the whipping strap of the Bible Belt, where acts of God come in the form of Dorothy-and-Toto-style twisters, challenging the Midwest's black-and-white order with the full-color chaos of two-hundred-mile-per-hour winds, the kind that can pluck a small house from its foundation intact and redistribute it across the land: torn shingles in a neighbor's mailbox, canned food rolling like marbles on the road, forks and spoons and shattered windowpanes stabbed into a garden on the other side of town.

Jason clicked on his weather radio, tilting closer to the speaker to hear the National Weather Service's computerized announcer. A quick, robotic, male voice, it sounded piqued, struggling to form a full sentence as if gasping for air: *Warm temperatures. Will begin to cool. This afternoon and. Converge. Along. The dry line. Will cause. Thunderstorms to form. Large hail and damaging. Winds. Storms will move northeast. Into. Central Kansas.*

Directly ahead of us clouds had begun to gather; Jason popped open a can of Diet Pepsi and poured it into a purple travel mug big enough to hold a brick. "Looking at storms, there are certain features that come up again and again," he said after a long draft from his cup. "They tell you an incredible amount about the storms themselves. And that's one of the things I really like: I like seeing the patterns, finding the flow. Like language." He nodded at the word. "Language flows," he said. "And it flows in a very distinct way." He sipped his soda. "I like seeing how words flow. And I like seeing how storms flow." He sipped again. "And how medicine flows. Finding the patterns."

• • •

We met up with Jason in a restaurant called Meridy's, somewhere on the Colorado side of Kansas. Bible tracts by the cash register; American eagles on the place mats; a good BLT for two dollars and change. Jason didn't want any of what the diner usually offered. All morning the clouds had been shifting outside the plate-glass windows. He wanted to look at them from above.

"Excuse me, ma'am?" He leaned in close on the cash-register counter so he wouldn't have to raise his voice for the big woman standing there to hear him. This was a mom-and-pop establishment; we took her to be Mrs. Meridy. She kept her eyes on her blue-and-white order pad, totaling our bill.

"Would it possible to borrow a phone line for just a moment?" Jason asked. A purple computer the size of a steno pad appeared from his fanny pack. He set it between the Bible pamphlets and a bowl of pastel after-dinner mints. "A toll-free number, I swear."

Mrs. Meridy glanced up without moving her chin. Every spring the locals endured a small siege of former science club types like Jason, tearing down their back roads in search of the thrill of seeing a tornado. The thrill: Stormchasers called it a "stormgasm." Last time Jason had had one was in West Texas, a year earlier. "It was an extravaganza," he'd told us. "Four tornadoes touching down at once, kicking up beautiful walls of red dirt." He hadn't been able even to think about how to film it. He'd just kept staring, mesmerized.

Mrs. Meridy looked back to her pad and shook her head as if to say, "Must be easy to get turned on by tornadoes when it's not your restaurant standing in their way." There were only a half dozen other paying customers in the place. "Well, all right," she said. "It's the only line we got, though."

Jason formed his hands into a prayerful steeple and put them to his goateed chin. "Thank you, ma'am, thank you. It won't take a minute." He unfolded his computer and began tapping its screen with a stubby plastic stylus. A few seconds later, he had what he wanted. "Okay, I've got the satellite."

Though standing just a few feet from us in jeans, sneakers, and a green-and-black windbreaker, when he stared at the screen Jason seemed to be in two places at once: down on the ground but also flying over it. His eyes grew wide behind his glasses, focused like lasers on the newly downloaded satellite map. Colored splotches and symbols spread out on the screen, jigsaw puzzle pieces waiting to be assembled. If you knew how to read it, the map told the story of everything around and above us.

"See here," Jason said, waving his stylus over the upper left corner. "These cold fronts will bring the moist air up to the higher atmosphere. As it pushes up, the air gets colder, eventually it condenses." He leaned in closer, almost pressing his glasses to the screen. "Looks like thunderstorms in a prefrontal trough in western Oklahoma. This area is very ripe. When a big storm system forms, cold, dense air forces surface moisture up into the atmosphere." He tapped the corner of the screen like the X on a treasure map. "My bet is that's where things are really going to fall." He pointed to what seemed to us an empty expanse on the Kansas-Oklahoma border. "That's where we're going. Could be pretty exciting."

We leaned in toward the map to see what his big grin was about but saw nothing.

"Don't worry, you will soon," Jason said. "When you first show med students an X ray, they all say the same thing: I don't see anything. I see the heart, and I see the lungs and the ribs, but I don't see anything else. And then you'll point out a feature to them and they'll say, My god, how did I miss that? I mean, it was right there in front of me and I didn't see it at all."

Jason's patients, for the most part, were people with cancer. His practice, for the most part, consisted of watching them die. "Doctors tend to think we control destiny," he said. "We don't." But as much as he wanted to remember that simple fact, he couldn't stop trying. He was a "hospitalist," which meant that he kept tabs on every field. "Medicine evolves," he said, and it was his job to keep track of its adaptations, to communicate one specialist's innovations to another. "I am flamboyantly smart," he said, knowing he sounded arrogant, smiling because he was arrogant enough not to care. "I am built to memorize things with no apparent pattern, and to discover the pattern."

He was small man, trim and compact. After chasing storms for fifteen hours and sleeping for four, he'd be up at seven, his jeans crisp and his plaid shirt tucked in and unwrinkled. He smiled and frowned like anyone else, but his dark brown eyes were always earnest and intent. As a religion, the Judaism of his youth dissatisfied him; neither chaotic like a storm nor black-and-white like an X ray. Its 613 commandments seemed to him like so many quick fixes. "Religion" struck him as a means for imposing patterns, not revealing them.

Jason had a black belt in tae kwon do, and he'd begun studying a fighting system devised by the Israeli military called *krav maga,* Hebrew for "explosive force." In college, he'd been a stand-up comedian. His routines worked, he said, because he knew how long to let the crowd laugh. As a doctor, he had an eerie sense of prognostication. He seemed to be able to just look at a patient and read the number of days. Valuable information; his colleagues called him Dr. Death, and meant it as a compliment. Everything Jason had ever done had taught him the same paradoxical lesson: Timing is everything; you can't control anything.

When he was in medical school, Jason would keep an eye on the TV weather and hop into his car to go speeding out onto the plains east of Denver whenever he heard about a tornado, which was like trying to catch a thief in the act after reading about the robbery in the paper. So he studied: weather maps and meteorology books, the coolness of raindrops, the different sounds made by wind, the underbellies of clouds. One night, he convinced his fiancée, Irma, to drive out into the aftermath of a storm with him. He suspected it was growing instead of dying, turning into a supercell, which is a weather system so vast—"a tower of water as tall as Everest"—that it seems to defy physics, to break any rule people could imagine. Jason guided his car into its heart, "core-punching." Out onto I-70, which had been turned into a black ribbon by the rain, driving from the time he saw the late news—on which he'd watched footage of the tornadoes he'd missed and the crowds that had gathered around their touchdowns—on into midnight and past. And that's when he saw it. Or rather, heard it. Humming, in the dark; roaring, beneath the drum of rain. Lightning flashed. "And there it was, lit up by four strikes, in front and behind," Jason recalled. "My own private tornado."

A bell alarm squawked in the minivan, a quick series of beeps followed by a long, high tone, rising from the dashboard. "Thunderstorm warning," Jason said, and turned up the weather radio: *The National. Weather Service in Hastings. Has issued a. Severe thunderstorm. Warning. Until seven-thirty P.M.*

We pulled over at an intersection and got out of the car to have a better look at the conditions. Ahead of us clouds had built to a tower, spreading out at the top like an anvil. On one side of the road, wheat lay down as if dead. On the other, a field of tall green grass rippled like a brushfire in wind so strong we had to shout. An oil well bobbed in the distance. The earlier, homogenous white sky was now a menacing palette of hues: To the south it was yellow; to the north, dark gray; it was brown on the horizon; and a nearby hill was silver-green. From the west, a still-bright sun hanging low in the sky made the dark cloud tower glow. We were nearing the "magic hour": 6:00 P.M., when, after absorbing eleven hours of sunlight, the ground gives off the most heat of the day. The heat ascends into the cooler, "virgin air" above, spinning as it rises, creating fuel for storms. If we were going to see anything that day, it would be soon. But would we know it if we saw it?

"Okay, Stormchasing 101." Back in the van, Jason picked up a pen and a notebook and started into a routine that was somewhere between a meteorology lecture and a high-speed game of Pictionary. He drew lines, circles, crosshatches, and arrows, pointing in every direction at once, at each other, off the page. He scribbled vocabulary and definitions in the margins: dew point, convection, dry line, convergence. Sketches and letters becoming indistinguishable, indecipherable, as they piled on the page. The most commanding picture looked like an elephant with wings about to blow the earth away. Another could have been Moby Dick with a harpoon pricking his hide. The whale-cloud on the page looked as mad as the cloud-tower above us, both ready to swallow us down.

"A lot of words people use about storms imply maliciousness," Jason said, defensively. "But that's not how storms are. They're no more malicious than a jaguar chasing an antelope. Really, they're no different from us. They're made of the same stuff. The molecules that make us started by being born within the stars. We're nothing more than recycled entrails of dead stars. A water molecule that's making up one of my brain cells could have been a water molecule in a stream during the Jurassic period, and before that it traveled through space to end up mysteriously right here in front of our boring little sun. That's cool shit. The fact that it all came together and formed what we call life, that's even cooler shit.

"Storms are very much like what I think God would be: plodding along. Existing on all the various parameters that exist around it. How could a storm be malicious? Good and bad are human-assigned values. They don't exist. In that way, storms are very much like religion. They're not here for good or bad. They just exist. No altar is going to make the storm less or more powerful. No amount of prayer is going to make the storm more real. No amount of energy on my behalf is going to make a storm form one place over another. And whether or not I'm paying attention to the weather, it's going to take place despite of me. That's one of the things that makes weather magnificent. You can try and predict it all you want. If you have all the math down and it still doesn't end up the way you thought it was going to end up, that's neat. That's what people dig. People dig a good mystery.

"A lot of my patients, those whom I help guide to death, they ask me about my spirituality. If they ask me to pray with them, I'll pray in any religion they have. But I think the world is as the storms are. It is. There's not even an agenda. There's just a tremendous amount of force."

Some doctors, he knew, thought of his prayers as placebos; other, more devout colleagues wished that he wouldn't sully the devotion of true believers with his atheistic imitations. As far as Jason was concerned, both types of physicians would benefit from more time studying the clouds. "What my patients are asking me to do is give them spiritual strength," he said. "I don't see that as dishonest. I can't predict what's meaningful for them. A patient's spiritual life is one area where I don't sense patterns." He paused. The minivan shook in the wind. "Storms give me the same solace. Sometimes I just get lost."

We weren't sure if that was good or bad, if the storm was the cure or the symptom, but Jason put the notebook down and shifted the van into gear. "We're done with the lesson," he said, pulling back onto the road, heading on a straight line for the storm clouds we'd been chasing all day. "Now you'll see things."

And if thine eye offend thee, pluck it out . . .

GOSPEL OF MATTHEW 18:9

GOSPEL

By Randall Kenan

SHE kept peeking through the blinds to see if they were still there, as if the situation could have changed in a mere five minutes. Every time she would see the vans with their gigantic white mushroom antennas sprouting up toward Heaven. CNN. NBC. MSNBC. FOX. BBC. CBS. BET. Piney View Lane had been clogged and coagulated with people and cars. The Orange Grove police had erected barricades and had taped off her yard with that yellow police tape Velmajean remembered from television police shows. But seeing the brethren—some full-time security, some volunteers from the church—made Velmajean breathe more easily. The sight of them reminded her that the Reverend was in charge. And he was going to make sure everything would be all right. Any minute now he would be arriving for the press conference at which they would announce Velmajean's next miracle.

On one of her compulsive peeking trips she was happy to see the Reverend's sleek black SUV pull up, a miracle in and of itself the way the crowd parted before it like the Red Sea for the children of Israel. It was one of those bright autumn days in North Carolina when the leaves swirl about like roan pixies. At first the sea of reporters engulfed the arriving dignitary, but thanks to the brethren a path was made, the tape was lifted, and an entourage from the church made its way to the house. Before he could knock, Velmajean opened the door.

"Oh, Reverend, I can't tell you how glad I am to see you."

The Reverend Jamie "Spike" Horowitz took off his shades, paused in his patented way, and opened his arms to the sixty-two-year-old widow. He flashed his cover-boy smile, which always made Velmajean more than a little giddy and wrong-feeling inside. It was the sort of smile that could cause her to write bad checks. "Sister Velma, how's our little miracle worker?"

As they embraced, and the Reverend whispered calming, dulcet-tone words into her ear, in filed five men: two lawyers and three equally suit-clad bodyguards. The Reverend himself was in his usual jeans and signature form-fitting sweater. He was easily the largest man in the room; his muscles visibly undulated underneath each time he moved. "Sister, the Lord's got big—big— things in store for you. Hallelujah!" He slapped his hands together with a loud slap, as if he were about to close some great deal. "Hallelujah!" That was one of the Reverend's favorite words. He used it the way gang members used the F word. He looked into her eyes, expectant perhaps for confirmation or outburst or questions or doubt. But Velmajean simply smiled. She wanted to get this ordeal over with. *General Hospital* was coming on in ninety minutes.

The Reverend Spike ordered everyone to get down on their knees. The men encircled Velmajean Swearington Hoyt, placing their hands on her shoulders and back; the minister laid his hand on her forehead.

He said: "Father God. Please bless this endeavor into which we—your children—are about to embark . . ."

"Praise God," said one of the bodyguards.

". . . and please guide my tongue . . ."

"Guide him, Lord."

". . . for the further glorification of your Kingdom. We ask a special prayer for your chosen vessel, our sweet sister Velma here, Lord. Hallelujah. That her heart remain pure . . ."

"Pure."

". . . and that you continue to use her as your sign upon this earth."

"Amen."

With that the men helped Velmajean to her feet.

"Do I look all right, Reverend? I mean, will this look okay on TV?" She wore a sky blue dress of conservative cut from the collection of one of her favorite designers that she'd bought at Hecht's department store a year ago. One of the women from the church had come by and touched up her silver coiffure.

Again the Reverend Spike looked at her as if she were the kumquat of his eye, the center of his universe. "You look positively radiant, sister."

With that, led by the Reverend, followed immediately by Velmajean, and then the five men, the group marched down the path from the split-level brick-and-beige house, built in 1976 and paid for in full by the death of Velmajean's husband, Parker Hoyt, in 1996, down to the horde and the lights in the middle of that Thursday afternoon, to the microphones feeding up to satellites informing televisions and radios and computers around the globe; where the Reverend Spike Horowitz, the former Internet millionaire turned Christian entrepreneur, announced that on the coming Sunday at a special service to be held at the newly completed Atomic Church of God and Worship Center ("congregation 20,000"), Mrs. Velmajean Swearington Hoyt, of Orange Grove Township, would be doing the Lord's work "by performing her thirteenth recorded miracle live on an international broadcast sure to reach two billion people, to convince them of the Almighty's presence in the world and in their lives."

Just as the Reverend had instructed, Velmajean stood and smiled for no more than two and a half minutes for the flickering barrage of lights, never uttering a word, whereupon two of the bodyguards escorted her back into her well-guarded four-bedroom home while the Reverend and his lawyers fielded questions for another twenty-seven minutes.

Velmajean considered watching the show on TV but reckoned it would be on—in an edited version—in heavy rotation well into the night.

As she took off her dress, looking forward to relaxing, to trying to put all this hoopla out of her thinking, she realized with a start that she had recognized a face in the crowd. That strange, beautiful man she had seen that day in the parking lot, the day she brought the little girl back from "the other side."

That day had been a Thursday too, and she had gotten to the supermarket early. She was feeling particularly proud of herself, for with the judicious and meticulous use of coupons she had purchased $201.29 worth of food for $79.82 ($25.25 would be in rebates).

As she labored to put the groceries into her six-year-old Oldsmobile—once upon a time bag boys offered to help, but those days were long gone—a young man walked up. "Please," he said. "Allow me."

"Thank you, young fellow." She was pleased and flattered. He was black—an African, blue-black—and basketball-player tall. He was smartly dressed in a black suit, over which he wore a long black coat that almost touched the ground—odd on a pretty spring day. And he wore shades. His head was clean as an eight ball and just as dark. For some reason he reminded her of the Secret Service agents who surround the president, and for that reason, or so she told herself, she felt safe around him.

When he was done he closed the trunk. The grocery cart was gone.

"Where—"

"You are blessed among women, Velmajean Swearington."

At first, so perplexed by the disappearance of the cart, she had not registered what he had said. She looked at her African chieftain in his expensive suit. "Yes, young man, I know. Have we met?"

"No," he said. "I mean you are truly blessed."

With that he reached out and took her hand. The feeling was warm at first, then noticeably hot, her hand tingled, her face flushed. She could not move, only stare at the stranger. To this day she could not swear on exactly what it was she felt, only that it felt better than sex, sweeter than love, stronger than the will to live. Or maybe it was just the spring air and his warm hand and smiling face.

Just as quickly the man let go and stepped back. He spoke only a few words after that, before he walked off into the highway to melt into the traffic as if he were some human sports car.

He said: "His wonders to behold."

Looking back on it, Velmajean marveled at how easily she had brushed the entire incident aside. Laughed it off. Thought nothing of it. Straightaway. "Good Lord," she had told herself, "there are some crazy folk walking around here." As for the touch: He sure was warm-blooded.

Perhaps, again in hindsight, she might have thought on it more had not, no more than twenty minutes later, she turned onto Kensington Road: a beige Suburban SUV rolled over. An ancient Dodge Dart on its side, the wheels still spinning. A man, distraught, standing, pacing. A man and a woman on their knees. Lying prostrate and motionless before them a child, bloody and twisted.

Velmajean rushed from her car and toward the people as if by instinct. "Oh no. Oh no."

Both the woman and the man were crying and clutching each other, a portrait of kneeling sorrow; pitiful, tear-soaked visages, bodies quivering with sobs.

The standing, hippie-looking man, his long hair flaring out in all directions, was possessed by a wild look of despair. "I didn't see your turn signal, man. I didn't— Oh, God. I didn't—"

Velmajean had been ordered to take rudimentary first aid and emergency skills classes as part of her job as office manager at Deco Furniture long before she retired. She asked if an ambulance had been called. If the girl had been moved. No one answered her.

She knew to check for vital signs: the eyes, the breath, the pulse. At first things seemed dire. There was a lot of blood. She could not see where the blood was coming from. But as she touched the girl, by and by the little one began to stir. First her leg, and then a piercing cough. With flutters the girl's eyes opened, and she lifted her head, at first tentatively, and then with the full strength of youth. "Daddy?" She began to cry.

"Oh, my God!" The woman grabbed the girl up into her arms. The man literally yelled.

"She must have just been knocked out. But don't move her," Velmajean said.

"No," the man finally said, as he too rushed to his daughter. "She was dead. She was dead."

"You must have been mistaken. See. She's right as rain."

Down on her knees next to the father, both smothering their daughter in hugs and sobs, the mother finally raised her head and said, "You don't understand. My husband's a dermatologist. She was dead."

Still and all Velmajean drove off that day convinced that things were never as bad as they looked.

Velmajean Swearington Hoyt had belonged to the St. Thomas Baptist Church of Orange Grove Township all her life. In her youth the church, just outside Durham, had been thriving, the center of a small crossroads community not even listed on most maps. The minister, the Reverend T. T. Bryant, had been a theology professor at Wake Forest Seminary and had as much charisma and warmth as he had theological knowledge and wisdom. Folk always said his sermons were like an angel's home cooking. Velmajean had been baptized in that church, she had been married in that church, and both her parents, and finally her husband, had been funeralized in that church.

By that time the congregation had dwindled almost to the point of extinction. The community had been engulfed by building, and what had once been a village on the outskirts of a small North Carolina city had become a bedroom community full of apartment complexes and strip malls and oil change shops, grocery stores, fast-food restaurants, movie theaters, and gas stations. When, at the ripe old age of ninety-three, the Reverend Bryant passed on to his reward, the board of trustees were faced with a sad fact. They had only seven members left. All of them sitting in the same room with a lone real estate agent with a bad hunger for land, the land under their church. Now, seven years later, where St. Thomas Baptist Church once stood loomed a vast car dealership shaped like a hog.

For several years Velmajean wandered from church to church on Sunday mornings, looking for what people called a spiritual home. She preferred to call it a church. She had tried the high-tone, Sunday-Go-to-Meeting Baptists, the Speaking-in-Tongues Holy Rollers of the Pentecostals, the casserole-toting Methodists, the choir-besotted AME Zionists, the Hat-Happy Church of God in Christs—but none of them felt right to her, felt comfortable. Each was like a pair of shoes she admired until she tried them on.

One fine Saturday morning there came a knock at Velmajean's door. There before her stood that nice couple who lived five doors down, Philip and Amanda Witt. He was black, she was white, both so young and handsome, she thought, they should be ashamed of themselves. And they had a toddler too cute for words. Simply adorable. She had offered to look after the child if they ever needed a baby-sitter. She thought they had come to ask for her services. She looked forward to having a three-year-old around, even if it were only for a few hours.

"How are you two today?"

That was when she heard about the Atomic Church. In truth she had heard of it before. It had been all in the news when it first opened, and she remembered scoffing at the notion. A failed shopping center refurbished and rebuilt as a single mammoth church with just as mammoth a congregation. The New City of God their minister liked to call it.

"We'd love it if you came with us on Sunday. We think you'd enjoy it."

They were oh so nice, so gentle. She couldn't tell them that was not her sort of place.

Nothing could have prepared her for that odd gathering. More like a nation under one roof. Never in her sixty years had she been among so many human souls at once. The rumblings alone sounded like thunder. The main auditorium held ten thousand people and was sandwiched between two vast wings containing, among other things, a nursery the size of a small school, a "worship gym" where one could work out while watching the sermon on jumbo monitors, four small theme chapels, several suites of administrative offices, a bookstore and record store, a gift shop, a café and a restaurant and a sandwich shop; an infirmary; and a children's recreation room that resembled Disneyland. The Atomic Church of God and Worship Center boasted a credit union, an employment agency, a marriage counseling service, a culinary school ("learning to cook for Jesus!"). There were six choirs, four Christian rock bands—the Rolling Tongues of Fire, Loaves N Phishes, the Adam and Eve Project, Psalmsmack—and an inspirational rap group, Boyz 4 da Cross, which had a best-selling CD entitled *Gangbanging 4 da Lord*; there were four services on Sunday, and at least one major one every day, not to mention endless Bible studies and support groups, and a flotilla of outreach programs and lectures and encounter gatherings and forums that resembled activities aboard a luxury cruise ship. In fact, that was what the entire operation reminded her of: one vast ocean liner on land, afloat from the rest of the world. She would get through this service.

After musical numbers and skits that made her think she was first at a rock concert and then a Broadway play, and then a stadium-size group therapy session, with the uproar and flash of a rock star cum head of state, on center stage rushed the Atomic Reverend himself, Reverend Spike. ("Are you ready to get nuclear for Jesus?")

Aside from the physique of a professional wrestler and the good looks of a movie star, and a platinum tongue, the Reverend Jamie Horowitz's mystique was bound up in his past.

His father had been a famous physicist and his mother, part Japanese, part Hawaiian, a concert pianist. He had gone to excellent schools and at a tender age made a fortune in computers, which he lost, and then another one with an Internet company, which was in turn wiped out like so much goofer dust. All before he was thirty. But did that stop Spike Horowitz? No, brothers and sisters. The Lord had an appointment for him stored in His great celestial PalmPilot. Hallelujah! The Lord told him to build him a city, a City of God, just as St. Augustine has written about. And the Atomic Church was that city.

The standing applause took a while to die down as the great tree trunk of a man stalked back and forth across the immense stage, white teeth flashing, eyes manic with glee.

"Praise be to God, saints," he said as the crowd finally took their seats, though the mass of worshipers never quieted, always there was the hum and the occasional ejaculation of agreement, communication back and forth from the high-tech high priest and the pulsing Army of the Lord. The spectacle made Velmajean smile despite herself. This wasn't church, this was a movement.

"I'm happy this morning, saints. I've been talking to the CEO, the Chairman of the Board, the President of the Universe—hallelujah! And do you know what He told me?"

The response was akin to a thunderclap.

"That's right, children. Hallelujah! Our annual report's good. Our soul-stock is up! Our major asset—our Atomic Faith in Christ Jesus our Lord—is through the roof! Hallelujah!" With that, balloons and confetti fell from the air like manna, and the response was seismic. The band struck up a disco version of "Soldiers of the Lord," and people not only leapt to their feet but danced, and for a time there was rejoicing in the aisles. Velmajean spied the frenzy the way a rabbit watches foxes frolic.

"Hug your brothers and sisters. Amen. Amen. Amen!" The Reverend led the worship pep rally for a good twenty minutes or more before the lights dimmed, the stadium hushed, and the hulk from Honolulu settled down to his sermon, "God's 401(k) for You!" (which would be available at the next service on audiotape, videotape, CD, and DVD).

By and by, somewhere in the midst of his message, long after the cute catchphrases had subsided and the laser lights took a break, Velmajean found the Reverend downright moving. It was not his ocean-deep, river-smooth voice—the sort of voice that made you want to believe, to follow; after a spell it was hard to conceive that this voice did not know what it was talking about, did not come from another place; or the fact that he was simply riveting, difficult not to watch. But his words, tender, healing, inspiring, touched her. ("God's retirement plan is a Welcome Table of love, dearly beloved. The meek, the weak, the halt, the lame, the peacemakers and the sinners—hallelujah—will all be fed. Cleansed. Wrapped up in his bosom . . .") This, Velmajean thought, is how a sermon should make you feel.

At the end of the sermon, Velmajean was on her feet along with the crowd crying Hosea.

Make no mistake, Velmajean Swearington Hoyt was as levelheaded and as sensible as they come, not easily swayed by a good-looking man, no matter

how well he filled out a pair of jeans. Yes, she liked the Reverend, could listen
to him all day, could watch him for the rest of her natural life. But it was not
the Reverend's good looks and sermon that convinced her in the end, that
swept her along—it was the people. The overwhelming sense of fellowship, of
belonging, of congregation in the truest sense: She felt as if she were becoming a member of a new nation, something fresh and wonderful, and she
wanted to be a part of that new happening.

In fact, she had been a member of the church for close to two years before
she personally met the Reverend Spike. That occurred the day after the turkey
barbecue incident.

He had actually been scheduled to be there that day—the Annual Thanks-
giving-in-May Celebration to feed the homeless at a strip mall in Durham—
but on paper the Reverend Spike was always overbooked, double-booked, as
if, one fine day, the Lord would see fit to actually split him into eight men to
accomplish all the works necessary in his ministry.

Velmajean arrived at the parking lot early that day. There were to be fifteen other workers from the church to dispense the food. A poultry processing
plant had donated turkeys galore, and the women and men in the Reach Out
Program had spent days roasting turkeys, frying turkeys, making turkey
casseroles and turkey salads and turkey soup—gallons of turkey soup, as the
chairperson reasoned, depending upon the turnout, the soup could be
stretched (and ultimately frozen) yet remain filling and nutritious. Four fat
gobblers had been left over. Velmajean had volunteered to take them home to
barbecue. She'd spent hours that night and the next morning slowly grilling
the butterflied birds, deboning and hacking the meat into two large plastic
tubs of delicious chopped barbecue with a strong vinegar-based sauce sure to
please a crowd. Her wrists and forearms were still sore from the work. She had
also stopped by on her way to pick up a gross of bread loaves donated by a local
upscale French bistro. Her car smelled of toasted sesame seeds and new barbecue.

Thirty minutes before the appointed hour, a small group of men had gathered, smoking and milling about, talking loudly. There was no sign of her fellow church members. Velmajean sat in the car, her mouth watering from the
smells of piquant barbecue sauce and the loaves of bread, pungent even from
the trunk. She listened to the all-news radio station.

She didn't get worried until fifteen minutes before the meal was to be
served. The two vans with the Atomic Church of God and Worship Center
logos were nowhere to be seen. A crowd of men and a smattering of women

had gathered now. For the first time in many months, Velmajean regretted that she had not knuckled under and gotten a cell phone.

Then came a knock at her window. There stood a youngish man, chestnut brown, in a frayed-collar shirt and green fatigues. He had a several-day growth of beard, and his teeth were Ivory Snow white. He smiled at Velmajean as she rolled the window down.

"Miss, some of the guys were wondering if we got the wrong day for the Thanksgiving thing."

"No, no," Velmajean said. "It's supposed to be happening right now. I don't know where everybody is."

The man licked his lips. "Mmm, that smells good. Barbecue?"

"Yeah, turkey barbecue. Made it myself."

The man paused and stared at Velmajean. Of all the things that occurred that day, the look on that young man's face abided with her. Not a look so much of hunger, or of longing, or of weariness, though to be sure these powerful ingredients stewed there; but there was also an admixture of sadness and shame, the desire to request, yet a deeper need to be understood, not pitied. Most powerfully there was a sense of a man clinging to his dignity, not to be melted for barbecue.

Later, when asked what had moved her to get out of her car, take out the two tubs of barbecue, retrieve the 144 loaves of bread from the trunk, and begin, one by one, to serve the throng, she could only shrug and sigh. "It seemed like a good idea at the time."

She knew the real reason but felt she could never find a way to properly articulate it, to make anyone understand: She did not want that young man to have to ask.

Ninety minutes later the two vans from the church arrived, heavy laden with their cornucopia of turkey cuisine and condiments and Kool-Aid. They saw Velmajean Swearington Hoyt, alone and armed only with a spoon and a knife, cutting open loaf after loaf of bread, scooping up a decent amount of turkey barbecue, patiently feeding an entire tribe of men.

Perhaps that would have been the end of the matter, people might have spoken of the incident with warm hearts and glowing tones in that way one speaks of dedicated teachers, but she kept on and on and on. Despite the brothers and sisters hurriedly arranging the tables and fare, and now-tepid soup, for some odd reason the crowd gravitated around Velmajean, wanted to taste and be fed by the woman who had been serving them singularly from the beginning. The loaves did not run out; the tub of barbecue never went empty. Each and every person in the crowd was filled.

Later accounts put the number of people at over a thousand, which was not merely unrealistic since the program had never served more than five hundred people at one time. Mrs. Frederica Stanforth and Mrs. Nellie Mae Washington both reckoned the crowd at more like one hundred fifty to two hundred. But how the flesh of four turkeys and a big bag of bread could feed such a number escaped even their eagle eyes. Moreover: Velmajean never opened the second tub.

Velmajean understood that something had occurred but tried not to name it. She went home, tired, and fell into a cotton candy sleep, gauzy, sweet, luscious, buoyed, and serene.

At first the rumors and talk percolated only among the Atomic saints, but given the number of witnesses and the sheer size of the congregation, soon a new urban legend arose: This woman—her name, fortunately, had been lost in the translations—had fed an entire crowd of men with a tub of barbecue and a basket of bread at the Quail Dale Square at Broad and Hollywood in Durham, North Carolina, a legend now being repeated all over the state. It was at Bingo Night that Velmajean first heard the word *miracle* applied to the incident. That was the first time Velmajean Swearington Hoyt began to feel, instead of blessed, afraid.

Depending on the scholar one asks, the Christ performed somewhere in the neighborhood of thirty-five miracles. By the time the Reverend had contacted Velmajean, inadvertently four more incidents had befallen her: dancing with her nephew on the pond at Abendigo Park; delivering a nonagenarian woman from Alzheimer's with a hug; touching the cheek of a young man who suffered from acute paranoid schizophrenia and watching him walk away smiling and whole of mind. She shook hands with a woman who suffered from carpal tunnel syndrome and the shooting pains vanished.

By and by her name had been divulged, and crowds appeared along Piney View Lane. The doorbell rang constantly. After six people—a blind man, a woman with kidney failure, a deaf boy, a quadriplegic man, a woman with breast cancer, and another with multiple sclerosis—her neighbors declared they had had enough and put a stop to the steady stream with a barrage of calls to the police department and the sheriff. By that point Velmajean had already become more and more disturbed. People turned up asking her to pay their Visa bills, to be cured of sexual addictions, for winning lotto numbers, and to

palliate penile dysfunction. When she heard the sirens and the official barking on electrified megaphones, she felt two things: relief and shame, more
than she would care to admit. To be sure there was a great joy, a deep, exhila-
rating sense of awe at the works being performed through her—not once did
she take responsibility for the changes—but with each new face, with each
new begment, she had experienced a creeping sadness and confusion.

"I'm looking for a miracle," the song went. For as long as she could remember, Velmajean had believed in miracles. Small and large. Mysterious and
homegrown. She believed angels walked among us. She believed that folks
were inexplicably healed of dread ills. That prayers were answered. Only now
the purpose of miracles among men was less clear to her. Were they to demon-
strate God's love, the power of faith? Or to do good? Was one better than the
other? Was it more important to have faith than to be made whole? She had
not reckoned on the differing views—if indeed there was a difference. And
frankly, the contemplation made her head hurt.

The police and state troopers set up barricades and stood guard, and Velmajean was left to worry and fret. Part of her, roaming about the empty house,
vacuuming, dusting, defrosting the freezer, was secretly terrified, though she
did her best to hide it from herself. Theretofore she had been successful in not
asking questions about what was happening to her. But no longer: Why me?
What have I been chosen to do? What have I done to deserve this? That night
she did not sleep well at all. Her dreams were beyond baffling: She dreamt of
being in a choir of gorgeous, multicolored, naked angels, singing hip-hop
songs in a language she did not understand; she dreamt of frantically trying to
finish a supper for Jesus and a party of twelve, who were going to arrive at any
minute and the damn turkey was raw; she dreamt she was watching television
with a roomful of long-dead people—her mother, her father, her cousin
Agnes among them—but everyone ignored her and left her to watch 60 Minutes by herself. She missed her husband as if he had died the day before.

Demonstrating that he was well brought up, the Reverend Spike had the
good manners to call first. Overwhelmed by calls, Velmajean had broken
down and purchased an answering machine. It was lucky she had picked up
the phone.

She served him tea on her sunporch and was bemused and delighted by her
pastor, the pastor, curiously enough, who had paid her no attention in twenty-
four months after her joining his behemoth church.

"You aren't getting bored in this big house all by yourself, are you?"

"No more than usual, Reverend. And I have all these nice men to play pinochle with at night. Not for money, of course."

They chitted and chatted. Velmajean found it difficult to put her finger on what made this gigantic figure so attractive. ("More tea, Reverend?") Not merely the composition of his face, the symmetry, the rich salmon complexion, the intimidatingly white and well-formed teeth, the ink black eyes. ("Thank you, sister.") No, it was the way he insinuated himself upon the individual you ("Did I ever show you pictures of the new baby?"), the self-possession, the self-power, the self-projection of self into yourself. ("Isn't he a little cherub? Look at that.") Your self was locked into his self when he spoke with you—it was a presence that told you: Don't worry. You're with me.

"I was wondering, Sister Velma, if you would feel more . . . well, secure, more comfortable, in a hotel. You know, we have nice guest suites down at the church. You might—"

But Velmajean demurred. She felt better at home. "Honestly, Reverend. I don't know what I'd do if I didn't have a floor to mop or some dusting to do. Keeps me in my right mind, if you know what I mean."

"Okay. For now, Sister Velma. I understand completely. But you might start thinking. . . . There may come a time when you absolutely have to be in more secure quarters."

With her permission, he had enlisted members of the church and a professional security team to guard her home. He could not stress enough, he told her—her hand resting in his palm—how much he was concerned about her safety.

With studied finesse, he pulled from his leather valise a sheaf of impeccably typed pages—itineraries, schedules, flowcharts, contracts—and he told her about the Plan. It was a dizzying outline of the church's, i.e., the Reverend Spike Horowitz's, plan to help Velmajean Swearington Hoyt "manage" her miracles. There was talk of power of attorney, profit-sharing ("with the church, of course"), of media deals and S corporations.

"I'm certain, Sister Velma, that this is the Lord's plan for you. To show that His power is here among us. And we must act quickly. The telecast is already scheduled for next Sunday."

"Telecast?"

"Yes, both network and cable."

"I know I shouldn't ask this question—shouldn't ask it ever—but do you have any idea why me?"

"The Lord works in mysterious ways, His wonders to behold."

Velmajean simply fixed him with a cold stare, more than a little weariness knit across her brow.

To his credit, the Reverend cast his eyes down and sighed, as if to acknowledge the fact that Velmajean Swearington Hoyt was in no mood for easy Bible quotations. "Sister Velma, I have no idea. Maybe a reward. Maybe a curse. Maybe it will be revealed to you, to us, one day. Maybe it will go down as another of His mysterious manifestations. Another episode of *Unsolved Mysteries.*"

He gave her that underwear catalog smile, and she felt better. Not because of the charisma but because of his seeming honesty. She felt a smidgen less alone.

The day didn't approach quickly. It seemed she was a prisoner in her own home, which was at least now spotless. There was no doubt in her mind that the Reverend Spike had her best interests at heart, and was about God's work. A panel of doctors and scientists and skeptics had been invited to examine, in advance, and to testify to the global public afterward, as to the states of the infirm, followed by the laying on of hands, and the reevaluation of their situations.

"And what if the Lord is offended and decides not to heal them?"

"I have faith He will, Sister Velma."

Was it better to work miracles quietly, to heal the sick, fix the wrongs of the world? Or lead the masses to the Holy of Holies? That was the debate roiling through the late-night radio talk shows and Internet chat rooms and cable programs, and in the mind of the Deacon Wilford Brown, late of St. Thomas Baptist Church, when he came to call.

Dusk had just inked the air when one of the bodyguards told Sister Velmajean there was an elderly gentleman out front who said he was an old friend and insisted he had to see her.

He was in a wheelchair and rolled by his niece, Hettie, whom he had called from the bed of his nursing home in Raleigh, telling her she had to take him to see the woman he had known from the cradle.

Wilford Brown was now eighty-seven and had lost a leg to sugar diabetes. Velmajean had known him all her life, and for as long as she could remember he had been chairman of the deacon board of their now-erstwhile congregation.

"Sister, girl," he greeted her with wide-open arms. He felt frail in her arms, though all his life he'd been a tall, sturdy, bullish mechanic of a man. His fingers were still sausage thick, though she could never remember them being so immaculately clean.

Over decaf he inquired about her family and her health while his niece watched TV. He seemed loath to jump right into the business that had brought him to Piney View Lane, Velmajean could see. But could it be more obvious?

"I'm a little worried about you, baby girl. Looks like you got ahold of something—or something's got ahold of you—and it's running away with you. Is all this talk true?"

"I can imagine you've heard a bunch of mess, but a lot of what they say is true."

"That little girl? The one in the car crash?"

Velmajean nodded.

"The barbecue?"

Again she nodded yes.

The old gent took a long silence, rubbed his face, and looked away. Velmajean felt more than a bit uncomfortable. Requests always made her feel uncomfortable.

But what he said next took her off guard: "And what do you reckon Reverend Bryant would say about all this foolishness?"

"Foolishness?"

"Oh, come on, Velmajean. All this mess with the TV, and that jack-legged, wrassler-looking, no-good, lying car salesman of a preacher got his claws all up in this. What do you think I'm talking about, baby girl? I've known you all your born days, and the Lord knows I figured you to have more sense than to let yourself be *used* like this."

"If anybody's using me, I'll tell you: It ain't Reverend Spike Horowitz."

"Listen at you. 'Reverend Spike.' Is you blind?"

"The Reverend might be . . . unconventional, but he's sincere. I know it in my heart. He's for real. I really do believe that."

Wilford snorted. "Unconventional." It was as if the word were a sour taste on his tongue.

The crash through the window was not what Velmajean would remember. She heard the glass sunder and tinkle on the floor, the wood split and crack and splinter as the body hurtled through her kitchen door. But the way Wilford jolted and then tried to get out of his wheelchair, and the look upon his face when he realized he was trapped, made her want to cry. Velmajean did not scream, but the deacon's niece did— How did she get to the kitchen so quickly?

The man was wearing the same black overcoat, now slightly torn, though it was his face, sans sunglasses, that she fixed upon. Whereas before he'd had a kindly visage, he now seemed to be frothing, and his bloodshot eyes leered. He smelled awful, like spoiled milk mixed with overcooked cabbage. In fact, Velmajean soon realized he was wearing the same suit as well, now torn, leaf and straw mottled.

Wilford hollered at first. Then said, "Get," as if he were shooing away a puppy.

The knife sliced through the air, not with a singing sound but with a bat wing's flap. Twice he slashed at Velmajean, who just stood there afraid to leave Wilford and fighting the overwhelming need to pee, and pee bad.

The other thing that surprised her was the sound the gun made. Nothing like the loud bang she had heard at the movies or on TV. More a pop, like a firecracker.

On the floor the stranger convulsed and held his wounded shoulder, the blood—prune juice dark—fanning out caterpillar speed onto her yellow tiles.

The security guard told her to stay away, but it seemed so patently, so light-bulb clear what she had to do.

As she bent over him, her hand moving toward the bleeding spot, her former African chief, her fantasy Secret Service agent, stared at her and mouthed: "Who said . . . Who said . . . who said . . ."

"What? What are you saying?"

"Who said it was from God?"

ENDING 2

Wilford's niece's high, piercing scream seemed to go on forever—How did she get into the kitchen so fast? Velmajean had only seen the knife flash, once, twice. And then he stood still, staring at her. That pain was on the outside, as if she had received a long paper cut on her belly. On the inside was only a dim pressure, and a throbbing, and then a pouring. In some dull, still-functioning, stubborn place inside her brain, she understood in a crystalline way that she was in shock. And she had to pee, and pee bad.

He stood there staring at her, and she wondered why she had ever judged him as being beautiful. His jet lips, now parched, ashy, and cracked, moved, but it was only after the pop of the security guard's gun brought him to his knees that she finally made out what he had said to her: "Who said it was from God?"

ENDING 3

The security guards—the paid one, Fletcher Cross, a fat white man with cherry cheeks, and a young man from church, Buzz Terrington, bear-big and the color of a fine leather jacket, and with a penchant for video games—tackled the intruder simultaneously. Limbs and fists flew in such a blur that Velmajean soon turned away. Wilford's niece had wheeled him from the kitchen as he called out to Velmajean in confusion and fear, "Are you okay? Velmajean? Velma?"

After wrecking the dinner table, two chairs, the coffeemaker—the glass carafe simple exploded—and the cabinet door under the sink, the two bodyguards subdued the smelly man.

His face bloody, tears wetting his cheeks, he snarled and struggled to get away. It was not at all clear to Velmajean that these two men could hold him down.

"Call the police!" Buzz said. "Nine one one!"

"I already did," Wilford's niece said from the doorway. "They'll be here any minute. Hold him!"

Velmajean took a step forward, trying to see the man's face clearly, to understand. He fixed her with a glare so intense it almost made her cry. He spit at her, making her jump back.

"Who said it was from God?" he hollered. "Who told you that lie?"

ENDING 4

Apparently the guards had warned the man. They would later tell the police they had called to him as he ran toward the house, but he would not stop. Fletcher Cross, licensed to carry a gun, fired only once.

Now the floodlights were on, and in the middle of Velmajean's deck lay writhing her Secret Service agent, her black angel-helper, her once-vision, now nowhere near angelic: he wore the same thick coat, the same suit, tattered now, smelling like rotten cabbage and piss. Buzz Terrington held him down, but he gave little resistance, instead growling like a wild animal.

"Shut up," Buzz yelled. "Keep still. An ambulance is on the way, you dumb shit." Velmajean could smell the fear on the other two guards, who had come round to watch.

The man had been shot in the shoulder and was holding it with his right hand. The hand was wet with blood, and between grimaces and snarls, the strange man sucked air as if it were hard to breathe.

Heedless of any potential danger, in fact convinced of some plan, divine or otherwise, Velmajean made her way to the fallen trespasser.

"Don't touch me!" The man's words were distinct, clear and loud. "Don't you come near me, you whore."

"Wha——"

"I know who you are." The man winced but tried to slide back from Velmajean. He began to cry. "It was not meant to be like this."

HEARTLAND, KANSAS

There is no fear of God before their eyes.

PSALM 36:1

PAGANS aren't supposed to tell their Craft names to strangers, but Candy Ayres, also known as Elowen Graywolf, was a "crone," already a senior witch and a grandma at forty-seven, which meant that even though she couldn't twiggle her nose to make the dinner dishes disappear, it was in her power to grant an exception with the help of a little magic.

"That's m-a-g-i-c-k," Elowen told us.

"What's the *k* for?"

"Keep David Copperfield Away."

No hocus-pocus for her, no card tricks. To cast the spell needed to let us in on her magickal identity, Elowen simply shook her hands and shook our chakras and, presto chango, right there in a Denny's in Durango, Colorado, we were initiated as observers into the outer edges of her witch group, the Salene Circle/Dark Moon Coven/Fort Riley Pagan Association.

Durango was not where Elowen lived, but that was where her husband had been transferred for Wal-Mart management training, so that was where she was for the time being, and it suited her—there were nearly as many pagans in Durango as there were in her hometown, Miltonvale, Kansas, where 20 out of 240 families practiced a faith that monotheistic America might describe, at best, as "Other."

Elowen's daughter, Kim, worked at the Durango Denny's with an all-Pagan waitstaff, their Mormon manager keeping an open mind so long as the witches kept the customers' coffee mugs full. There were gothic types with pale skin and pentagram necklaces, there was a gray-bearded regular at the counter who said he'd learned the Craft in the Navy during the Korean War, there was a clean-cut jock working the register who said he practiced "Syrian magick." When we asked him why, he shrugged. "I dunno. That's just what my family has always done." And there was Kim. Elowen had three children, but it was only her eldest who was her "witch daughter," just as Elowen had been witch daughter to Kim's grandmother, and her grandmother to her mother before her. It goes like that, generation to generation and, in Elowen's family, green eyes to green eyes. Elowen's own were emeralds set in rosy skin beneath platinum white hair, cropped to bangs in the front and falling like an avalanche over her shoulders. Kim had eyes of a darker shade, more like the green of a bottle. Her mother was stout and strong, but Kim still held the shape you could tell her mother had once owned: lean and smooth—which you'd better be if you're going to go around calling yourself Willowdancer, which Kim did. She had two names too.

Willowdancer was twenty-five, twice-married and twice-divorced with two kids, Zoë, two, and Ian, five. Magick, she said, was mostly just common sense. "Wear rose petals around your neck for thirty days"—a beginner's love spell—"and I don't care how ugly you are, *someone's* going to start associating you with sweet things." Most of the witches burned at the stake in the Middle Ages, she said, were just really good cooks. Or they were curious, like her: As a teenager, Willow had tried out Christianity, only to be kicked out of three churches for asking too many questions. She'd run away from home, hit the other end of the virgin-whore spectrum—"literally," she said—and survived to join a religion that didn't bother with such distinctions. She'd made it to the promised land and found her mother there, waiting for her all along.

Naturally, she was a bit defensive, protective of her family and of their beliefs. She sat in on our lunch with Elowen as if she was a lawyer at a deposition. Were we trying to "save" her mother? she wanted to know. Elowen answered for us: "They can't, dear, I'm already Christian, in my way." Were we Catholics? Elowen answered again: "Kim, don't be rude. They clearly don't know what they are."

"Do you even know what a Pagan is?" Willowdancer asked.

"Of course they don't, dear," her mother said. "*Paganism* is kind of a silly term. There are too many different kinds of magick to use just one name."

Elowen proceeded to draw for us an umbrella labeled PAGANISM, with a spoke for each of its subsets: a curving line for Shamanism, another for Druidism, one for Wicca, one for witchcraft, and finally, confusingly, one for Paganism as well. She looked over her diagram, carefully rendered on a Denny's napkin, and then declared that it wouldn't tell us much.

"I guess you'll just have to see for yourself," she said.

Willowdancer groaned, rolling her eyes.

"Honey, they can't understand without seeing."

"There's nothing to see," Willowdancer said.

"I disagree, dear. There's lots to see."

Elowen shushed her daughter and insisted we be their guests at the Heartland Pagan Festival, an upcoming camp out for witches and assorted other heathen in rural Kansas, on a big patch of land a group of Pagans owned collectively, a nation unto itself amidst miles of corn punctuated by equal numbers of grain silos and church steeples. Willowdancer agreed we could come, promising to show us around and make sure we saw the right things.

This is what we saw: There were many, many witches, not to mention troll-people—those who believe they are "part troll," the way some people say they are "part Cherokee"—as well as vampires and halflings and full-blood Vikings, radical faeries and mischievous elves, and strutting around in kilts and tartan, communicating by walkie-talkie, some big, bad-ass druids providing security. Some of the druids were bikers; many of the magick people were military: lifers and grunts and NCOs. There were also construction workers, Jiffy Lube mechanics, a major contingent from Kinko's. They came to the festival in campers and rusty RVs and souped-up Chevy two-tons; they camped in pup tents and under tarps and in some cases under trees; they brought toddlers and teenagers and their grandmothers.

All told, there were well over a thousand Pagans gathered for the festival's opening ritual, standing in a circle around the makings of a serious bonfire, a cabin-size column of heavy timber which the "keepers of the flame"—sooty, muscular, bare-chested men with axes—had been hewing and stacking for days, and which they had topped with an enormous, hollowed-out log carved with a bearded face, a likeness of the "Horned One" to whom they prayed. There were also worshipers of the witch goddess Hecate, and of the Norse trickster god Loki, more popular among gay Pagans than his straight-arrow brother Thor. There were devotees of the Ancient Mother and of the Roman war god Mars, of the Green Man and of Isis, of Herne the Hunter and of the Bitch Goddess, she of uncountable mammaries. There were women in black velvet robes and men with great, gnarled staffs, and despite the mist of precipitation, the fog of cold breath, and the two days of rain and mud—a *lot* of mud—that had preceded the opening ritual, there were naked Pagans everywhere. Some whose nudity seemed like a gift to all who beheld them, others whose raw nakedness was just plain raw. There were drums, constant, unrelenting. And there was chanting, some like the barking of congested seals, some like the singing of drunk midwestern angels. Bells tinkled, a little boy riding on his mother's shoulders shouted "Yay!" with genuine joy, and through the throng of revelers the prayer of a man standing in front of the bon-fire-to-be filtered out to the margins.

"Desire! Warmth! Light!" he called.

He waited, as if there was supposed to be a reply, but the crowd barely mustered a murmur, so he continued: "Wisdom! Passion! Join us and protect us in this our rite!"

It was clear he wasn't talking to us, we of the great, half-nude army surrounding him; he was talking, actually, to the Horned One; but he wanted our help, our amplification. Despite the crowd's good intentions, though, this Pagan priest could not get an Amen. So a priestess took over, and directing the crowd like it was a grade school choir, coaxed out a chant:

Fire of passion,
fire of light,
fire of knowledge burning bright,
fire of heart, fire of mind,
fire of soul throughout all time.

The first time around, she was pretty much on her own. The second time wasn't much better. But by the third rep, most of the Pagans were shyly following the words, as if in a contest to see who could say them the quietest, with the least inflection.

"Yay!" shouted the little boy, the only audibly eager heathen in the crowd.

Except, of course, for the loudmouthed woman next to us. She had a mane of red hair that drooped down to the middle of her back, and she wore a green robe with a gold belt beneath a patchwork parka. She had a lovely alto-soprano voice. What she didn't have was a spot close enough to hear the chant leaders. She kept trying to sing along with the priests and priestesses in the center, but she couldn't really make out what they were saying, so she fudged it: "Fire of passion, fire of light, fire of hmm-mm. Ooh, fire . . ."

When a group of Native American singers entered the circle and began a wailing, all-vowel song, she seemed relieved; as far as she was concerned, there were no words to this one, and she could wail with the best of them. But wailing, like ritual, is trickier than it seems; you can't just moan like a cat in heat and expect the Goddess to appear. On the edge of the great circle a small ring formed around the "ooh, fire" woman. She drowned out the Indians, and then, magickally, she mangled the next prayer, though it was the only one in the ritual everyone seemed to know. Even we understood that the words were "Earth my body, water my blood, air my breath, and fire my spirit," but still Ooh-Fire sang it as a litany of imperatives: "Lift my body! Water my brood! Hear my breath, fiery spirit!"

And then, as if in answer to her command, there *was* a fiery spirit. During the chanting and the prayers, the keepers of the flame had been getting busy with long metal prods and torches doused in gasoline, and now the fruit of their labor blossomed into the darkening sky; we felt its heat before we saw it, and then we saw it too, licking over the heads of the crowd.

"Yay!"

We wanted the fire as much as the nakedest Pagan, as much as the man with the biggest rack of antlers. He, we, all of us—we wanted the flames to transform this drizzly, schleppy event into something with heat, with energy, with the old, scary gods the Pagans kept insisting were coming to the party. The flames reached the hollowed-out log perched on top of the bonfire, and it exploded with light. The fire turned from yellow to deep, dark green, roaring through the log and around it, a trick devised by the keepers of the flame. It was an answer to our prayers: big flames, big logs, century-old wood sizzling and popping, calling out, crackle, crackle, boom, boom, boom. Even on the edge of the circle, we felt the reverberations in our sternums, and the heat washed our faces like a baptism.

Yay!

A chorus of drums leapt up to join the flames, bongos and tablas and dhokals, bells and flutes and rain sticks and maybe some pots and pans. Cacophony. The man standing next to us—skinny, short, and sharp-faced, his head hairless but for a white goatee, a bit like an elvish Freud—began stripping off layer after layer, sweater after sweater, then his T-shirt and sarong, folding them neatly and piling them until he was down to nothing but bright red bike shorts. Then he peeled those off, too. Naked, he seemed less skinny; he was nothing but muscle and bone, powerfully built for his size. With his bike shorts folded and topping his pile of clothes, he leapt toward the flame like a white-tailed deer. No one knew who he was, but everyone stared. He may not have been a manifestation of Loki or Thor, or the Stag King, he may have been a bookkeeper from Wichita or a truck driver from Kansas City or a schoolteacher from Abilene, but something supernatural had to explain the—what else to call it?—the *broomstick* between his legs. We had never seen anything like it. No one had. "Yay!" The little kid shouted, and his mother's eyes grew wide; people laughed and put their hands to their mouths, delighted with this miracle, transfixed as Skyclad—so we named him, in honor of the Pagan term for nudity—began dancing around the fire, dancing not with his hips or his ass or his shoulders but with his whole body, in the air as much as on the ground, his eyes black and huge, his arms akimbo and passing through the flames. Most of all, he danced with his penis, trailing behind him and swinging in front of him like a giant gong. Regardless of your sexual preference, regardless of whether you worshiped the Horned One or the Goddess whose flames engulfed him, regardless of what name you chose to call or not call the divine, it was amazing to behold.

There are many kinds of magick, Elowen had told us. Too many for just one name.

The altars at Heartland—some, smoothed-down tree stumps; others, half-buried circles of stones—were meant for leaving gifts to the gods, but kids at the festival insisted they were more like bartering tables. Leave a pretty rock, you can take a Sacagawea dollar. Leave a hemp necklace, you can take a rusty knife. Some of their parents liked to pretend magick was all goodness and light, but the kids knew otherwise. Make a bad trade, something bad will happen. Just look at the altar. Stacks of keys: Those were from people who'd left home and wouldn't go back. Dog tags: Those were for people who couldn't go back.

Later we joined the Salene Circle/Dark Moon Coven/Fort Riley Pagan Association at its camp, a dozen tents set apart from the crowd in an embrace of trees. We sat with a score of witches at Elowen's campfire, passing a bottle of mead, waiting for the dedication ceremony, or "wiccaning," of an infant girl named Aliyah. Her father, Kal-el, an artillery sergeant at Fort Riley, had missed the birth of his first child, Logan, because he'd been in the DMZ in Korea—"It's a live-fire area. No family allowed."—and now he was going to miss Aliyah's first year because he was about to be shipped back overseas. Kal-el sat by the fire wishing witchcraft was what outsiders imagined it to be. "But I can't stand up there popping off fireballs," he said. "I really wish I could. Yes, that would be really nice, because that would end a war really quickly, a guy blasting off fireballs, people running away, people saying, 'Okay, this is not good for our reality. We surrender.' Then I get to go home." He kissed Aliyah good-bye even as he dedicated her to the Goddess, rocking her in his arms.

A little bowling ball of a boy, black hair, a dragon on his T-shirt, a Charlie-Brown-striped sarong, rolled down the path toward us. There was a snake in the dirt, but he stepped right over it and stomped up to us, fingering a kid's bowie knife, cheaply made but impressive-looking, with a serrated edge on one side and a compass in the hilt. He asked us if we'd seen any Dungeon Masters. "We're not Dungeon Masters," we answered. "I *know* that. That's not what I asked," the boy said, rolling his eyes. Later we spotted him showing off his knife to a smaller boy, running his finger down the dull blade, finding true north with the compass, expounding on the virtues of a leather grip. He had clearly earned his Pagan badge. "There's more than monsters out there," he counseled his younger friend. "You have to be prepared."

On a grassy peninsula reaching into Heartland's lake, the site of an altar to the hunter god Herne, the trickster god Loki, and the thunder god Thor, there was a man watching us who was so frail he looked like he might snap his fingers and disappear. Red goatee, pale skin, holding on to his cane even when he sat down on a stone. A sad, kind, quiet voice. He said he was admiring us in the sun. "Your sarongs are see-through when they're backlit, you know." He'd been a witch for twenty-five years and was the last one alive of his original coven. He talked to the dead, but they didn't answer.

"Frankly," he said, "it's not part of my craft to be all oogie-boogie. It's about recognizing the gods." He paused, reconsidering. "And it's about remembering the ancestors."

"The witches?" we asked, thinking of what we'd read about Paganism's fixation with the "Burning Time," when witches were burned at the stake.

He tilted his head and looked at us as if we were helplessly naïve, or just too young to understand.

"AIDS," he explained. "Queers. Remembering *them*."

There was a girl at Elowen's campfire named Mary Dragon, daughter of a witch called Crow Wolf and stepdaughter of a biker named Cat Johnson. Crow and Cat had not had an easy time of it in life. They were friendly but a little shy. Mary Dragon was smart as a whip, college-bound for sure; they let her do most of their talking. She explained their religion thusly: Monotheism is a mirror that offers only one reflection; Paganism is a spinning disco ball, a thousand glittering possibilities.

Not long after Skyclad began his dance at the opening ritual, storm clouds plowed in and spattered rain and hail down on the fire. The drummers didn't seem capable of tapping out "Yankee Doodle," much less a rhythm that could summon up gods, or forces, or just that feeling in the gut that makes you want to move or howl. Skyclad danced alone in the rain. Later that night, though, when the sky turned clear and cold as metal, when the drums thickened, when beautiful women unveiled themselves and old men hobbled around the fire like they were marking time, we stripped down to our sarongs and joined Skyclad and several hundred others weaving loopy circles around the fire. We dipped and twirled and skimmed the flames, shuffling in the mud and the heat to polytheistic polyrhythms. A couple of skeptics made to dance like holy fools. If that wasn't magick, it was a hell of a trick.

"What did you guys think of the opening ritual?" Elowen asked us. She meant the question pleasantly, but maybe because Willow muttered and rolled her eyes, and because we could still hear the herky-jerky bongos back up at the big circle, we told her the truth: We'd liked the fire but were disappointed with the words, the silliness of the chanting.

Elowen nodded. "That's all right," she said, "magick is individual. When we do our own rituals it's not like that at all. Would you like an example?"

A tall redhead called Velvet jumped up from beside the fire. "Ooh! Do we get to do an example?"

"Yes," Elowen said, and at her declaration several witches stood, pulling fleeces over their sarongs. A cold wind was blowing, pushing the clouds westward and making the evening even cooler. Only Elowen remained mostly naked.

"We're going to name the elements," she explained. "By calling to the powers found in each direction, we invite the presence of the Goddess, who oversees them all."

Willow, who besides being a witch and a mother was also a belly dancer, was standing with her butt to the fire, casually twitching her hips and shaking her belly-dancing bells. Other than her chain-mail skirt, she was naked, her stomach a tanning salon bronze, her breasts pale and petite as any you'd find in a high school locker room.

Her bells trilled as she turned away. She disliked the talk, the explanations. She might be willing to act as a guide to the best Paganism had to offer, but she couldn't forget we were outsiders who were there to work magic of our own: the kind, she thought, who steal stories and make the world smaller than it is; the kind who scoff at naked Pagans and their unsuspecting mothers; the kind who make so many possibilities wear the same drab name.

"Kim, do you want to call North?" her mother asked.

"I'm not calling anything with them around."

"Suit yourself. Just stand back out of the circle then. We don't need your negativity."

Kim seemed to consider storming off but then decided to follow the group up to an empty field lit by a brilliant, nearly full moon. Her mother took up a position in the center of a circle made mostly of her fellow witches.

Velvet stood in the southern position. She'd come to Heartland this year to talk to a man named Owl, who besides being a Pagan was successful in business and knew how to get things done; he'd pledged to help Velvet win back custody of her baby son, granted to a fundamentalist uncle because the judge deemed Velvet Satanic. "As if I'd even talk to a Luciferian," she'd said. She was an elf witch.

In the west position stood Night, a raven-haired Latina who'd retired from the army and now worked for McDonald's and somehow managed to support several children. In the middle with Elowen stood Lady Keltic, who had asked Elowen for a spell to help her conceive. Elowen was the conductor; we were North and East.

One by one we called out the names of our elements—fire, water, earth, and air—and of our directions, free-associating on their attributes like we were gently speaking in tongues.

In the distance, a woman roared like a lion; a man walked by singing "Sitting on the Dock of the Bay"; the wind smelled like incense and Porta Pottis; we were freezing. We looked at Elowen, her white mullet glorious beneath the moon, her naked torso seemingly impervious to the cold, her feet bare in the mud, and couldn't help ourselves: We laughed. She looked at us, in our muddy sneakers and double-knotted sarongs, shivering with notebooks in hand, and she laughed, too.

Willow didn't get the joke. "I can't believe you're showing them this. They just want to make you look stupid," she said. "To make fun of all of it. Can't you see that?"

We started to tell her she was wrong, but Elowen had a better answer. "Kimberly," she said. "They have no power over me. Over any of us. They've come here to learn about how we live and worship, and we are going to show them. What they do with that experience is on them. I don't believe they want to hurt me, or any of us, but they couldn't if they tried."

Willowdancer uncrossed her arms, then crossed them again, biting her lower lip to keep it from shaking in the cold.

On the far side of the field we could see torches being juggled over the heads of the crowd that had lingered at the opening ritual; a tipped-over trash can added the sound of a cymbal to the drumming. The dancers still were circling the bonfire, all together, each alone.

Elowen took Willow by the shoulders and pulled her close. A mother warming a daughter with her heat, she swallowed Willow with her body like a flame wrapping a log.

"Do you really believe some silly book could have more power than we do?"

Seal not the sayings of the prophecy of this book:

For the time is at hand.

Revelation 22:10

REVELATION

By Haven Kimmel

PART ONE

There is a place outside the Franchthi Cave site in the southeastern Argolid, across a small bay from the modern Greek village of Koilada, where her bones reside, so deep beneath the surface of the rocky ground that she will not be found for approximately 237 years (three months and sixteen solar days into the year). The current scholars say there were no burials at the Franchthi Cave, that the Neolithic people who lived there made beds, they hunted and gathered, bred and gave birth, but did not bury their dead. On the whole the scholars are correct. But *she* is there, the one We loved. She was called one thing by her parents, another by her husband, and would have had yet a third name if any of her children had lived. We cannot repeat those names, but We can say that in the Holy Order each sound is assigned a number, and one day (while We were actually thinking about something else), We realized that if We added up the sounds of her three known names We got good old Lucky 7, of course. We don't name them, but We do pay attention. Some come by the name honestly, some are so called but undeserving (millions, actually), for some it is the natural name but they do not know.

We loved watching her. They tell us Time Has Passed and We believe

Them, and We know it must be difficult to imagine a genius in the Neolithic era, no arts and letters, no mucking about with the atom, no *cinema*. Hard to picture her there, rocked back on her heels at the edge of the water, contemplating the sublime and recognizing it as such without access to German philosophy of the Enlightenment period, but that is what she did and who she was. No Hegel, but she both recognized cause and effect and *simultaneously doubted it.* [Italics Ours.] No Virginia Woolf, but she thought more than once, I would need to sew rocks in my pocket if I wanted to sink. We paraphrase. She had no word for pocket. She trusted gravity before Newton and recognized that the speed of light was constant (in general), and there are two ways she anticipated Giordano Bruno (she also died by fire, incidentally), and one of them We cannot report because it hasn't been discovered yet. She questioned what was Inside, and what was Out. There was even in her physical comportment a harbinger of evolution not yet registered in the earth's mechanics: her forehead was smoother than her mother's, her arms were shorter, her back straighter.

But the moment We are thinking of, the one that caused Us to let go a collective sigh that raised a tidal wave in an unoccupied coastal inlet in China, was the afternoon she sat on the beach with the small stones. She was solitary. She loved the company of her own mind, and rightly so. On this afternoon she was grieving the death of her third child, a hydrocephalic daughter born lumpen and covered with hair; the birth had split her mother stem to stern. During each pregnancy Our Beloved had searched for a stone, one as close to perfectly round as she could find, and before the stone was located she sat and drew circles in the sand with her fingertip; she drew them until a stillness settled in her solar plexus, quieting her, and she stopped when the stillness flowed down her arm and into the sand, and as soon as she had drawn the perfect circle the stillness flew into the air like a flock of startled seabirds, she could see them go, white, the sun a shock against their wings.

The stone for her first child, a boy, had been obsidian, and she had found it in a pool where over millennia We had allowed it to roll against the sand. We put it there for her before the dawn of time, as some of Us like to say with a wink. (Ask *her* if time had a dawn.) The second stone, for a girl who died of a fever after what you call two years of perfect health, was coral. The third was gray. A sad, gray pebble. She sat at the edge of the sea, still burning from the delivery (she would never fully recover, she knew, We knew), and rolled the stones. The first child had been on time, and big; she remembered the watery burst of him into the midwife's hands, how for a moment she had seen stars on the ceiling of the cave, constellations she had named after dead elders and old loves. We cannot repeat the names. She saw the boy's head, well-formed, his blue lips, the cord tight around his neck. Her people believed the baby's father had been X, but really it was Y. No harm there.

The coral stone had been prescient, for that daughter had loved the water, had danced like sunlight on water, laughing, for two years. Our Beloved had been pregnant a third time when the coral-colored girl died in the fever that swept through them like a hot wind, and in her grievous rage Our Beloved had poisoned the baby she was carrying, too, lost everything, or so she believed. There is no such poison. Even geniuses are wrong about many things. She rolled the stones a foot or so in front of her, then picked them up and tossed them again; they weren't in a race as such, but she was interested in the way the little gray pebble always fell behind. But of course, she thought, it would be last because it is the smallest, and without the weight to propel it, it would give way much faster to inertia. These weren't her exact words; the task of the Translator is formidable. Energy = mass X a constant, squared. If there is a constant, and We aren't saying yes or no, one candidate is this grief of mothers; why, it has hardly changed at all, and some of Us can barely stand it, we have formed a Committee. To no avail. We watched her sitting there, They tell Us it was long ago, and We felt her wretchedness, her sinking, the burning tear between her legs, she rolled the first stone and imagined her first child, the boy, had lived, the way things might have been different for her, she saw him growing up and older and away. (We felt for her, We admit that at one point We raised a wing, just slightly—We thought to offer her comfort—and accidentally swept clean an entire civilization, one that had been struggling for a thousand years and was just about to really get going. Very sorry; entirely Our fault.) She rolled the second stone not quite as far and saw the second child, her daughter, reaching the climacteric, aged seven, then fourteen. The third stone was the furry baby licked clean, her head recovered to some unknown perfect state, and the three children stood a moment in front of their mother, then turned and walked into the sea. Our Beloved thought: They are both living and dead. She thought, It is as if the world is made of parallel lines, and here I live with my dead babies, but if I could merely step over . . . And at that moment We called the Others, We felt something tick like the wheel in a watchworks, and the Others were already gathered. (How many rational creatures can exist in one place if They do not occupy time and space? A tricky and well-organized question, much belittled of late.) She looked at the stones and thought of the babies, and just like that, she thought, *Three*. And from there it happened so quickly, she thought of the seven elders who carried the sacred fire, she looked up at the sky and recited the names of the twelve caves:

The Cave of Running.
The Cave of Dreaming.
The Cave of Sex.
The Cave of Loss.
The Cave of Hunger.
The Cave of Plenty.
The Cave of Remembering.
The Cave of Rain.
The Cave of Winter.
The Cave of War.
The Cave of the Dead.
The Cave of . . .

. . . she paused, it was the last one, some in her tribe couldn't speak the word because it had no correlative except itself, her grandmother had passed it to her . . .

. . . of *Becoming*. Oh, for Us it was a majestic moment, the way she held the little round stones and looked at the sky, and realized that there were three, seven, twelve, and that the universe was turning according to a principle within her grasp, because the universe was outside, in the form of the stones, and inside precisely the same, the Self is infinitely expanding and infinitely receding, which direction We are not at liberty to say.

We said, "Let it be this one, she is the One!" But the Others shook their heads, after a fashion, and said no, and for quite good reasons. The circles she drew in the dirt were not enough, your world was too young to change. But some of Us could not resist, and We breathed into her ear, *The Kingdom of Heaven is Before You*. We have tried every combination in every language, we have rolled Time up like a blanket and shaken it out again, We mean to say We have made the Holy Effort, and finally *The Kingdom of Heaven is Before You* is the absolute best We can do. The numbers add up, it translates well, it is both concise and true. But We said it wrong to her, Our Beloved; for one thing we called her John, and that was a muddle. And We lost her. The fire took her, we'll say no more. Her husband was to carry her to the Village of the Dead, miles from the caves, or he was to give her to the sea, but in his grief he began instead to dig, and he dug for days, and he placed her in a hole and buried her, and later a rockslide covered her ever more finally. To the tribe he made the gesture of ascension, *she simply flew away.*

She'll be found, it's not so long now, and there will be some academic careers solidified over her remains, certainly so. What to make of that cranium in light of the carbon dating? What of her eloquent bones?

In every language there are names that add up to seven. You are very good at figuring such things out, at zeroing in on them and clinging to them without ever knowing why you do so. There are other things you suspect as well but cannot prove. For instance, humans love to sit facing enormous bodies of water, and one of the things they invariably do is pick up a handful of sand and let it sift through their fingers. Why? Because there is a point, midway between the gathering of the handful and the sifting back to the infinity below you, when you are holding a *number* of grains of sand, and it equals the number of times the average dog wags his tail in an average life. You are a clever species.

For a while there were variations in your heritage: Jonah, Joan, Joshua, Yeshua, Jesus, Miriam, Esther, these are all sevens. But at some point you settled in and decided to give a single name to many prophets: John the Baptist, John Who Was Jesus's Favorite, John at Patmos, countless saints, priests, men and women of the cloth, John Keats, John Lennon, John Crowley, John the Mechanic up the Road (who is a man of few words and all of them uncanny), not to mention John your favorite horse, who carried you seven miles through a blizzard in the jubilee year. One of Us, Who is Funny and Too Clever, thought of introducing into your population (randomly! through dreams and the media!) some of our other favorites: Ain Soph. Kether. Chokmah. Binah. Chesed. Geburah. Tiphereth. Netzach. Hod. Yesod. Malkuth. Da'ath. Finally We agreed they wouldn't work well on a playground.

So much water under the bridge, or so they tell Us, and you have come to believe the Books were written as they appear, and they were written in a certain order, and that order was preordained. Matthew Mark Luke John. A lot of letters from Paul, who was also a seven but troubled. John John John, Jude, John. In the Beginning was the Word. But what was given to John on the island of Patmos, wracked with fever and unable to hear Us clearly, was not the end, and had it been up to some of Us it wouldn't have been included at all. He moved Us to Love and Pity; We could not intercede, even when he misunderstood and got it all wrong, and threatened the course of human history. But it makes for a good story, the way he told it. Beasts! Whores! The Rising of the Dead! The End of the World! (Ask *her* if the world has an end.)

There is The One, but The One does not speak. It is We Who do all the work, Who adore you, We hover, you sense Us again and again. How else to explain this feeling, so common among you, that everything you do is seen and recorded and treasured as if in a Holy Book in which you are the main character, the sole point of view? You are the hero, the victim, your parents didn't love you enough, the traffic conspires against you, your little acts of kindness, when you can afford them, seem so significant. Who indulges you so? *The One*? You cannot imagine and We cannot describe the distance between you and what you seek, Him, Her, The Father God, The Mother. Is He so close to you that you cannot see Him? Is She so far away that your most brutal metaphors couldn't carry you there? Beyond the Dark Matter, beyond the expanding and contracting limits of the universe, imagine a photograph taken in an easy time, when your land was prosperous, perhaps between wars. The photograph is of a dance floor (black and white diamonds), and two people are laughing and dancing, he in a slim, black, perfectly tailored tuxedo, she in ivory silk that spills down her narrow shoulders like a bright, liquid accident. Their affair has endangered them, has separated them from their clan, but it has brought them here, to this beautiful night, and their bodies are in motion (little is more pleasing to Us). The shutter of the camera opens and closes, the moment is captured on a delicate slip of film, the photograph is given to the couple as a gift. They marry, have a family, they grow old, the photograph is placed in a box and tucked away in a closet under the stairs. They die, the wife first, the husband soon after; before their children can decide what to do with the remnants, a fire consumes the house, a fire will take everything. The ground is razed.

Where is that dancing couple? That is what you must decide, that is what you all have to contend with, because once you know it, you know the way to The One, the mansion with many rooms. Close? Or Far?

• • •

There is The One, but The One does not speak. And We are manifold, indeed, We are Legion, and can agree on almost nothing, which causes no end of trouble. We apologize. Time, for instance, moves too quickly for you, the swiftness leaves you *unhinged*, and that was a mistake on our part, but there is no going back. Some of you perceive that there isn't room enough between events to navigate the information contained within the moment consumed and the moment anticipated. We call this, among other names, The Dilemma of the Bullet. The contraindications of The Dilemma give rise to terror, dread, and nausea. But those of Us Who suggested slowing time down were outvoted, on the pretense that a perception of time moving thick and slow, manageable but sticky, would give rise to torpor, dread, and nausea. Oy. And We know that there are eras, there are, We might say, acres of time where the veil under which you live (and which protects you) grows very thin, it becomes little more than a scrim through which you glimpse the Ineffable, and amazing things happen in those years. We see it coming from far away, and We see, too, those Who carry the light that will lead you to safety. And those poor mortals! every day pricked by the quills of Our monstrous encouragement! That Magician, for instance, wandering through Palestine, performing His feats and rattling the bones of all who looked upon Him. He was great! He was fantastic and doomed, and He took it on the chin, We could hardly have loved a Man more. But every time He spoke or raised His hand, sometimes even when He *blinked*, the veil grew more sheer; sometimes a corner grew tattered and lifted off the earth like a circus tent in an electrical storm, the carnival of that man! All around Him people were puzzling over yeast or no yeast, cloven hooves (not good, they were right), what to do about beards and tattoos, the Law, the Law, the Law, and here He is, a sudden Baal Shem, and everywhere He steps the world flips! upside down. The sky becomes a bowl that men may fish in; love grows sharp as a sword; the unseen radiates up and outward, and no one can tell anymore the difference between speaking and singing, what they dream or what they hold. You like, We think it's safe to say, for *inheritance* to have *mass*, but He says no. You may not keep your treasure, even from one moment to the next. The blind will see, yes, and the dead sit up in the stained chair, but what, bear with Us now, is the point of all that? Because the blind man, the soldier's daughter, the hemorrhaging woman, crusty Lazarus himself, where are they now? Dead and gone as if He'd never touched them at all! Trickster! Look what He buried in the heart of His argument! Your own (at least We think he was yours) Emerson said that prayer for any commodity is *vi-*

cious. Sight, health, wealth, a harvest, a son-in-law: vicious. But if that's how you want it, He said, shrugging His shoulders. If that will get your attention, okeydoke. And He used His magic in the service of Our message, that song shaken off the wing: *The Kingdom of Heaven is Before You.*

Not enough! shouted the fan club.

Who could say such a thing? rumbled the gathered throng.

Only the Messiah, was the decision; only some mess of finitude and eternity. "For Pete's sake," We said, rolling Our eyes. Fully Human and Fully Divine, like a cookie recipe. (You didn't understand about Him at all then, you understand less now. He was an impatient man, driven. Imagine Him boarding a train right now, *a train you are on,* the sinister cut of His suit, the look in His eyes. Maybe He's dangerous, or maybe He's just the man to share a dry martini with: He passes you, you cannot say which He is, and then He's gone. A sexy, impossible, impertinent man not prone to suffering fools.) But He listened to Us, in a way He was One of Us, and We said, "Fine, fine, stop trying to explain. *Blend.*" You know where that ended up. Sort of Our mistake. We might have pushed the envelope, as you say. We might have allowed Him to rumble the oversoul too much, too soon. Never in the history of You Know What have people grieved so mightily, and for so long. You're grieving still, aren't you?

You wouldn't know Him if He tipped His hat to you on the street. He would terrify you.

PART TWO

Apokalypsis. Revelatio. The words sound so grave now, with good reason, but what We mean to give is simple as a sigh. The bridegroom lifts the gauze, and there She is. She was there all along. You're rumbling around in your boxes, heartbroken, tooth-grinding, and you hate the way you spend your days and how you ruined your life by having healthy children and all the ways your mate does not understand you. A voice which is not a voice and doesn't actually speak reminds you to eat your sandwich. Daily revelation, the most quotidian of all. And then there are the other ways it arrives. A heron sails close to a cold stream, a black cat leaps on windblown leaves. A tired woman rests her fingers on her face. In the words of one of your poets, *The man in the black coat turns.* Gracious, We love Poetry here, We take turns reading Our favorites, but one of the problems with you, We've been trying to say this for some time now, is the old vaticinia ex eventu. You conflate your personal history with Everything Else. For those of Us Who wish to give you a gift, this Kingdom-of-Heaven-is-Before-You token of Our esteem, no defect in your evolution could be more ironic. Imagine offering a treat to a dog with no mouth.

Stay inside your skin and figure it out, We urge this upon you in your sleep. Be radically negative: not this, not this, not this. The Kingdom is not *your* clan, your country, your meetinghouse. The Conflict is not *your* government, your enemies, your struggle with entropy and degeneration. Use your history only as metaphor, koan, or parable.

We chose John even though Exile was his middle name. We chose him to say a little something about the Magician, because we thought he Got It (not the Magician per se, but what the Magician pointed toward). John had been treasured by Some of Us from his youth, because he dreamed in numbers and had a keen eye. We spoke to him annually, beginning when he was small. We said, Look! And there, gathered around the well for just a moment, seven women bending from the waist at once, seven cats on the wall behind them. Delightful. Easy joy. He loved the light of a hard summer sky, the blinding crests of waves at midday. It seemed he was a natural follower (he took extensive notes), and so when We decided that perhaps a book could be written— We have a weakness for books—he naturally came to mind for one of the chapters. Not the last, for Heaven's sake; perhaps the first. Perhaps he would provide a map for everything that followed.

But by then there had been the storm in the desert, and the Magician was gone, the apostles scattered, some in prison. Domitian ordered John to the island, and We thought, That's fine, he can use the time like a retreat. He was sick when his boat docked, and he grew sicker each day, and by then Some of Us thought We should turn Our Faces away. The ill invariably speak from their condition, and he was filled with rage and shame. Don't judge Us for miscalculating how to treat him; We've seen mothers make similar mistakes every day. Of course you can have ice cream if your stomach hurts, they say, All Love. And so we sent him this: $(\log (K)) * 666 = 25919.99787$. The Platonic cycle. This seemed to go over so well with him, at least in sleep, that We got a bit carried away and sent him the values of harmonics, the Aztec equivalents of the Brahmic cycle, the height of the Cheops pyramid, the descending sums of stacks of square roots, do please understand that this was like play for Us, like showing a child a group of nesting dolls, infinitely nesting. All We meant to say is that the Root can be stripped of history, of mythos, of pathos, and will shine up bearing a remarkable resemblance to other things you know and love, and then the Root can be clothed again in particulars and We're all the richer for it. Imagine Us giving this to him in the night, put your best spin on it, as you say. Imagine what it sounded like to him, an inflamed, dehydrated man.

It is the case that, speaking mathematically here, all sacred texts are preserved, and none are. We maintain sangfroid easily in the face of this basic discrepancy. So we said to John that Inanna's sacred number is 252, and he wrote, *The name of the star is Wormwood. A third of the waters became wormwood.* We shook Our heads, tried again. We asked him, What is the basic unit of truth, John? He groaned in his sleep. We said, What happens on the day that, hypothetically, others of your own kind begin forcing whole families into ovens? What is True on that day, on the days to follow? And he wrote: *Then from the smoke came locusts from the earth, and they were given authority like the authority of scorpions of the earth.* We said, Sweetheart, do you remember the night years ago when you became so frightened, and you wandered out into the garden and found your mother there? She was weaving a dress for her sister, and had torches lit against the midsummer darkness? Do you remember what you saw in that moment? And he wrote: *So he carried me away in the spirit into a wilderness, and I saw a woman sitting on a scarlet beast that was full of blasphemous names, and it had seven heads and ten horns.* We said to Each Other, he doesn't need Us, he needs a *doctor.* And as We talked among Ourselves, the volume not quite down far enough, John continued writing. He wanted to see, We realized, the earth as scorched as his own mouth. He wanted the world to end, he wanted to cease grieving and complaining, he wanted more power and liberty, to be less afflicted by the vagaries of this experiment; simple, childish things. All over your world, in every given moment, boys are knocking down blocks and log buildings, they're smashing against dams built for good reason and against floods they can't imagine. They are jumping up and down in fury and swinging their little fists. And if those children manage to grow up, they invariably run for public office, offering their lives to the world like a humble sacrifice. Inside, they are voracious. We are Pensive about this trend, and We've given it a name: TABB. We offer them a prophecy, but They All Become Bureaucrats.

• • •

John wrote, and We indulged in Our own weakness: comedy, and cheap imitations. Well, they'd have to be cheap. Not One of Us has a dime. Some of Us are really good at doing animals (you try imitating a giraffe), others love a Broadway tune. One joker is especially good at Random People in Big Cities. Everyday it's someone else—a homeless man, a tax collector, a prostitute, a grocer. John wrote all night, and We grew giddy, as if We were reading a fabulously skewed translation, and toward dawn We chose a couple to watch, and they were so fun We reared back with laughter and repeated their exchanges. They were middle-aged and cranky, an Italian cobbler and his wife living in a railroad flat in Brooklyn. Sal and Rosa, two 7s. Three children. We'd watched them before; they had the timing of old radio stars. On this morning Sal was sitting at the kitchen table waiting to start his breakfast, and Rosa was in the bathroom combing her hair. Sal yelled, "Rosa!" She ignored him. He yelled it a little louder, his toast and coffee growing cold. "Rosa!" She ignored him. Finally, he shouted, "*Jesus Kee-rist!* Get in here!" We can do him perfectly. Rosa sighed, rolled her eyes, shouted back, "I'm coming, I'm coming, I'll be there soon!" Oh, it was funny.

GENEVA, ILLINOIS

The voice of the Lord causes the oaks to swirl,

and strips the forest bare;

and in his temple, all say, "Glory!"

PSALM 29:9

SHE called herself Dina, but that wasn't her real name. She was a stripper, but there was only so much she could reveal. She would have liked to show us more, but she wasn't allowed—there are rules about revelation in a "bikini bar." *Thou shalt not show more than six-tenths of thy breast, that portion which is revealed to exclude thy nipple; thou shalt not show more than four-tenths of thy ass. Thy legs must be hidden, but thou mayest use sheer nylons that giveth the appearance of flesh; this deception shall pass, sayeth the Lord and the state of Illinois.*

"I'd be raking it in," Dina told us, "if I just flashed a little." She grabbed her left breast, smallish and firm, covered by a white bikini with red crosses over each nipple. "But one of the other girls would rat me out."

The other girls strode by on towering Lucite heels and in thigh-high, black leather boots, their bikinis plunging up when they passed one way, down when they passed the other. Outside it was five degrees, and the one-story cement-block bunker that housed the dark cave that was Club Exotica provided weak insulation. The girls kept moving not just to satisfy the management—a pale, fat, hairless snowball of a man who stood watch from the

bar—but also to keep warm. They were like sharks—if they stopped swimming, they'd freeze and die.

But we all knew who the sharks were: the men in the plastic lawn chairs
Snowball had set out for his customers; watching it all with gazes sharper
than the wind screaming outside.

Some sharks. There was a guy in a leather Blackhawks jacket who occasionally approached the stage, dollar in hand, as if he was going to buy a
"dance," which was the word the club used to describe what happens when
the stripper humps the stage in front of the customer, then swings around and
drapes a leg over his shoulder, thrusting her pelvis in almost close enough for
a kiss. Blackhawk blushed every time the humping began, and instead of
staying through the mock cunnilingus to slip his dollar into her garter, left his
crumpled bill on the rail and ran back to the bar, where he ordered a Coke he
slurped through a straw while he waited for his embarrassment to pass.

Then there was a table full of drama club geeks, all of them either small or
round, their hair dyed black and shaved close in back, cut in long diagonal
bangs up front; they looked like sheepdogs. And there was a long-haired guy
with a beard who everyone called Jesus. It was Jesus' birthday, so Big Snowball sent him onto the stage, where three girls surrounded him, bumping him
back and forth between their hips like a pinball until Jesus, laughing despite
the alarm in his soft eyes, looked ready to escape to his cross.

Dina didn't call him Jesus; that was on account of the fact that she was
Jewish. Well, half-Jewish, because her mother was from Spain and was, she
said, "Roman." When we mentioned it, she was sure she'd heard her grandmother say something once about Marranos, the "hidden Jews" who went
undercover to escape the Spanish Inquisition. She crossed herself and named
the Father, Son, and the Holy Ghost in Spanish, and said hiding might have
been a good idea for her father, whom she never knew—he'd been a Polish
Jew, escaped the war by an inch and, from what she'd heard, never really
seemed to recover from the scare. He died when he was fifty-nine, a few
months before Dina was born.

"People gotta hide who they are," she said. Then she asked us who we
were.

So we told her what we'd been doing, about making this book.

"What's a heretic?" she asked.

"You are," we said.

"Me?"

By dint of circumstances if nothing else, she was; Club Exotica was six miles from Wheaton, Illinois, which along with Colorado Springs and Lynchburg, Virginia, is a point on the Bermuda Triangle of fundamentalist America, the metaphysical zone in which shades of gray disappear and God is a cross between Jimmy Stewart and Genghis Khan, wholesome in every regard but for the fury with which he regards sinners. And no sin is greater than the revelation of His creation. We were in Club Exotica because we'd been in Wheaton. We were at Club Exotica to see some flesh and movement because we'd earlier seen the stone-still face of Billy Graham a thousand times in repetition at his official multimillion-dollar museum. We were at this temple of cheap caveman thrills because it was there, in the middle of a dark ocean of flat land at the heart of the country, because a freight train without end had cut off our path back east and made Club Exotica a dead end with a brass pole and a disco ball.

We thought of the disco ball Mary Dragon had told us about at Heartland, her idea of God, an endless number of reflections. We mentioned it to Dina.

"Totally," Dina said. Then she asked us what we had seen when we'd looked into its mirrors. Stories, we said, and found ourselves nearly speaking in tongues, telling Dina about the smoke in the air when we'd left New York City, and Isshizean Zean and her heart tattoo, and about the choir that wore red and sang for blood. We told her about wishing we could speak Spanish in Los Angeles and listening to people speak Elvish in Heartland. We told her about Skyclad, and Dina's big brown eyes went wide, her shoulders slumped, her professional sex kitten pose for a moment abandoned. She stripped for a living, she said, but she was an exhibitionist at heart, and she loved the idea of a bonfire surrounded by naked bodies dancing; her eyes swung around the room, undressing everyone in it, even Snowball, and setting them in motion.

We told her about Buddhists marching around stupas, the witch shaking her hips in Crestone. We told her about the buzzards we'd seen circling, the Dickheads laughing, the doctor who hunted tornadoes—

Dina took a drink of the kamikaze we'd bought her and leaned back in her chair, a clear plastic heel in each of our laps.

"I'm a writer, too, you know," she said, and then she told us about the things she had written, reciting poems and letters and stories, some of it funny, some of it sexy, some of it sad, a lot of it lousy, a little bit of it, like that of any writer, very wonderful. She was hard to follow over the sound system—AC/DC's "Dirty Deeds Done Dirt Cheap" and Prince's "Darling Nikki" and Elvis's "Fever"—but we caught a story about her junkie cousin—"she gets up in the morning and pushes her life into her veins"—and a sweet-natured poem about Hell, and a wistfully pornographic story about a man in a shower, "every bead of water like a jewel," that Dina said had won her a state prize when she was thirteen.

"Do my stories sound like prayers?" she whispered, leaning forward, her long, bleached hair like a veil of smoke and incense between us and the rest of the club. She didn't wait for our answer. Instead, she undraped herself from us and stood, her heels so high she towered above us.

"Don't go."

"I have to," she said. "He's watching." We followed her eyes back into the corner, catching Snowball's evil glare directed at our table. "You're not buying," Dina said. She meant private dances. "But that's okay. I'm not selling." She winked. "I'll be back."

And just like that Dina set off into the current, shrugging off the gauzy shawl she'd wrapped over her bikini, her fingers drifting behind her across the shoulders of men until one snapped to attention, standing and taking her hand as if at a ball, leading her to the back of the room, where he traded her ten dollars for a song's worth of tits and ass, heavy whispers and almost-kisses. Then ten dollars for another song and ten for another, until we realized we might not see Dina again.

A tall blonde who called herself Kennedy ("Because I wish I could've slept with Marilyn," she said) asked us to buy her a drink. We waved to the waitress and Snowball sent over something pink with a whisper of vodka. "You boys just passing through?" she asked. We weren't ready to preach another sermon so we said simply that we were writers, we wrote about religion.

"Well, you came to the right place," Kennedy said.

"A lot of true believers here?"

"You're looking at one."

Kennedy said she was a Calvinist, raised in Kearney, Nebraska, by parents who home-schooled her and forbade even the blackberry wine her uncle made for Thanksgiving. She knew doctrine and theology and every good reason why her Lord didn't want her to be sitting across from us in a sparkly silver leotard that scooped down to her pubic hair. "But I can't help it," she said. The money was good, but that wasn't all. When she was a girl she'd rebelled—"You know, sex in a cornfield"—and it was only when she broke the rules that she felt like she loved God as much as He loved her.

She glanced over at Snowball. "Here," we said, opening our wallets and passing her two tens so that the fat man could see the transaction. "Keep talking."

Kennedy relaxed, signaled the waitress for a Coke. "I dream about God all the time," she said. "You know, what He wants."

"What does He want?" we asked.

Kennedy frowned, an expression that for a second seemed to send her hurtling back to Nebraska, her face dour and serious, her black eyes frustrated and angry. "I don't know," she said.

In one of Kennedy's dreams, her mother shared the stage with her at Club Exotica, praying while Kennedy danced. "And she's making more money than me! They're slipping twenties between her tits and I'm doing pole tricks and flashing my pussy but nobody's watching.

"In another, my dad's car breaks down across the road from the club, so he has to come here to wait for the tow truck. But the tow truck comes and takes his car away, and he still stays. He has his Bible, and he takes dollars out of it to tip me. The other guys want to tip me too, and he's passing pages around. And this one guy slides the Gospel of John into my garter.

"I have crazy fucking dreams. It's like I'm a kid, when your dreams are too real, you know. That's how Christianity fucks you up, it's like, you get too much of it and you never stop dreaming. And they're not good dreams. Like for instance the dreams I have about tornadoes."

"Tornadoes?" we said.

"Yes, tornadoes," she said.

In the dreams, Kennedy is back in the cornfield, only now there's no sex, and there's no God. "He's not there," she said, "which really upsets me." And there are tornadoes all around her. "You know how they call them 'fingers of God'?" we said. "Yes," Kennedy said, "but that's stupid. Have you ever seen what they do?" We admitted that we had not—we never did catch that storm. "They ruin everything," she said. Then she paused. "But they are beautiful." Before a tornado, she told us, the sky turns green, the color of the sea ("I've seen the Pacific *and* the Atlantic," she boasted). "And it crushes you." She reached out with flat palms on top of our heads and pushed us down into our chairs. "That's the dream," Kennedy said. "Green and crushing and a dozen tornadoes spinning around me."

"Kennedy!" Snowball's voice boomed over the sound system. *"On stage now! Put your fucking paws together, gentlemen!"*

"I'm sorry," Kennedy said and strutted away to the stage. Her first dance was just hip swinging to hip-hop, but then Snowball cued the Who's "Baba O'Riley"—a song written for Meher Baba, whose compound we had lived in for a while in South Carolina—and Kennedy looked confused. Big guitar chords, arena-rock drums, a fiddle solo—it's not really a bump-and-grind. Kennedy straddled the pole in the center of the stage, tried to make like it was the biggest dick in the world and she was loving it, but the illusion wouldn't take, not for her, not for the audience, not even for the pole. "Out here in the fields I fight for my meals . . ." sang Roger Daltrey. It was like a bad dream, she was in the cornfield, naked, and He wasn't there. "I don't need to be for-giveeen. . . ." Only Kennedy felt like she did, so she started spinning, holding her breasts in her hands as if they were offerings and occasionally running a finger down to her crotch and back up to her lips as if she was tasting herself, moaning and shaking her head as if she'd just sampled manna. She grabbed hold of the pole with one hand and started swinging around it, faster and faster through the violin solo, until the crescendo. When it was over, she stopped and stood center stage, slump-shouldered, lit by two rinky-dink red spotlights, framed by two artificial palm trees, dappled by the disco ball, sur-rounded by applause for the undeniable truth of her skin and bones, real here on earth.

"Dina!" Snowball called. Now Dina was dancing, first to "Relax," by Frankie Goes to Hollywood; then to a song that seemed less like a song than the soundtrack to an industrial assembly line. It began as nothing but the noise of gears grinding, gates slamming, booted footsteps stomping up steel stairs; then all the noises gathered into the boom-clang-boom-clang of a radi-ator banging, accompanied by two deep piano chords, each allowed to res-onate until it faded away. The music of a factory eating itself: first the relentless pulse of its labor, then the rumble of its rhythmic destruction, like electric can openers gnawing into an oil drum.

It was a very slow song, and Dina didn't so much dance as die slowly for each man in the room. "All the other girls hate her," a woman called Carmen, who'd seen us talking to Dina and claimed to be Dina's only friend, told us. "She makes too much money." It seemed to be true: Blackhawk was wearing a path between the stage and the bar, the drama club pooled its cash and gave her a fistful of dollars, and even Snowball presented an offering, heaving his bulk to dead center in front of the stage, stripping a twenty off a roll, put-ting it between his teeth, and standing between the small crowd and Dina with no respect for the view. Dina tugged the twenty from his teeth with her own. When Snowball turned away, she spat it on the ground.

After her dance, Dina returned to us. "I thought of a story for your God book," she said. "It's about a tornado."

She took the doctor we'd mentioned and remade him into a hero of a romance novel, a tall, powerful man who nonetheless goes weak in the knees for tornadoes. He has a wife, of course, and he loves her, too, and she loves him. "Now, you know how a woman gets when she really loves a man—he's her whole world, he's the moon in front of the sun or the sun in front of the moon—you know what I'm talking about?"

"An eclipse," we said.

"Yeah," Dina said. " 'Clipped.' That's what the wife is, clipped by her love for the doctor who loves tornadoes. She can't stand it, he runs away from her, he chases storms, he could die. 'Who do you love?' the wife demands. The doctor doesn't answer— This is the sexy part," said Dina. "He strips her and starts kissing her all over, he's licking her, you know, and touching her, and it's just one orgasm after another, it's fantastic. And then she gets it, I mean, she gets what's going on, 'cuz she's so in love with this man she knows all about him."

"Gets what?" we asked.

Dina rolled her eyes like we were fools. "He's fucking the tornado, you dummies! Didn't you ever read Danielle Steel?

"So he's shtupping the storm and the wife can't figure out whether she should be happy or sad. It almost doesn't matter, because it's the best fuck of her life. They're both covered in sweat and the bed is shaking, and her man's eyes look black and huge like the sun in front of the moon or the other way around. Which isn't so great because in the dark who knows what's what? So she tries to uh, uh, what's the word? *Clarify.* 'I'm your *wife,*' she says.

"The doctor doesn't say anything. He howls like the wind, and she wonders, Well who are *you?*"

Dina stopped. "That's as far as I got," she said. "I don't know what happens next. I guess the wife gets angry, 'cuz her man has a mistress, this fuckin' tornado."

"Maybe," we said. "Or maybe the wife is really the mistress."

"*Yes,*" said Dina. "That is it exactly. The wife is the mistress and the tornado is the doctor's real lover. Ooh, this is so hot, 'cuz, 'cuz, you know what happens next? The woman, she grabs her man by his shoulders and she says to him, she says this: 'You, you, as long as you keep chasing *her*'—the storm, the sky, God, whatever—'you're gonna keep loving me because I'm your mistress, my flesh and bones are your secret. And you know what's gonna happen? You keep chasing the storm, you're gonna make me into a fucking hurricane.' "

Dina sighed. "Isn't that beautiful?"

Yes, we said, scribbling the Book of Dina on cocktail napkins, *A Heretic's Bible*'s Apocrypha: adultery redeemed, humanism made holy, big-tent polytheism, everyone a god by no grace of his or her own but through the love of another—

"Put that crap away," Dina said, slapping our hands. "The boss will think we're trading phone numbers, and he says nothing that happens here goes out the door. Besides, it's your turn to tell a story."

Dina hailed the bartender for a round of kamikazes. She lit a cigarette and blew the smoke into the air above us, her breath joining the ashy cloud that hung there. She pulled her chair in close and lowered her voice.

"So that big trip you took," she said. "What *else* did you see?"

The sound system banged and pulsed, in the back a man grunted with pleasure, onstage the slap of flesh on the brass pole sounded like a congregation clapping in time. Hard to tell if she could really hear us over all that noise. But what did that matter? We told her everything.

ACKNOWLEDGMENTS

This book grew out of a web magazine, *KillingTheBuddha.com*, launched in November 2000. Jeremy Brothers, a brilliant designer and a funny, funny man, built the site and continues to design it to this day. There would be no *Killing the Buddha* without him. Many others have contributed their editorial talents to the website and thus shaped the ideas in this book, among them Patton Dodd, Irina Reyn, and Jeff Wilson, and most of all Paul W. Morris, our adviser, fellow traveler, and friend.

Our agent, Kathy Anderson, understood this book before we did. Not only did she open doors, she pushed us through them.

Tess Bresnan; Fiona Burde; Clare Burson; Molly Chilson and John Kearley (and their son, Sam); Mark Chilson; Jessica Christensen; Ingrid Ducmanis; Betsy Frankenberger; Sara Jaye Hart; Sean Manseau; Alane Mason; the late David Miller; Fred Mogul; David, Don, and Jude Rabig; Jennifer Ruark; Gary Shapiro; Phil Shipman; Diane Simon; Kio Stark; and Paul Zakrzewski asked us tough questions. Ben Weiner was our rabbi.

Jocelyn Sharlet and Baki Tezcan (and their son, Teoman) sold us the car that made it possible for one dollar, and felt bad for taking our money. Kathleen Manseau gave us a shiny Shiva sticker for the windshield and a travel pillow filled with beans.

More people than we can name gave us shelter; following are some of those whose houses we consider holy: Victoria McKernan in Washington, D.C.; Ray and Brenda Hurst in Bridgewater, Virginia; Justin Faerber and Rachel Ingold in Durham; Jen Ashlock in Chapel Hill; Emily Missner in Nashville; Leah Hochman in Gainesville, Florida; Doug Hadley in Dallas; J. C. Conklin, also in Dallas; Judy Cayce in Breckinridge; Brandon Bonneville and Nina Montemarano in Crestone, Colorado; Lisa Anderson in Colorado Springs; Jason Nutile in Santa Monica; Jim and Rich Marnell in Venice Beach; Jordan Cushing in Toronto; Christina Stanton in Great Barrington, Massachusetts; the Seznec family in Annapolis; and Colleen Clancy and Elana Wertkin in our sometimes hometown of New York City. The Jazz Inn, in Albuquerque, New Mexico, gave us a great place to write at special Buddha-killing rate.

In Chicago, where much of this book was written and compiled, Bridgette Buckley, Atakan Guven and Arielle Weinenger, and Tom Windish provided sanity-saving interruptions to the work. In Hamilton, New York, where much of this book was written and compiled, Lesleigh Cushing endured too many overheard arguments and cooked too many wonderful meals to ever be thanked sufficiently.

In our introduction, we write that this book has fifteen authors; even more people bear responsibility for its existence, and we intend to name names: Philip Rappaport, the brave editor who first took a chance on us; Amy Scheibe, the editor who took the leap of faith necessary to make the book a reality; Chris Litman, who guided us through the details; Dominick Anfuso, who laughed when we proposed the book (which we took as a good sign); Elizabeth Keenan and Carisa Hays, publicist-commandos; the designer, Karolina Harris; the production editor, Philip Metcalf; the copy editor, Susan Brown; and Stephanie Fairyington.

The scholars Jose Lopez, Steve Prothero, Terry Rey, Mercedes Sandoval, and Diane Winston provided us with intellectual guidance, though they should not be held responsible for what we did with it. Early lessons in the flexibility of religious tradition and literary form came from Julius Lester at the University of Massachusetts at Amherst and Michael Lesy at Hampshire College.

Shaiya Baer and Gary White at Vanderbilt University; Bar 13, in Manhattan; Chi Cha Lounge, in Washington; Halcyon, in Brooklyn; JCC of Manhattan; Sam Israel and Locus Gallery, in Manhattan; the McSweeney's Store, in Brooklyn; Byron Nichols at Union College; and Joanna Yas of *Open City* and the KGB Bar, in Manhattan, provided us with the opportunity to test much of this book on a live audience. David Isay and David Miller of Sound Portraits lent us recording equipment.

This book would not exist without all the people who shared their faiths and doubts with us, among them Rabbi Chaim Adelman; Reverend Oliver Barnes; Sister Connie Bielecki; Sheriff Thomas Breedlove; Daphne Bowe; Mel and Victor Chavez; Jonathon and Kendra Crossan Burroughs; Clarity; Larry Deutsch; Dina; Mary Dragon; Elowen Graywolf; Jim Evans; Reverend W. G. "Buddy" Faucette; Debra Floyd; Isis; Cat Johnson; Steve Johnson; Kal-el, his wife, Lumen, and their son, Logan; Dharma Kavr; Elizabeth Kay; Lady Keltic; Kennedy; Gail Scout Lopez; Tony Lowe; George and Stacy McVay; Midnight; Jacob Morris; Pablo; Dr. Jason Persoff; Reverend James E. Pettaway; Prem; Sparky T. Rabbit; Ramloti; Ani Rinchen; Robert K. Ritchie; Julie Schure; James Simpson; Sat Nam Singh; Sotantar Singh; Hanne Strong; Yesshe Thomasch; Geraldine and Desiderio Trujillo; Velvet; Greg West; Liz Wilcocks and her daughter, Zoë; Willowdancer; Crow Wolf; and everyone else we met along the way.

Many religious and spiritual institutions opened their doors to us, including: Belmont Church, the Billy Graham Center, Capilla del Santo Niño de Atocha, the Carolina Miracle Shack, Circle of Love Ministries, Church of the Rising Daughter, Church of San Lazaro, Club Exotica, Confessions, Dick's Last Resort, Dolores Mission Catholic Church, Dragon Mountain Zen Center, Faith Tabernacle Pentecostal United, Haidakhandi Universal Ashram, Ivanwald, Jacob's Well Outreach Ministries,

Kane Street Synagogue, Kunzang Palyul Choling, the Los Angeles Catholic Worker community, Meher Spiritual Center, the Manitou Foundation, Nashville Cowboy Church, Nashville Muslim Community Center, New Market Church of the Brethren, Prairie Station Cowboy Church, Santuario de Chimayó, Sanctuary House, Schenectady Hindu Temple, Shinji Shumeikai International, Shrine of Our Lady of Exile, Spirit Life Dome, Spiritual Life Institute, St. Luke-in-the-Fields, the Tennessee State Museum, Trinity Full Gospel Chuch of the Living God, the Twenty-First Amendment Liquor Store, the Twenty-third Psalm Café, and the Washington, D.C., Scientology Center.

Our parents, William and Mary Manseau and Robert Sharlet, provided the logistical support and absurdly unwavering confidence that made our creedless crusade possible. Nancy Sharlet was always with us.

Peter would like to thank especially Gwenann Seznec, who watched this book begin from the other side of the world, and saw it end from across the room.

Jeff would like to thank most of all Julia Rabig, his wife, who let him kill the Buddha, took him back when the Buddha kicked his ass, and made the attempt worthwhile.

ABOUT THE AUTHORS

Peter Manseau and Jeff Sharlet are founding editors of the online magazine KillingTheBuddha.com, winner of an Utne Independent Press Award. They began working together at the National Yiddish Book Center, where they helped rescue old Yiddish books from the trash. Peter studied religion and literature at the University of Massachusetts and Boston University. He lives up and down the eastern seaboard, from Charlottesville, Virginia, to Boston, his hometown. He is currently working on Vows, a memoir about the relationship his parents, a Catholic priest and a former nun, have formed with each other and their church. Jeff, a graduate of Hampshire College, has written about God, gods, and godlessness for numerous publications, including Harper's Magazine, The Washington Post Book World, The Dallas Morning News, Chicago Reader, and The Baffler. He lives in Brooklyn, where he edits TheRevealer.org for New York University's Center for Religion and Media. He is currently working on Power in the Blood, a history of American fundamentalism. Peter and Jeff can both be reached through www.KillingTheBuddha.com.

CONTRIBUTORS

A. L. Kennedy was born in North East Scotland. She has written four collections of short fiction and three novels, along with two books of nonfiction and a variety of journalism, including a column for *The Guardian*. She has won a number of literary prizes. She also writes for the stage, radio, film, and TV. She has sold brushes door-to-door, but now lectures part-time in the Creative Writing program at St Andrew's University School of English. In 1993, she was listed among *Granta's* Best of Young British Novelists. She is now ten years older and is listed again.

Francine Prose is the author of ten novels, including *Bigfoot Dreams*, *Primitive People*, and *Blue Angel*, a National Book Award finalist in 2000, and the recent nonfiction work *The Lives of the Muses*. Her short fiction, which has appeared in such places as *The New Yorker*, *The Atlantic*, and *The Paris Review*, has been gathered in two collections, *Women and Children First* and *The Peaceable Kingdom*.

Michael Lesy is the author of eight books of literary journalism and photography, including the classic *Wisconsin Death Trip*, *Visible Light*, *The Forbidden Zone*, *Dreamland*, and *Long Time Coming*. His writing has appeared in *The New Yorker*, *The New York Times*, *Aperture*, and *DoubleTake*, for which he was a columnist. He is the recipient of two NEA grants, and his book *Visible Light* was nominated for the National Book Critics' Circle Award. He lives in Amherst, Massachusetts, where he is a professor of writing at Hampshire College.

lê thi diem thúy is a writer and solo performance artist. Her performance works are *Red Fiery Summer*, *the bodies between us*, and *Carte Postale*. She is the author of *The Gangster We Are All Looking For*.

April Reynolds, a graduate of Sarah Lawrence College, was born in Dallas, Texas, and moved to New York in 1997. She now teaches at the 92nd Street Y and Sarah Lawrence College. Her short story, "Alcestis," appeared in *The Bluelight Corner: Black Women Writing on Passion, Sex and Romantic Love*. Her fiction will also appear in the anthology *Mending the World*. Her first novel, *Knee Deep in Wonder*, which won a Zora Neale Hurston/Richard Wright Foundation Award, was published in 2003.

As the child of a Holocaust escapee and a grandchild of Holocaust victims, **Peter Trachtenberg** grew up suspecting that the world is unfair and its presiding spirit capricious if not actively malign: Hence his enduring interest in the story of Job. He is the author of the memoir *7 Tattoos: A Memoir in the Flesh* (Crown, 1997) and of stories and essays published in *The New Yorker*, *Harper's*, *Salon*, *Chicago*, *TriQuarterly*, and *BOMB*. He has been the recipient of the Nelson Algren Award for Short Fiction and an Artist's Fellowship from the New York Foundation of the Arts. He has performed as a monologist at Dixon Place, P.S. 122, Hallwalls, and the Museum of Natural History, as well as on National Public Radio's *All Things Considered*.

Darcey Steinke is the author of two novels, *Jesus Saves* and *Suicide Blonde*, and coeditor with Rick Moody of *Joyful Noise*. She frequently writes for *Spin* and *The Village Voice*. She lives in New York.

Charles Bowden is the author of fourteen books, including *Blues for Cannibals*, *Blood Orchid: An Unnatural History of America*, *Juarez: Laboratory for the Future*, and *Blue Desert*. His essays have appeared in *Best American Essays*, 2001 and 1998. He is a contributing editor to *Esquire*, a frequent contributor to *Harper's* and *GQ*, and a winner of the Lannan Literary Award for Nonfiction. He lives in Tucson, Arizona.

Melvin Jules Bukiet's ninth and most recent book is *A Faker's Dozen*. He teaches at Sarah Lawrence College and lives in Manhattan where nothing bad ever happens.

Eileen Myles is a poet who lives in New York and a novelist who teaches fiction at UCSD. Currently she's working on a novel called *The Inferno* and a libretto called *Hell*.

Rick Moody is the author most recently of *The Black Veil* and *Demonology*, a collection of stories.

Randall Kenan is the author of a novel, *A Visitation of Spirits*; a collection of stories, *Let the Dead Bury Their Dead* (nominated for a National Book Critics' Circle Award); a biography of James Baldwin for young adults; and a book of nonfiction, *Walking on Water: The Lives of Black Americans in the 21st Century*. He lives in Hillsboro, North Carolina.

Haven Kimmel is the author of two novels, *The Solace of Leaving Early* and *Something Rising (Light & Swift)*, and a memoir, *A Girl Named Zippy*. She studied theology at the Earlham School of Religion, never imagining that she would one day wrangle the Book of Revelation.

A CONVERSATION WITH THE AUTHORS

1. What was the most valuable thing you learned about God while writing this book?

We learned that God might be what the book itself is: a collaboration, a collage, a call-and-response. Our favorite thing about *Killing the Buddha* is that a single reader can have such a wide range of responses to it—you might love parts of it, hate others, or see yourself in many of the people we write about and yet be frightened by a few as well. That seems very much like the way we often experience life and shape our religious (or irreligious) understanding of it: The world is beautiful and ugly at the same time, opposites piling up on top of each other. Not harmony but cacophony. And yet it can sound beautiful. Maybe what we call God is the same way: a hermaphrodite terrorist angel (to put it in the terms of our story from Henderson, North Carolina), or a collection of attributes and characteristics that shouldn't fit together, but do, despite all our assumptions.

2. When you went back out on the road to promote the hardcover edition, did you reencounter any of the people you met the first time out?

Debra Floyd, the witch we met in Crestone, Colorado, was excited to sell *Killing the Buddha* in her magic supply store, right there with the love potions and the tarot cards. Jason Persoff, the stormchasing doctor we traveled with through Tornado Alley, wrote to annouce the birth of his second child. Naturally, he related this life-changing news in the form of a weather report: "DUE TO UNCHARACTERISTICALLY STRONG INFLOW . . . LRG DMGING DIAPERS HAVE ALREADY BEEN REPORTED." And Elowen Graywolf, the military pagan grandmother of Heartland, Kansas, actually wrote a review of the book online. The phrase she used to describe *Killing the Buddha* was "a wonderful mixture of truths and humor." It was a great compliment, especially since "truth and humor" are the first words that come to mind when we think of her.

3. Can you tell us what it was like to work with such amazing contributors?
To give up control of the direction of the book was really to take a leap of faith in the project and to give ourselves over to the idea of creating a congregation within these pages. Later when the book was done, the paper congregation we'd created became a real one when a number of our contributors joined us for readings around the country. Peter Trachtenberg flew across the country to perform his Book of Job with the aid of a PowerPoint display. Mel Bukiet joined us in New York, and when April Reynolds had to cancel at the last minute, Mel's teenage daughter stood in for April and gave probably the most popular reading of the tour. In North Carolina, Haven Kimmel and Randall Kenan joined us. Hearing Haven read aloud from her Revelation was truly a religious experience — confounding, beguiling, mesmermising. It reminded us that scripture when it was first created was oral, and it must have had that same quality — the immediacy of words so sublime they seem to have come from God.

4. What was one of your oddest road encounters?
In northern New Mexico we spent a week at the most popular religious pilgrimage site in America, Santuario de Chimayo, which is a Catholic shrine where people eat dirt. Really: The faithful line up to enter a small church through the back door, file past abandoned crutches and walls covered floor to ceiling with pictures of people who have been healed there, and then they crowd into a tiny room with a hole cut in the concrete floor. They reach in and grab dirt by the handful, or else scoop it into Ziploc bags for later, and then they eat it. People say part of the miracle is that the hole is never empty — no matter how much is scooped up, it always stays full. We asked the priest who runs this place if that were true, if the Lord keeps dirt in the hole. "Do you think God would have time for such a stupid miracle?" he said. "I buy this dirt. Twenty-five tons a year!" He took us to the pile in the back where a dump truck had dropped a recent load. He showed us where he kept the shovels and the buckets. And then he let us fill the hole.

5. How has writing this book affected your own spiritual quests?
All we really did with *Killing the Buddha* was gather stories, compiling many ways to think about God, death, life, and all the rest. Basically, we took what

most Americans are already doing with their lives and put it in book form. These are the last pages of that book, but there are too many stories out there to stop looking.

6. What did you miss the most about your homes when you were out seeking?
Clean socks. Seriously. It's hard to keep your clothes clean when you're constantly on the move. We ended up buying disposable wardrobes. Clean socks in every town, and then the sorts of things that normally live in the back of the closet. Flipflops for walking around Little Havana in Miami, looking for Santeria priests. Stiff, dark, blue jeans from Sears for Texas, when we realized our "city pants" made us suspect in the eyes of the cowboy Christians we were visiting. At the pagan gathering in Kansas, our hosts required us to buy—and wear—sarongs. Now all those things actually are in the back of our closets. They remind us of what Debra Floyd, a witch in Crestone, Colorado, who made her own clothes, said to us about how different names for God are costumes we use to dress up the divine. Same with people, our fashions and trends and styles—they're costumes we use to talk to one another. On the road, we missed the certainty of the same kind of clothes every day, the unchallenged identity that's as comfortable as old jeans. But looking back it might have made our job easier. We had fewer barriers to new experiences with our usual habits left behind.

7. Do you believe in having a "calling"?
It can happen. Sometimes it's as simple as the family business. Peter's father is a priest, his mother a former nun. Everyone in Jeff's immediate family makes books of one kind or another. But a "calling" is more complicated than that. If we claimed that we had a divine invitation to make this book, we'd be setting ourselves up as a couple more Buddhas, and we know what happens to them. Yet it probably is true that we were driven to make *Killing the Buddha* not just by the usual incentives, but by a sense that something like it was needed and that a strange set of circumstances had put us in the place to make it. All of which points to the accidental, contingent nature of a calling, whatever it may be. It is something shaped not so much by a divine voice but by all the voices you've ever heard.

A GUIDE TO SCRIPTURE IN *KILLING THE BUDDHA*

Mortal, Eat This Scroll!—the title of the introduction to *Killing the Buddha*—is a phrase taken from the biblical Book of Ezekiel.

Genesis contains not only the tale of the creation ("In the beginning . . .") but also many of the best-known Bible stories, including those of Adam and Eve, Cain and Abel, and Abraham and Isaac.

Exodus is an account of how Moses led the Hebrews in their escape from Pharaoh, a story which became the basis for the Jewish holiday of Passover.

Leviticus is the law book of the Bible, a set of harsh codes embraced by the Hebrews during their desert wandering. Many of the fiercest injunctions of the Bible are to be found here, as well as many of the strangest.

Ruth is a story of mothers and daughters. When Ruth's husband dies young, she vows loyalty to Naomi, her mother-in-law. The bond between Ruth and Naomi is stronger than any either has ever known.

The two books of **Samuel** in the Bible tell the story of the beginning of politics. The Israelites, thinking that the key to survival is to emulate the surrounding nations, ask God to give them a mortal king. Samuel, the alleged author, follows God's instruction to anoint a man named Saul. The Israelites live forever after afflicted by political infighting.

The Book of **Job** tells the story of a good man named Job who becomes the object of a wager between God and Satan. Satan bets that Job will curse God if afflicted, and God accepts the bet, allowing Satan to throw his worst at Job. The Book of Job becomes a chronicle of suffering endured by Job.

Song of Songs, also known as the Song of Solomon, is the most erotic book of the Bible. It's the story of young lovers who take turns describing their adoration for each other and the joys of sexual union. Many scholars interpret it as an analogy for the relationship between God and humanity.

Isaiah is the prophet best known for predicting a time when the lion will lie down with the lamb, a beautiful world in the future when all things will be at peace with one another.

Ezekiel is one of the strangest prophets, given to visions of mythical beasts circling him, much like the carousel in *Killing the Buddha*'s "Ezekiel," and of a scroll handed to him by God with instructions that he learn its contents by literally eating it. Like Bukiet's Ezekiel, the biblical Ezekiel is obsessed with why and how to worship a God who permits so much suffering.

The Book of **Daniel** tells the story of a young man, Daniel, brought against his will to the court of the king of Babylon. Daniel is favored by God with the vision of a prophet, but when the Babylonians discover that Daniel still prays to his God, he is thrown into the lions' den. Never losing his faith, he escapes without a scratch. *Killing the Buddha*'s Daniel, brought against his will to Long Island, is not so lucky.

The biblical **Jonah**, like Jonah Feldman in *Killing the Buddha*'s "Jonah," is a reluctant prophet who tries to escape his calling. God sends a storm to threaten the boat he flees on and, after the crew throws him overboard, a whale to swallow him and bring him to his senses.

There are four **Gospels** in the Bible, by Matthew, Mark, Luke, and John; there is one in *A Heretic's Bible*, by Randall Kenan. Like the originals, Kenan's "Gospel" is a story of a miracle worker, and as in the original, the miracle worker attracts a lot of attention, not all of it desirable.

Revelation, the last book of the New Testament, is a dense, surreal vision of apocalypse, fiercely narrated by a man named John of Padmos. *Killing the Buddha*'s "Revelation" is told in the collective first person voice of a choir of angels, reflecting on how hard it is to accurately communicate visions to us mortals.

The Book of **Psalms** is not a narrative but a collection of poems. Nonetheless, the psalms do tell a story—many stories, in fact. Between the lines can be found true tales from the emotional history of a people. Full of praise, lament, anger, and hope, the psalms have been called a catalog of the states of the soul.